UP THE CREEK
an Amazon adventure

To Richard & Claire,

with best wishes,

John Ha~

BRADT PUBLICATIONS, UK, &
HIPPOCRENE BOOKS INC., NEW YORK

UP THE CREEK
an Amazon adventure

JOHN HARRISON

First published in 1986 by Bradt Publications, 41 Nortoft Road, Chalfont St Peter, Bucks SL9 0LA, UK

British Library Cataloguing in Publication Data

Harrison, John, 1950—
    Up the creek : an Amazon adventure.
    1. Kayaks—Amazon River   2. Amazon
    River—Description and travel
    I. Title
    918.1'10463   F2546
    ISBN 0-946983-07-0
    ISBN 0-946983-05-4 Pbk

Photographs by the author
Front cover and map by Martin Jordan
Line drawings by Peter Strub
Designed and typeset by Allset Composition, London
Printed and bound in the UK by A Wheaton and Co Ltd, Exeter, Devon

Back cover photo: the author with payara fish

Contents

	FOREWORD by Dervla Murphy	vii
	ACKNOWLEDGEMENTS	ix
	MAP	x
Chapter 1	PROPHECIES AND PREPARATIONS	1
Chapter 2	DEPARTURE	7
Chapter 3	EARLY DAYS	20
Chapter 4	SLOW PROGRESS	35
Chapter 5	MALARIA	41
Chapter 6	BURNT FOOT CAMP	50
Chapter 7	BACK TO THE BEGINNING	64
Chapter 8	UP THE CUC	83
Chapter 9	THE JARI AGAIN	104
Chapter 10	CHOKED WATERS	116
Chapter 11	DIRE STRAITS	126
Chapter 12	DILEMMAS	138
Chapter 13	THE RETREAT	149
Chapter 14	THE LONG WAIT	156
Chapter 15	CHRISTMAS	168
Chapter 16	LAST DAYS	175

Foreword

During recent years a sinister shadow has fallen across the world of travel and travel-writing. Its name is 'Sponsorship'.

The quest for sponsors was, I suppose, inspired by the example of mountaineering expeditions. And its rapid spread may not be entirely dissociated from those State-dependent attitudes so dismally prevalent among the post-war generations. Even in modern Britain the State is not expected to subsidise long trips abroad; but the notion of someone else paying for one's thrills is lamentably congenial to a certain type of young traveller. During the 1970s more and more firms advertised their goods by backing phoney 'adventures' and 'expeditions'. These much-publicised stunt journeys, televised at appropriate stages, have all too often been followed by lavishly-illustrated books of remarkable tedium and questionable veracity. Such volumes are presented to the public as 'travel-books', which does no good to the blood-pressure of genuine travel-writers. Happily their numbers seem now to be dwindling: perhaps a beneficial result of the recession. Or it may be that publishers have discovered sales-resistance to the latest heavily-hyped account of descending the Indus in a beer barrel with an outboard motor or crossing the Gobi Desert in a golf-buggy.

In the course of duty I have been compelled to read many descriptions of sponsored expeditions. These develop one's sensitivity to travel pseuds and heighten one's appreciation of authentic adventurers like John Harrison, whose unsponsored Amazonian journey is recounted here with humour, honesty and enthusiasm. This is a thoroughly satisfying description of a hazardous and gruelling canoe trip on one of the more obscure tributaries of the Amazon — an adventure undertaken just for the hell of it and completely convincing in all its details. John Harrison uses vigorous, unpretentious language and has blended his ingredients most skilfully. We have good old-fashioned suspense (if anything does seriously go wrong hundreds of miles from the nearest village no sponsored helicopter will fly to the rescue) — and marvellous descriptions of Amazonian wildlife (sometimes viewed from the inside, as when John observed that a certain species of monkey, a favourite for the pot, was always riddled with worms) — and witty analyses of how and why things went wrong between John and his companion (he had two companions over different stages: there may not be any other man who could have withstood all that hardship, disease and danger).

By the last page one's strongest feeling is of sheer admiration for this traveller's courage. It is the courage of a sort not often found nowadays, because not often needed. John Harrison was born a century too late. He should have been out there with Livingstone, Speke, Selous and all that lot. For people like him, our shrunken planet offers too few challenges. His readers, however, will hope that he soon finds another — and writes about it.

DERVLA MURPHY

Acknowledgements

I wish to thank the following for their valuable contributions and encouragement.

Martin and Tanis Jordan who never lost faith, who helped so generously with illustration and typing, and who share my obsession with Amazonia.

My Mum, June Harrison, for her practical and moral support always.

Peter Strub for being in the right place at the right time and for saving the trip, and for illustrating our adventures so vividly.

Granta Boats Ltd, Ramsey, Huntingdon, Cambridgeshire, for their help and advice.

Heather Barrett for all her help, encouragement and love.

Hilary Bradt for her ruthless attack on the first draft and for her help since.

EQUATOR

SOUTH
AMERICA

SURINAM

FRENCH GUIANA

Mapaou

Ximim

Cuc

MOLOCOPOTE

BRAZIL

Jari

Ipitinga

E Q U A T O R

CARECARU

Jari Project

MONTE
DOURADO

River Amazon

|←SCALE: 400 KILOMETRES ≈ 250 MILES→|

1 Prophecies and preparations

'I'm a father at last,' he beamed proudly, blocking my path, 'and in my country it is a custom to invite a total stranger to a meal so that the child might grow up strong and healthy.'

It seemed a charming and commendable custom, and with nothing but the welfare of his son in mind I accompanied him. As we walked he told me he'd come from Khartoum so that his wife might have the baby there in Cairo, and this was his first visit to Egypt.

'In Khartoum I live in an apartment where the balcony overhangs the Nile. In the evenings I can sit up there getting splashed by crocodiles slapping the water with their tails.'

We stopped at a street stall and he bought me a cup of coffee and a dirt-encrusted honey cake. No expense spared here. He did not seem concerned that his son might grow up to be a sickly runt.

Having nothing better to do I let him lead me round the alleys of Cairo where for a visitor he seemed to be extraordinarily well-known by all the shopkeepers and passers-by. He tried to lure me into all the shops to gain a commission, offered me hashish, girls, boys and semi-precious stones, and as we passed an old man sitting on a doorstep, he suggested I have my fortune told. After establishing a price, I agreed and sat down.

The old man looked unblinkingly into my eyes before reaching for my hand to read my palm. It was a relief that his piercing eyes left my face since his stray, dead eye wandered in different directions from the other. He had a wrinkled, authoritarian face, a white stubbled chin, and the hand that held mine felt leathery and dry. I waited impatiently for his prophecy, my guide chattering irritatingly all the while.

'This man is very wise. He can see into the future: your life next year, twenty years, even fifty years ahead!'

The old man was silent, bent myopically over the mysteries of my palm. I was not expecting much revelation and the pretence at thoroughness was a tedious delay.

'This old man told me two weeks ago that I will have a boy. What did my wife give me this morning? A boy! He is very, very wise!'

'I thought you told me you only got to Cairo three days ago,' I reminded him maliciously, and he looked embarrassed.

The old man finally sat up straight, looked into my face briefly, painfully uncoiled himself from the doorstep and said something in Arabic.

'What did he say?' I asked.

'He says that the things he can see are best left untold,' said my companion, looking genuinely perplexed as the old man began to shuffle away.

'I bet that is just a ploy to squeeze more money out of me,' I thought, pursuing him much as I'd chase an evasive doctor after a chest x-ray.

'Tell him I want to know, whatever it is.'

They talked gutturally while I studied their faces. If this was play-acting they were very, very good. My guide turned to me.

'He says it is better not to know. You're very young. How old are you?'

'Twenty.'

'Twenty. That's very young. When you're young you need hope, and you think that you will live for ever and ever. It's not good to learn bad news. Best forget it.'

'Tell him I want to know. I prefer to know.'

'You'll regret it if you do.'

'That's my worry – now go on and tell me.'

'You're going to die young and it will be death by water.'

'At what age?' I asked, half-hoping this time he would refuse to tell me.

'When you're thirty-three,' translated my crooked friend, and the fortune-teller disappeared into the crowds, not even accepting payment. In Egypt that was cause for concern in itself, and I stood in the alley feeling goose-pimply even in the Cairo heat.

Never mess with fortune-tellers. Once threatened with a prophecy like that how can you forget it? You ridicule the idea of seeing into the future as hogwash, superstition and baloney, but the memory stays and subtly comes to alter your life. In my case that prophecy led to much misspent youth. I could never make any long-term plans and that included a career. What was the point of spending six or seven of the last years of my life cooped up securing a profession if it only led to the Big Gurgle at thirty-three? Or would it be my thirty-third year? This distinction did not seem particularly important when I was merely twenty, but assumed major significance on March 21st 1983 when I celebrated my thirty-third birthday. Was I already safe, or was the fateful year just beginning?

Certainly it was not the time for canoeing in Amazonia, thought my friends. Why the hell was I going to one of the most watery places on earth when I shouldn't even be filling the bath more than one inch? And what about water-borne disease? We all know that every glass of water in South America is a cocktail of death.

'Stay at home,' I was told, 'No swimming, no deep baths, only drink Perrier and you'll be alright.'

I tried to convince them, and myself, that it was mere coincidence that I felt the urge to return to Amazonia during this particular year. Really, of course, I knew that staying at home would afford me no protection if the fates were out to get me. I might spend a year living timidly in London, only to fall over on my way home from a party and drown in a puddle. To die in an Amazonian rapid or from Amazonian typhoid seemed a touch more stylish. A dubious distinction admittedly, and as I made preparations for the trip I did my best to put the prophecy out of my mind.

This was to be my fifth Amazonian river journey, and I had a pretty good idea of the sort of river I wanted to explore. The previous trips had started as simple apprenticeships on easy rivers – the Branco and Guapore – and gone on to harder stuff, the Verde and Teles Pires. This time I wanted a river with very few people living along its banks, a river where the wildlife would be abundant and the jungle undisturbed. That meant a river with rapids.

Before the road-building programme of the 1970s the pattern of population along Amazonian rivers used to depend on the ease, or otherwise, of river travel. Rivers free of rapids on their lower or middle reaches – the Madeira, Purus, Tocantins, Jurua, Branco, Amazon and Solimoes, for example – carry a scattered population of perhaps one house every kilometre on either bank, and have communication by riverboats with nearby towns. This is a tiny population density, but enough to banish two of the main attractions for me – isolation and the chance to see a lot of wildlife. Now, of course, the new roads have increased the population along those rivers where in the past rapids made travel too difficult and deterred settlers.

Another important consideration to me was the size of the river. Personally, I find huge wide rivers boring to paddle on, and in Amazonia more than 1 kilometre is a common width. You can see only one bank clearly at a time, the water conditions are often choppy and tiring, and there are few things more psychologically withering than to see the river in front of you endlessly, merging with the sky kilometres away. Twists, turns, islands, shallows, narrows and a few rapids are what I need to keep my interest.

As the states of Mato Grosso, Rondonia, Amazonas and much of Para are already too developed to meet these requirements, I concentrated my attentions on northern Brazil between the Amazon river and the borders of Venezuela and the Guyanas. Here were several possible rivers – the Trombetas, Paru d'Oeste and Jari – all descending from the Guyana shield, some of the oldest highlands in South America. All of them have rapids which deter settlements. They flow from one of the last truly virgin areas of rain-forest in Brazil and are relatively small rivers in comparison to those of south and eastern Amazonia. I say 'small' in strictly Amazonian terms: the Trombetas is 750 kilometres long, and the Jari 600.

Where to end this trip posed a problem. I did not relish paddling all the way up a river only to paddle all the way down again, but as there were no towns or roads in the north where we could leave the rivers I began to consider a more ambitious project. The headwaters were up in the Tumucumaque hills, and these hills mark a watershed with rivers running north and south. If it were possible to paddle to the top of the Jari, for example, it might be feasible to portage over the top and descend the river Litanie into French Guiana, or cross from the Paru d'Oeste to the Tapanahoni in Surinam.

The idea was exciting. It would give a real goal to the trip, and be an enormous challenge. The distance between one river and another looked on the map to be about fifteen kilometres on average, and from the comfort of an armchair in England such distances seemed trifling. A week or two of reconnoitering to find the other stream, a week or two of cutting a trail through the jungle, and a few days of humping the canoe and gear across. Easy.

I finally decided on the Jari. It seemed to provide all the necessary ingredients for an exciting trip and to have a few less rapids than the others. It 'connected' with rivers in French Guiana, which was a more politically stable country than Surinam or Guyana, and it had the added interest of Daniel Ludwig's Jari project on its lowest reaches. This pulp and timber project has aroused such controversy I was keen to have a look at it for myself.

As for a companion to go with, that was a problem. On previous expeditions I made a few preparations in England, and then flew out to Brazil and hung around the cheaper bars and hotels until an interested traveller appeared. That way I had done canoe trips with a Chilean, an Australian and an Italian which had all worked out well. None of my companions had ever paddled a canoe before (neither had I on my first river trip), but something had lured them to Amazonia, they had got there through their own initiative and even the brief look they had had when travelling to Manaus by river-boat or along the transamazonian roads had given them some idea of what to expect.

In England I never know where to start when recruiting a companion. Canoe clubs seem a possible source, but I find that the average canoe enthusiast and I don't speak the same language. They are usually kayakers whereas I have always used local dug-outs or 'Canadian' canoes. They are passionate about technique and white water, and their vocabulary is full of 'stoppers', 'slapping for support', and 'graded rapids'. Between trips to Amazonia I never canoe. I find white water sometimes exhilarating, sometimes downright frightening and a bloody nuisance the rest of the time. It is like talking to a rally driver before setting off on a motoring holiday around Europe. You are both using cars, but enthusiasms, language, type of vehicle and passions are different.

An alternative method of recruitment is putting adverts in several journals and newspapers, and sitting back hoping to be swamped with applicants. But then how do I select one? Do I take them all on some outward bound endurance tests and spot their strengths and weaknesses, or meet them one by one in a pub where a beery evening can easily give us both the wrong impressions? Unless a similar trip has been done before, the uncertainty remains. I could lay it on thick about the dangers and discomforts and a few would run away thanking their lucky stars for their narrow escape, but the majority would insist that they could handle it.

When preparing for a long and ambitious trip like this one, I chicken out of the option of hanging around in Brazil until the right person appears. There's too much to be done in England and it's more fun to plan and prepare with a companion. There are expenses I couldn't meet alone, and altogether there is too much uncertainty when relying on casual contacts. Suppose, for once, no one appeared, because everyone had an intractable schedule or the number of travellers had declined since I was last there? I would be left with a pile of gear and a canoe, forlornly scouring the streets for gringos, with dwindling funds and growing desperation.

This Jari trip was going to be extremely tough. I needed to find someone to match. Paddling up against the current would be a continual slog, the rapids would entail long portages and danger. The trip could go on for a minimum of five months – possibly up to a year. Where could I find the right sort of idiot? I contacted one or two canoe clubs without any joy, and was reluctantly facing the necessity of inserting some adverts when Mark was introduced to me. Mark was a stringy Australian of well over two metres who had done the overland route from his country and was therefore familiar with travel in the Third World. That seemed to be the sum of his relevant qualifications, but he was enthusiastic, capable and keen to go. No one else was. So I agreed to take him.

I had reservations about Mark from very early on, and a hunch that things might not work out smoothly. However he seemed tough enough, and that was my prime concern. I made a point of warning him again and again of the physical hardship of the expedition. I didn't want him taken by surprise. I exaggerated the monotony of paddling, the heat, the insects, the bland diet, the slow progress, and the long, back-breaking portages. He seemed to lap up my descriptions, confident of his own stamina and endurance.

My reservations were over our incompatibility of character. Meeting once a week in a London pub in the months before our departure, I think we both found each other's company a bit of a strain. Conversation would lag, and it was hard to find topics of mutual interest. It is foolish to embark on an expedition with such doubts, but time was running out. So I put it down to our difference in age (Mark was twenty-two) and got on with the preparations. As I expressed it to a friend, 'The chances of finding the ideal combination of wit, raconteur and beast of burden in one powerful body are remote. They must have thrown the mould away after I was made. But better a humourless beast of burden, than an unladen wit.'

Incidentally I never mentioned the dreaded prophecy to Mark. I did not think it would improve his concept of the trip knowing he would have to share a canoe and drink out of the same water container as someone condemned to die a watery death.

One problem was whether we'd find a canoe to fit him. On previous trips I had used either local dug-out canoes bought for a few dollars at the riverside, or – on three occasions – plank canoes that I built myself at the nearest saw-mill to the river. These were pretty basic constructions but very strong and stable. Their big defect, as with the dug-outs, was their great weight. Any portage over long distances or over rough terrain was out of the question with only two people, and on the Jari I knew we would frequently have to portage past rapids – and of course there would be the 15 kilometres of carrying at the headwaters. Also for the first time I was planning to paddle upstream, and the lighter the canoe the easier it would be to make headway against the current.

We decided to take a canoe out with us from England. We considered four types. First, in the kayak range, there were folding models that could take two people and a lot of gear. They had the advantage of being light, strong, easy to repair and could be folded up and taken on the plane. But they had disadvantages. First, all my canoeing experience had been gained in 'Canadian'-style canoes with a single-bladed paddle. Second, although they could reputedly carry two people and 200 kilos of gear, they would be tedious to load and unload with everything crammed down the bow and stern. Third, to get in and out of them you really need shallow water or 7 metres of clear bank that you can pull alongside, neither feature being typical of Amazonia. Generally you nose your canoe into the bank at right angles and walk along the canoe to get out. Finally, these kayaks were lovely pieces of craftsmanship and very expensive.

In the 'Canadian' style of craft there were aluminium and fibreglass models, which were attractive, light and strong. The fibreglass ones were easy to repair, the metal ones less so and also very costly. What really put us off were the prices quoted for shipping the canoes to Brazil: at least £600 one way, and God knows what customs problems. Also, after paying £900 for an aluminium canoe, you would no doubt want to take it home with you after the trip was over.

At last we hit on the perfect solution — a wooden 'Canadian' of nearly 6 metres that was in kit form. Since it cost about £200 it would not break our hearts to leave it behind at the end of our journey, and it was within the size limitation for luggage on the plane. The manufacturers were Granta of Cambridgeshire, and we were able to consult Ken Littledyke, the designer, who advised certain strengthening modifications. As the canoe was to be assembled using fibreglass, there was a worry as to whether polyester resin would be available in Amazonia (airlines do not accept it except as cargo because of its flammability), but correspondence with an acquaintance in Brazil assured us that we would be able to get it in the cities of Manaus and Belem.

Mark and I drove up one beautiful June day to try out one of the canoes and were relieved there was no one around to watch as we launched it onto a dyke near the factory. Mark had never paddled a canoe before, and for some reason I ended up in the bow when I'm accustomed to the stern. In a 'Canadian', the man in the stern controls the direction, while the one in front supplies the brawn and only helps with the steering in tight manoeuvres. We launched off, turned in a circle, and ran into a nearby bridge. After changing over in mid-stream and performing a giggling dance as we passed in the violently-wobbling craft, we got sorted out and paddled a few miles. We ended stiff and tired, but pleased with the responsiveness of the canoe.

2 Departure

London life always improves enormously just before I leave on a trip. I make more effort to get together with rarely-seen friends, and use the last few weeks as a pretext for parties, rowdy restaurant meals, and nights on the town. The grind of work and routine is ending and the anticipation of escape is at hand, along with feelings of regret at leaving and certain fears of what lies in store.

Most books one reads about expeditions talk about the months of hectic preparation before the trip: the leader tirelessly chasing up last-minute supplies, giving press conferences, raising sponsorship money and joining the other team members on a punishing training schedule. His house has crates of equipment spilling out of every room, and rugged super-fit expeditionaries sleeping in every nook and cranny. The leader's wife (who usually stays at home) must heave a sigh of relief when hubby, his boring cronies and all their bloody gear have gone, perhaps never to return.

I am afraid I usually set off overweight and out of condition. I may have made a practice of cycling to work instead of driving, but nothing more. I figure that two weeks on the river will make me lean and fit, and the tropics will soon sweat off the paunch. As for all the other preparations they don't seem hectic at all. A few letters, phone calls and a few days' shopping and it's all done. It's all so easy that I lie awake at night worrying about the dozens of things I must be forgetting. Nice though it would be to receive sponsorship and backing, life is a lot simpler without it. To stand a good chance of eliciting funds or materials, you need to mount a formidable public relations exercise. I've always preferred to finance a trip myself. After all, it never costs more than £2000, and that's a sum that can be saved in a year or two.

In a pamphlet that gives advice on how to approach firms for help I note the following tactics. First you give the expedition a glamorous name, 'Tumucumaque Traverse 1983' for example, and have some notepaper printed with the title and a little logo. Then you discover the name of the individual in each firm that handles requests for sponsorship so you can address your correspondence to him personally. Finally your chances are improved if you say you are undertaking some sort of research. This gives the enterprise the stamp of serious endeavour. Without it a trip is regarded merely as a stunt or an adventure. Yet the unsponsored venture is much more fun — and it's so much simpler to keep the trip cheap and small, unpublicised, unauthorised, flexible and unscientific. Escapism, pure and simple. Aren't many expeditions escapist? How many devoted lovers of the pink-eyed toad are there who after discovering its natural habitat think fearfully 'Oh dear, I'll have to go to Amazonia to study it?' No, I believe that nine times out of ten it is the place that attracts. All of us wandering maniacs are map and atlas freaks. We spend hours considering little jungle rivers, tracks in the desert, or distant mountain ranges, until finally we choose one. Perhaps after that we search around for some scientific pretext for going.

So the end of June we were finally on our way. Travelling with us were Martin and Tanis Jordan, old friends who have travelled on many rivers in Venezuela, Peru and Surinam using inflatable craft. This was to be their first trip to Brazil where they planned to travel up the Mapuera river — a tributary of the Trombetas. It was great for all of us to set out together and we assembled at Heathrow in high spirits.

The dominant item in our luggage was, of course, the canoe kit. Its box was 2.5 metres long, 75 centimetres wide and 15 centimetres deep (7 feet by 2 feet by 6 inches approximately) and weighed 40 kilos. Mark and I weighed it in as joint luggage and managed to get on three extra bags with no charge.

Mark had planned to join the army in Australia when he returned home, and he had a passion for anything military. To start the trip he sported a haircut that would have pleased a marine sergeant, with 'white-walls' running 5 centimetres above the ear. He also wore an olive-green combat jacket, stuffed with a lot of our medical kit: syringes, ampoules, bottles of pills and lotions. He looked like a dog of war off to another hot spot and the security guards quickly pulled him to one side and gave him a search. Fortunately we had persuaded our doctor friend to write a letter to say that he had prescribed us all the medicines.

After an apparently uneventful flight to Cayenne, French Guiana, we were informed that one of the engines had developed a fault, and we were blessed with what I had always dreamt of: two nights in a luxury hotel with a swimming pool and good food, all at the expense of the airline. Most of the other passengers with pressing engagements were impatient and irritated, but we felt our rivers would wait for us. We sunbathed, ate hugely and prayed that the engine would not be fixed for five or six days.

In fact Air France were not able to repair it in those two days so they chartered an old crate from one of the least illustrious Peruvian airlines to take us on to Manaus. It was one of the most unnerving flights of my life. On take-off all the ceiling panels groaned under the stress and large gaps appeared between them. Our oxygen masks kept popping down in front of our faces, and throughout much of the flight there seemed to be a crisis on the flight deck. Taut-faced stewardesses raced to and fro along the aisle clutching fire extinguishers, with no attempt to dispel our alarm by breezy smiles.

'Not much chance of finding us, or the black box, down in that lot,' said Martin, staring out of the window at the unbroken jungle below. It was a very relieved group that arrived in Manaus, and we looked on in pity at the poor passengers who had to continue on that plane over the Andes to Lima.

Visitors who reach Manaus by plane are often disappointed in the city. Because of its location 1,200 km up the Amazon they expect to find a small river settlement fighting a losing battle against the encroaching jungle and termites. The reality of course is quite different: a busy town of over half a million people, which because of its free port status has shops full of cameras, calculators and stereos, and the attendant traffic problems and skyscrapers.

For the new arrival to the Amazon the port area on the Rio Negro lives up to some expectations. It is crowded with river-boats and jostling humanity, there is a powerful stench of rotting fish, fruit and vegetables, and the roof-tops are lined with *Urubus* — the black vultures that do more to keep the rubbish from over-running the port than do the municipal authorities. Manaus has to be seen for what it is — a centre for quick profits, and a place of rest and recreation for combatants of the interior.

After weeks or months of deprivation and craving here is satisfaction: women, cold and reasonably-priced beer, a bed instead of a hammock, cinemas, crowded streets, a good time, and a rest from mosquitoes, rice, beans and *farinha*. If you manage to arrive feeling like a combatant yourself, so much the better. If all you have seen for weeks has been jungle or dusty little frontier towns, Manaus will seem like heaven. It's all there for a price, and the fact that it disappoints tourists because it's so easy to forget that you are in the middle of the world's largest rain-forest is an added bonus.

Arriving in 1983 at the international airport we lacked that combatant mentality, but it felt good to be back in Brazil with a new river to explore. The customs officers did not spoil that pleasure by asking us to open the canoe box, or Tanis and Martin's large holdall, or questioning us about the pharmacy of medicines we were carrying. Nor did the taxi drivers moan, complain or charge us extra for the problem of getting our bulky gear to the city centre.

During the taxi ride I noticed how the city had grown, and that much of the new suburban sprawl consisted of additions to the motels catering for sexual liaisons. These hotels charge by the hour, and generally have circular beds, orange lighting that is reckoned to be the most flattering to one's skin, luxurious bathrooms, and ample TVs or radios so that unfaithful husbands who are supposed to be at the football match can return home at least knowing the score. Video cameras are also on offer to record one's performance.

We had a lot of preparations and shopping to do in Manaus and that meant a lot of walking. The heat was unbelievable and our activities too hectic for gradual acclimatisation. So we trooped around with sticking shirts and sweat running down our faces, and occasionally found that the only relief was to go into an air-conditioned bank on some pretext or other. Our appetites diminished, and over the next two weeks our flesh dripped away, leaving us leaner and more comfortable. Neither Tanis, Martin nor Mark had been to Manaus before, so we did the sights. There aren't many of them, and the opera house (Teatro Amazonas) is more interesting for the period it represents than for architectural merit. It was finished in 1896 in the extraordinary period when Amazonia held a world monopoly in rubber; an era of ostentation, extravagance and bad taste.

Of course the rubber tree, *Hevea Brasiliensis*, had always been in Amazonia, but apart from a certain curiosity value for the product in the shape of erasers and rubber balls, demand was very small at the beginning of the last century. However two scientific developments changed all that. In 1839 Charles Goodyear developed the vulcanisation process that kept rubber consistently pliable (before that it became stiff in the cold and soft in the heat), and more importantly, John Dunlop invented the pneumatic tyre in 1888.

Suddenly rubber was in huge demand, for footwear, raincoats and tyres for bicycles, as well as for the emergent motor industry. The collection of raw rubber from trees scattered through the jungle required a huge network of tappers and traders, covering almost every tributary from the mouth of the Amazon to Bolivia. Local Indians were used, but the drought-ridden northeast of Brazil provided most of the work force. These men fell easy prey to the rubber bosses, and were tricked into a form of debt dependency that was little more than slavery. To get to his new place of work and equip himself with a gun, machete, hammock and staple foods, the tapper or *seringueiro* needed an advance from his boss. After that, however much rubber he collected, he never quite managed to erase the debt because he periodically needed to make new purchases (from the company store of course). And instead of making the fortune he had been promised, he never broke even.

The life of the seringueiro was, and still is, a hard and lonely one. Usually on his own up some pestilential tributary, perhaps with hostile Indians nearby, his days began before dawn. He followed the hilly, swampy trail from tree to tree, cutting a 'V' in each trunk and placing a cup underneath. Several hours later he would return home for a quick lunch and then it would be time for him to go round and empty the latex from each cup. Finally, before he could rest, he had to sit over a fire for an hour or two solidifying the latex on a slowly-rotating ball in the smoke. His life was usually short, and the chance of escape almost nil.

From all this forgotten, unacknowledged labour, however, Manaus and a new breed of foreign and Brazilian rubber barons made a fortune. In 1897 $49 million worth of rubber was shipped from Manaus alone, and the city took 20 per cent in tax. Extravagances had to be imported from Europe — the latest fashions, food, wines and building materials. The barons competed with each other to build the flashiest private residence, although the pièce de résistance was the baroque opera house.

Yet as the traders were lighting their cigars with bank notes, the seeds of their decline had been sown. Literally. An Englishman, Henry Wickham, spent a year in Amazonia, and in 1876 left Belem with 70,000 smuggled *Havea* seeds. After some initial setbacks at London's Botanical Gardens in Kew, the new seedlings were eventually shipped to be planted in ordered plantations first in Ceylon and Singapore, and later throughout most of South East Asia. In 1906 Ceylon produced its first 500 tons (as opposed to Amazonia's 35,000 tons that year), but by 1914 the Asians dominated the market. In 1918 the Amazon produced 30,700 tons as opposed to Asia's 256,000. An Asian tapper could cover five times as many trees as he went down the ordered rows than the poor seringueiro stumbling along in the jungle gloom. Asian rubber was 50 per cent cheaper, and Manaus' decline was abrupt. Attempts to try and organise the cultivation of rubber trees in Amazonia, particularly by Henry Ford on the lower Tapajos, were frustrated when a leaf blight attacked the young trees. Fordlandia was abandoned in 1946.

During our stay there seemed to be very few travellers passing through Manaus, and I was glad I'd brought Mark with me and was not sitting forlornly waiting for a travelling companion. We did meet a very interesting American who was returning home after ten years in Latin America. He had his own farm in Belize until it was destroyed by a hurricane and he was buried under the ruins of his house (he had malaria at the time and hadn't heard the radio warnings). Then he had gone to Nicaragua and worked with the Sandinistas as a nurse, before spending four years as an agronomist in Paraguay.

Dick had been with the Special Forces in Vietnam, and his platoon had frequently parachuted behind enemy lines to gather information. He had completed his year's draft and returned to the States, but like so many other veterans found he could not adapt to civilian life and re-enlisted for a further year. He had also felt strongly that he had a responsibility towards the new recruits.

'After all it was only the long-timers who'd kept me alive when I first got to Nam,' he said. 'How could I leave those green kids without passing on my experience?'

When he heard Mark was an Australian he told us this story.

'One night my platoon was on a plane for a night drop into the North, and found four Australian guys already on board with an amphibious vehicle.

'After a few hours' flight the light came on, too early to be our signal. The Australians got up, climbed in the vehicle, and one of them turned to me as they fastened their seat belts and yelled out "Clunk Click every trip", with a crazy grin. That phrase didn't mean much to me until an English newsman explained a few weeks later that it was a government advertisement for seat belts. Anyway, the big doors at the end of the plane opened, and with a whoop and a yell those Aussies just drove off the edge!

'My platoon sat there open-mouthed staring at the darkness beyond the doors. What a way to arrive in enemy-held swamps, tumbling down with only the vehicle's parachute! Shit, we thought we were a mean bunch of bastards, but those Australians were something else.'

Mark could have talked on to Dick for hours about the thrill of combat, the whiff of cordite and weaponry. I was to try many times to dissuade him from army life over the next few weeks, but made no headway. It was a mystery to me how someone could enjoy the freedom and irresponsibility of three years' travelling, and then voluntarily submit to the abuse of some square-headed drill-sergeant. Mark was determined he could. Anyway at that stage I was pleased to find riddles in Mark's character. Subject for future camp-fire conversations.

We didn't have much time for chatting: we had shopping to do. We were leaving the bulk of the food supplies for later, but in Manaus we had to buy polyester resin, tools for making the canoe, rope and machetes, plastic cups, knives, hammocks, mosquito nets, ammunition and shotguns. A few years earlier any foreigner in Brazil could walk into a shop and buy a firearm over the counter. Not any longer. Now it was a lengthy business that had us running from office to office, pleading and cajoling. A shotgun was an essential item. Without it we'd be unable to supplement our diet with fresh meat. We'd be unable to defend ourselves if attacked. We knew that supposing we couldn't get one legally, we'd have to find one illegally. However after two days we obtained the authorisation to purchase one.

In the evenings the four of us would have our large meal of the day and drink a few beers at one of Manaus' good restaurants. We savoured the last few days of comfort, varied food, ice-cold beers and above all, each other's company. We found ourselves clutching at pretexts for delaying our departure. We admitted to feeling a bit scared about what lay in store. We were well-prepared, with some experience, but obviously there were risks. We would be so far from help that even a minor accident could prove fatal. If unlucky, we might wreck the canoe in a rapid, or lose most of our equipment, get seriously ill or break a limb. We might be attacked by Indians. We joked about such fears, but our stay in Manaus lasted ten days instead of the five we had originally planned.

Finally we forced ourselves on to a river-boat going downstream. Mark and I were going all the way to Santarem. Martin and Tanis would get off at Obidos. We made thirteen trips between the hotel and boat with all our gear, and our manoeuvres did not escape the notice of the boat's captain. He informed me that he would be charging freight. How much he didn't tell us till the following day. 'Fifty dollars for the outboard motor,' he said, pointing to Martin and Tanis' new purchase, 'and twenty-five dollars for that long box over there' (our canoe).

'But that's ridiculous,' I exploded, genuinely shocked. This wasn't a ritual prelude to some good-natured haggling. Seventy-five dollars would have cleaned out our kitty.

'I have the right to charge fifteen per cent of the value of any cargo on board, and I know the cost price of that Yamaha outboard motor.'

'What's in the box then?' I asked, pointing at the canoe kit. Of course he had no idea, so I pressed on.

'You don't know what's in it, or what it's worth, so how do you arrive at the figure of twenty-five dollars?'

'This is my boat, I am the captain. You will pay or I'll call the police at the next stop.'

I consulted with Martin, Tanis and Mark. It was unfortunate that I was the only one in our group who spoke Portuguese, being the least suitable to handle delicate negotiations. Dealings with authority, especially with policemen, have got me into a lot of trouble in the past while travelling in the Third World. I find it very hard to be civil with such uncivil characters. I only have to see one of those swaggering, brutal cops with mirrored sunglasses and a sort of red mist descends. I want to go and knock his beret off. Fortunately Brazil is not notorious by Latin American standards. I spoke to the captain a second time, and this time he told me he had the right to charge 10 per cent of any cargo.

'Ah, come on, you're inventing the first number that comes into your head!' I yelled. We were on the bridge of the vessel, and our argument was watched by three of his crew who were on duty. One of them was grinning broadly at me as I yelled at his captain, urging me on with shadow-boxing encouragement from behind the captain's back.

'Just because we're gringos, you think we're made of money and are out to fleece us!'

The little man puffed out his chest.

'I've been travelling these waters for thirty years!' he shouted, quivering with rage. 'I've trained for this job, studied and know this river. I've transported hundreds of thousands of people safely up and down it. Never, never, in my twenty-five years of service, has anyone called me a *bandido* before.'

Impasse. We retreated to our respective corners and I calmed down. I decided on the psychological approach, shook him by the hand, patted him on the shoulder, and apologised for any offence, which of course had been unintentional. But surely he understood that we'd been shocked at those charges, that we hadn't budgeted for them (which was true enough), and that we were very short of money?

At this moment Tanis managed to squeeze out a tear, no doubt of pity at seeing me grovelling so abjectly, and the mood immediately became warmer. He had not realised we were English, he said. He thought we were Americans. The English had always done a lot for Brazil (he obviously had not heard of Henry Wickham), unlike those damn Yankees who only plundered. He dropped the charges to $20 for the motor and $10 for the canoe. Still too much, but it seemed we would get it no lower.

At 2 am on the second night we arrived at Obidos, and said farewell to Martin and Tanis. It was a sad moment. I was going to miss them. Also, as we embraced in the chill night as they stood surrounded by their piles of gear on the quayside, the focus of where we were going suddenly sharpened. It was no longer a mere jaunt. We were all thinking it would be a long time before we met again, and that, at the worst, we might never meet again.

Mark and I arrived in Santarem at dawn the next day. We checked into a hotel and began the quest for a place to assemble the canoe. One of the nice things about being a foreigner in South America is that people expect you to behave eccentrically. We spied some houses with good big gardens and knocked at the doors explaining our needs. We were regarded with no little suspicion. Not on their property thank you. They edged the door shut while dredging up numerous factors that made their particular garden unsuitable for our purposes. Undaunted we approached a large college on a hillside and spoke to a man sitting in the gardens. He let me explain my requirements in Portuguese before revealing that he was an American priest. The whole college was run by the Order of the Holy Cross with ten or fifteen Americans. They very kindly offered us the use of a thatched, open-sided shelter with a flat earth floor that was ideal. They also opened up a store room for us to lock away all our materials at night. We could not have asked for a better place, and the college was closed for the holiday so we would not be surrounded by hundreds of kids as we worked.

In England we had wondered how we would transport the assembled canoe from Santarem to the mouth of the Jari, 250 kilometres downstream. Perhaps we would have to take the Belem boat and be dropped off on the opposite bank to paddle right across the Amazon at nearly its widest point . . . not an idea that we relished. However, when we walked along the waterfront enquiring about boats, we found there was one direct to Monte Dourado (paper magnate Ludwig's town 100 kilometres up the Jari). Things seemed to be clicking into place.

We set to work at once. Neither of us had used fibreglass before and we were apprehensive that we would waste a lot of resin before we got the hang of it. The ratio of resin to catalyst was crucial: too much catalyst and the mixture would solidify in the pot before we had time to apply it. The ratio also varied according to the air temperature. We bought a calibrated baby's bottle and only in fact wasted about a quarter of a litre.

Assembling the canoe gave us a feeling of personal involvement in the project that we would have missed in buying a ready-made model. Moreover, talking to the manufacturers had led to modifications before we started, so that we could include water-proof hatches and extra strengthening, and position the seats just where we wanted them. But we were well aware that the finished craft was going to depend on our workmanship in assembly. We took our time over it.

Those kits are ingenious. The pieces of the hull are supplied cut to shape, and have to be joined together by a combination of stitching, wire twists and fibreglass tape. To make the canoe extra strong, we lined the inside with fibreglass matting. It is more effective inside than out since it stands less chance of being scraped off. It was fun and interesting to do, and pretty straightforward, and although it was hot, sweaty work and we were irked by inadequate tools, at the end of six days we had produced quite a fine craft.

Only one problem. We had underestimated the quantity of resin we would need for the job. We had bought two extra litres to allow for repairs on the trip, but the internal matting soaked up so much that to do the job adequately we had to use it all up. There was nowhere to buy any more unless we made a special trip back to Manaus or Belem.

We did buy some pitch to take with us, but that seemed a poor substitute. It would cover small holes and scrapes, but if something drastic happened, like the canoe breaking in half, it would be worthless.

I had a very narrow escape when we were tidying up at the college after finishing the canoe. We had a lot of liquid catalyst left over and I wanted somewhere to pour it all away. I found an oil-drum which was used for rubbish and I started to empty the bottle into it. Fortunately a little puff of steam gave me a second's warning. I stepped back just in time, as a mushroom fireball whooshed 10 feet above the top of the drum, singeing my hair and eye-brows. Then I saw the bottom of the drum still had hot ashes from a fire that morning. If it hadn't steamed and warned my turgid brain, I'd have ended up in the burns unit of Santarem hospital — if they had such a thing. I didn't know then that our trip was later to be drastically affected by a bad burn.

We carried the finished craft down to the river Amazon for trials, and the canoe looked very handsome with its coats of gleaming varnish. Would it float? In front of the crowd that had gathered we would look bloody silly if it didn't. We launched the canoe-with-no-name on to the Amazon, and to our joy and pride it floated without listing or leaks. Unfortunately the water-tight compartments were not quite water-tight, and, as we had no more fibre-glass to rectify that, we decided that instead of keeping cameras in them we would use them for storing tins of food. While making the canoe we had five or six kids who helped us, and a lovable bunch of rascals they were. We rewarded them with rides along the waterfront, and this was the perfect way to find out the canoe's carrying capacity without risking our belongings. We tested how many kids could be fitted in with the canoe still afloat, and then took them to a chemist to be weighed in on the scales. The canoe could take 400 kilos comfortably. Just as well, because our hotel room was be-coming congested with supplies.

When planning how much food you'll need for six months you have to think big, even if you plan mainly to live off the land as we did. We had to take rice, beans, spaghetti, oats, wheatflour, sugar, salt, coffee, tea, spices, cooking oil, garlic, onions, powdered milk, drinking chocolate and rum. Then there were pots and pans, torch batteries, water containers, machetes, rope, string, tools, clothing, spare paddles, knives, sharpening stones, books, mos-quito repellent, fishing rod, reel and tackle, shotgun, 200 cartridges, presents for Indians, plastic sheets, hammocks, mosquito nets and blankets, medical supplies, photographic equipment and other bits and pieces. It all added up to an alarming pile. Altogether would it weigh more or less than six kids? We would not know until we reached Monte Dourado and loaded the canoe.

I would have liked to take abundant reading material with me into the jungle, but the limitations of weight prevented such a luxury. It is difficult to choose the ideal book for a trip. We had brought a few hefty novels, but they would only last a few days each. We had also searched for something more substantial that could be read in fits and starts. I opted for 'A History of the World' by M. Roberts, a formidable piece of scholarship well over a thousand pages long. It was going to fill in a lot of gaps in my knowledge, and I'd be unlikely to read more than twenty pages at any one sitting.

Mark's choice was bizarre, and the source of a great deal of teasing on my part. In pride of place he had brought Debrett's 'Etiquette and Modern Manners'. A weird choice of book for the sort of trip where one generally goes naked, eats with one's fingers and becomes uninhibited about releasing wind and picking one's nose. I'd glanced at parts of it — what to wear at Ascot and Wimbledon, the duties of best man, how to handle funeral arrangements, and the correct way to tackle an artichoke and a plate of spaghetti. I wasn't sure whether I should be sufficiently bored in the jungle to face Debrett, but Mark clearly felt that spare time should be spent on self-improvement. Second on his list was an English grammar. Finally there was a depressing little manual on emergency war surgery. This was full of colourful descriptions of the devastation caused by tumbling high velocity bullets, and contained detailed instructions on how to carry out an amputation in the field.

Before we left England Mark had assembled an excellent medical kit. We had suturing for wounds, plaster for broken limbs, antibiotics for infection, ampoules for local anaesthetic and pain-killers, adrenalin to combat shock, anti-histamines for allergies, eye-drops and creams, multi-vitamins, pills for tape-worm and other parasitical infections, quinine and chloroquine for malaria, temporary fillings for teeth, and a large assortment of dressings. He also spent some time with doctors learning how to administer an injection, set a broken limb and so on. He told me that in cases of coma after a head injury a build-up of blood can occur in the skull, and that after a few days this should be drained by getting out the old Swiss Army knife and drilling a little hole in the skull. I drew the line there. I'd rather he let my coma run its course, thank you very much, I told him.

We had four days' wait before the river-boat arrived. In the Third World, travelling is often synonymous with waiting, and I find this harder and harder to take. They had told us the boat would arrive in two days, but it finally turned up after four. We had not pinned too many hopes on the original timetable so were not unduly disappointed. In South America two days late is approaching punctuality. However Santarem was a boring little place to spend our last moments in civilisation. We could eat well, swim in the river Tapajos with its beautiful squeaky sandy beaches and blue water, and get a little drunk each night, but time dragged and we were keen to get going.

At last we were strapping the canoe on the river-boat. There followed a pleasant and uneventful trip for a day and two nights to Monte Dourado. Compared to some Amazon river-boats this one was relatively empty, the food was edible, and the journey short enough to be bearable. Having spent a total of more than two months of my life on such boats, the thrill, if there ever was a thrill, has gone. The engine thumps, the jungle flows monotonously past, the kids howl, and waiting for your next bland meal is the highlight of the day. The ceilings are so low that after a few days you disembark with lumps on the head and curvature in the spine. Then there are competing radios and cassette players to contend with and the stinking toilets. What a disappointment Amazonia must be to the many tourists who confine themselves to a trip up the Amazon by river-boat and a stop at Manaus.

On both sides of the lower Jari lies the land of Jari Florestal e Agropecuaria – the concern headed, until 1982, by American billionaire Daniel Ludwig. He purchased 35 million acres in 1967 for $3 million, at a time when the new military government of Brazil was fully committed to a policy of attracting foreign capital. Ludwig anticipated a world paper shortage in the 1980s and the major part of his operation was the production of pulp for export. He cleared 250,000 hectares and planted them with three fast-growing species of tree: melina, Caribbean pine and eucalyptus. The former apparently grows to 6 metres high and 8 centimetres in diameter in a mere twelve months. To make these new plantations, he built 4,200 kilometres of road, 36 kilometres of railway, and three airfields. The pulp mill and power plant were assembled on barge-like hulls in Japan and towed 23,300 kilometres across the Indian and Atlantic oceans by tug – a journey that took three months. That was typical of Ludwig's style. Thought to be America's richest man, he pumped an estimated billion dollars into the project over the thirteen years before he pulled out. Apart from the pulp operations he planted a large area of floodplain with rice, and discovered the third-largest Kaolin deposits in the world on his land – a bonus he said he knew nothing about when he bought it.

The project attracted a lot of criticism from the beginning, chiefly from Brazilians who resented the acquisition of such a huge area by a foreign concern. As Ludwig refused to allow visitors during the first years of development, rumours abounded as to what was really going on there. Secondly there was criticism from ecologists concerned about the rapid deforestation of Amazonia. Would not Jari become a failure like so many other grandiose projects in the region, ending only in the bequest of useless, worked-out desert to future generations of Brazilians? When the delicate tropical rainforest was replaced with three species of foreign tree would not disease and blight run riot down the ordered rows – as had happened in Fordlandia? Surely the fragile soils would not be able to support single-species cultivation for long?

Many of the people who were initially hostile to the project seemed to change their views when they were finally allowed to look for themselves. Certainly Ludwig had the capital, resources and expert staff to assess each stage of development, and to research and have overcome most of the problems. The danger was that he would attract less than expert imitators in other parts of Amazonia. He employed over 13,000 people at the peak of the operation. But that was mainly for the temporary work of clearing, and the

BEIRADAO

number of employees dropped to about 4,000 as he was forced to make economies.

Most of Ludwig's plans for expansion failed to come to fruition. Power was generated by burning timber and the bark from the trees he was about to pulp, but he was applying for permission to build a dam on the Jari to provide hydro-electric power. He planned ultimately to extend the 10,000 acres of rice to 35,000, thus producing 140,000 tons a year, and by means of poultry-, cattle- and pig-rearing to make the project self-sufficient in food.

Yet despite all this huge investment Jari was losing an estimated $100 million a year by 1980. There had been setbacks with the melina which had not grown as fast as anticipated on the sandy soils. Hundreds of millions of dollars more would have to be invested before the project became viable, and even then there would continue to be uncertainty. Ludwig appealed to the Brazilian government to be guarantor for the import of a second pulp mill. It refused. It also delayed in giving him the definitive legal title to about half the land, and refused to grant him the necessary $6 million a year to pay for the running of the hospitals, schools and other social amenities he was providing.

In 1982 Ludwig passed control over to a consortium of twenty-three of Brazil's largest companies. The government itself put in $180 million. Yet that solved little except to save Brazilian face and pride. To be a viable concern the pulp output would have to be doubled or trebled. All Ludwig can expect to recoup is a small percentage of any profits from 1987 to 2021, and it seems unlikely that there will be any.

3 Early days

Mark and I would have liked to stay a few days at Monte Dourado to look around. However we had no letters of introduction or contacts and we were particularly nervous that some official might demand to see our authorisation to travel up the Jari. The longer we hung around, and the longer our canoe was left moored at the jetty, the more risk we ran of arousing unwelcome curiosity. We had not even applied for authorisation being certain it would not be granted. We were planning to canoe into a 'security area' (any of Brazil's border areas), thence to cross a frontier that had no controls – or so we hoped – and possibly to cross through an Indian area too. Even had we been a large and prestigious group I doubt whether permission would have been granted. Best, we felt, to go pleading innocence and ignorance, and hope to meet no officialdom.

As we unloaded the canoe at the waterfront of Monte Dourado that morning, we could see a police post only 100 metres away with a policeman lounging in the doorway. A crowd of onlookers was gathering.

'Where are you going?' one shouted.

'Oh fifty kilometres or so up there' we gestured vaguely, 'to make a camp and fish for a few weeks.' It must have seemed an awful lot of stuff we were loading into the canoe for a mere fishing trip, but we continued with indecent haste. The present financial state of the Jari project and the successes or otherwise of the operation since it changed hands, issues we were keen to look into before, held no further interest. We wanted to be off, round that bend, out of sight, out of mind.

We launched the canoe in trepidation, not sure whether the canoe would be able to take it all, and us as well. We dreaded climbing in and sinking to the bottom in front of all these spectators. However, much to our relief the water level rose to an inch below the gunwales and stayed there. We grabbed paddles, waved and departed. Past the police post we went, expecting every instant to hear a shouted command and see some uniformed figure coming down the bank. Nothing. Within five minutes we were round the bend and could breathe more easily. At least we had not been stopped before we started.

Fortunately for our debut the river was calm and slow-moving, and in fact with this canoe we seemed to go as fast upstream as I had gone down in the heavy plank canoes I used on previous trips. The river was about 100 metres wide, the water greeny-black, and apart from one or two glimpses of Ludwig's plantations on the hillsides the jungle along the banks was intact.

Paddling a canoe is hard work for the first few days. There can be few muscles in the upper body that are not called into play – but the back, shoulders and arms ache most. With the sun beating down it is not too much fun until the right muscles get into shape. It never becomes exactly fun, but one develops a rhythm that can be kept up easily for five or six hours a day. So that day we felt absolutely shattered by the time we stopped to make our first camp. We still had to sort out all our gear properly. The food (all treble-wrapped in plastic bags) we put into a large zippered nylon sack. That stayed in the canoe every night along with our two back-packs, and a polystyrene box that held our medical supplies and film. A large kit bag held everything we would need in the way of clothing and bedding each night. Another bag held small quantities of all the staples (rice, beans, sugar, salt, oil, coffee etc) that we would need for cooking at each stop. A third bag held our camera equipment, a small first-aid kit, books, notebooks, and shotgun cartridges. One final sack held all the cooking utensils.

As we stopped and brewed up a cup of coffee I felt an itching on my ankle, looked down and cursed.

'What's the matter?' asked Mark.

'That,' I said, pointing at my ankle.

'I don't see anything,' he replied, and then peering closer, 'you mean that little fly there?'

I explained about the pium fly: not much to look at admittedly, but the winged scourge of day-time Amazonia. It can make tough men break down and weep or leap fully-clothed into the river, and draw forth a string of obscenities from the lips of the saintliest man. They obviously did not have them in Africa — otherwise Katherine Hepburn would have gone through the film 'African Queen' fouler-mouthed than Bogart.

Mark's eyebrows rose in scepticism as he regarded the little speck that was now struggling to get airborne with its load of blood.

'Doesn't look much,' he muttered, but soon he was scratching his arms and legs where little spots of blood and welts marked each bite.

Pium flies had taken a lot of pleasure out of my trips in Mato Grosso, especially on the section of the river Teles Pires where they had forced us to travel fully-clothed with sleeves rolled down, trousers tucked into socks, and often towels wrapped over our heads. No fun in the heat. It was ominous to see them so soon on this trip, although they only attacked when ashore. Thankfully, after the first week we never saw them again. Their place was taken by mosquitoes. More about these little bastards later.

We slung our hammocks and mosquito nets, finding a 'triangle' of trees that allowed us to tie both hammocks to the same tree at one end and to different ones at the other. This is a sociable arrangement, and facilitates the use of the plastic sheet to cover us from the rain. We had brought two of the colourful local hammocks and they are very comfortable once you are accustomed to sleeping on your back. The mosquito nets, while stuffy on a warm night, are absolutely essential in most areas of Amazonia. They are specially made to fit the hammocks: you can tie the netting around the ropes to stop ants and other creepy-crawlies, as well as mosquitoes, from getting in. The chore is keeping them in good repair after nightly contact with thorns.

We cooked spaghetti for supper. We had no energy for fishing, and being so near to town there was of course no game. Once settled in the hammocks listening to the familiar jungle noises it felt good to be back after three years. All the aching muscles, the sting of sunburn and itch of bites could not overcome the feeling of excitement at being on our way at last.

The next day we paddled steadily, passing a few houses until in the afternoon we could hear the roar of rapids up ahead. We had been helped by the tide in the morning, which for a while kindly reversed the current for us. We were over 250 kilometres from the sea at this point, but the tide caused a rise and fall of at least a metre. A man fishing from a canoe told us that the sound of rushing water we could hear was the falls of Santo Antonio.

'Will we have to portage round them?' we asked.

He chuckled. 'Well, they'd be hard to paddle up.'

For 2 kilometres the roar increased, but the river twisted and turned and always hid the falls from sight. On one of these bends was a small cemetery, and towering over the humble crosses was one ornately carved and bearing a swastika. Curious, we stopped and went ashore, and found there had been a German Jari Expedition in 1932. This individual had died of fever. Either he had not got very far, or else had died on the way back with not much further to go. I remarked idly that the cross must have been erected later on: it was not the sort of cross expedition members could knock up in a day or so.

'Perhaps,' Mark said, 'they left Germany with one already prepared for each member just in case,' and our sacreligious laughter echoed across the graveyard.

Soon we saw the falls and understood why the guy in the canoe had laughed. The river dropped vertically for over 25 metres, and a haze of spray hung over the gorge. We passed the few dilapidated buildings of the village of Santo Antonio, and fought the cross currents below the falls looking for a place to begin our portage. We found an inlet on the right bank that looked as though it had been used for that purpose.

We made camp, and went for a reccy. From the water's edge there was a steep, vertical scramble up the 25 metres to the top of the falls, then 300 metres through jungle, followed by a tricky section through shallow water littered with slippery rocks, and then across an old clearing to finally emerge on a large track. We went no further that evening, assuming that the track would join the river upstream after a few hundred metres. Next morning we discovered how wrong we were. That track went on for over 4 kilometres — past another set of rapids, before finally reaching calm water. It was going to be a hard day.

We made four trips each with our gear, and what a lot of it there was. Filling our packs to capacity with 30 to 35 kilos, we struggled up the bank, clinging on to rocks and saplings, hearts threatening to burst, then advanced by hopping from rock to rock across the shallows and finally to the trail. Once there at least we were on level ground, but these were early days and we had been lazy about training for this trip. Rubber-legged we tottered along, sweat plopping steadily into the dust and pium and ticks feasting on our bare legs and torsos. Forty-five minutes later were would arrive at the end, drop the load and plunge into the river where we sat until we could face the walk back. We walked over 30 kilometres that day, half the time laden like mules, but by late afternoon we had everything portaged except the canoe. We struggled up the bank with it, which in our weary state was three steps up two back down, with the cheering possibility of toppling to the bottom and the canoe smashing on top of us. We got it over the other obstacles and a few hundred metres further up the trail before our muscles gave out and we abandoned the task till next morning.

Mark had come through the first test with flying colours. He had carried huge loads, and from his comments I gathered he was trying out the sort of burdens under which the troops had yomped in the Falklands. He was proving an excellent beast of burden, and cheerful company too.

It was nearly dark and we still had to make camp that night and cook some food, but the end of the trail was an open grassy bank with no trees for the hammocks. So we had to lay them on the ground, fix up mosquito nets with sticks, and put plastic sheeting above that. We were just in time, and before we started the cooking, down came the rain. Oh what a jolly end to a fun day! Uncomfortable, hungry and absolutely exhausted, we downed a couple of mugs of rum, sweating under our shelter as if we were in a sauna. The rum got us giggly and we forgot our troubles and laughed and joked. It rained all night. Some Brazilians passed – they had been out in a canoe to position fishing nets, and we all laughed together at our unorthodox shelter which was, moreover, proving to be ineffective, with water seeping upwards from our feet.

Next day it took over an hour to coax a fire into life using every trick in the book. On a past trip some Brazilians showed me the most effective and economical fire-lighters. An old inner tyre tube scrounged from a garage or bicycle shop, if cut into small pieces, will burn long enough to get a fire going in most circumstances. With dry kindling a piece less than a centimetre square is enough, but that morning we still had difficulties. We scraped the wet bark off twigs searching for the dry interior. We shaved off dry chippings. We got through a lot of rubber. Eventually we coaxed a reluctant fire into life. In all it took an hour and a half to get a cup of tea, and nostalgia was growing for the high-speed electric kettle. It needed several brews of tea and coffee to get us moving, and we used the excuse of drying out the gear before we went to collect the canoe. Meanwhile the fishermen returned bearing three huge armoured catfish which they tied to a pole and carried home on their shoulders with the tails of the fish dragging along the ground.

The next part of the river was full of rocks just below the surface, and there was not enough current to set up warning ripples. We paddled gently but rammed several and hit others with our paddles. These we had brought out from England and they were a joy to use — 1.5 metres long and very light. But we were worried that it wouldn't need many days of this sort to crack the blades. We strapped them with insulating tape to prevent splitting.

Officially this was supposed to be the dry season, which in Amazonia begins in May and ends in November or December. It was now the beginning of July and so it really should not have been raining at all. Yet rain it did almost every day for the first five weeks of our trip, and they were often torrential downpours lasting several hours. I have found that if a shower catches you while on the river it's no great problem so long as it stops before you get too chilled. The sun comes out, and everything steams and dries within an hour. The jungle, however, continues dripping for many hours afterwards and everything ends up sodden.

The dry season usually means day after day of cloudless skies. The jungle floor becomes tinder dry, and a plastic sheet is not necessary at each camp. However the Jari was never predictable as we were to learn over the next few months. Perhaps the extra rain was due to its proximity to the Atlantic? Certainly the bad weather came from the east.

We were without fish for the first few days. On previous trips I had relied on hand-lines with pieces of fish for bait. But you have to catch one fish in order to catch others. We tried water-snails, crickets, bugs and grubs with no luck, so we finally shot a medium-sized bird and used that to catch a 'pintado', a grey-and-black-striped catfish. However it was a long time before we started to catch fish regularly. I had decided for this trip that a rod, reel and spinners would make a less messy way of getting fish and be more fun. I wanted to avoid always having some rank piece of bait turning green and stinking in the bottom of the canoe. However during the first days the spinner did not seem to deceive the Jari fish, so instead we ate large quantities of rice, beans and spaghetti.

On the fifth day out we were getting the hang of it all. There was a strong tail of wind for much of the day, creating quite a swell and white horses, but we felt secure enough in the canoe. The river was wider here — over 200 metres — and seeing a large house ahead we stayed on the opposite bank still being paranoid about officialdom. We could see people waving at us, perhaps signalling that we should call in, and someone fired a shot in the air, but we just waved back and kept on going. Perhaps it was an invitation to lunch, but that did not seem worth the risk of too many questions.

To our alarm a few minutes later we saw a motorboat coming up behind us with a man in the bow training binoculars on us. They drew alongside, three men and a woman, and it was the latter who did most of the talking — or rather most of the questioning. We had no map of the first section of the Jari, since ours began at a point where a tributary called the Ipitinga joins, so we told them were were going up to near that confluence to camp and fish.

Amazement was expressed. 'Long way.' 'Lot of rapids.' But I was warily watching the man with the binoculars who sat there in silence regarding us unsmilingly. It was only through the woman that we learnt he was one of the two remaining American technicians working on Ludwig's project, and a surly, morose character he was too. When he did finally speak it was like an interrogation, punctuated by barks of scornful laughter at our plans. It was a sweltering hot midday, and the son of a bitch had the cheek to reach into a cooler and pull out a beer in front of us. Just the one. Plop, fizz, went the ring pull, and the can covered with pearly droplets as it came into contact with the hot air. We sat mesmerized as he drank deeply, sighed contentedly, and wiped the froth off his lips with the back of his hand. When it became clear that we were not going to be offered one we decided we had no reason to put up with his ill-mannered interrogation any longer and departed on our way. Later on, we discovered that he had reported us to the authorities in Monte Dourado for acting suspiciously.

We had, however, gathered a bit of information about the river from the Indian boatman. It seemed that the Ipitinga was a major gold-prospecting area, and that the section up to there had at least four major rapids. Also these gold fields were serviced by motorised canoes, so we were liable to see a lot of people in the week or so that he reckoned it would take us to reach Ipitinga. After that, on the Jari, there were no more camps and no more people.

I went for the first hunt of the trip that afternoon — clambering up the steep hillside behind our camp for over 40 metres. Naturally I made a tremendous din and all the animals scurried out of my way. Hunting in the jungle is a very tricky business, and I am full of admiration for those who do it well. Visibility is reduced to about 30 or 40 metres, often less, and if an animal stays still it is almost impossible to spot. Movement is the great betrayer, and as the hunter has to cover a large section of forest he has to betray himself all the time. Also he has to try and walk silently over a carpet of leaves and debris, forcing his way past bushes and creepers that clutch at clothing and rarely let him take an unhindered step. It seems an impossible task to me even now after many dozens of hours spent in the pursuit.

From speaking to good Amazonian hunters I have learned that they usually go barefoot, walk very slowly, about 5 metres a minute, and pause frequently to look or listen for movement. I have tried all that, but generally the only creatures I manage to slaughter are birds and monkeys, either too curious, or over-confident of their safety in the trees. As for deer which are common in the jungle, well I often see them bounding well out of range. How the hell do hunters manage to get within shotgun range of an animal that has all its senses in tip-top working order? Beats me.

I do find hunting quite enjoyable though, despite my lack of success. I have never hunted anywhere else in the world, and feel no urge to do so. Hunting for the pot, however, carries a degree of necessity and urgency and occasionally I do find myself moving well in the jungle. I seem to be flitting through it for a change instead of fighting it, and briefly I feel silent and deadly. I scan the forest with eagle eyes, my hearing acute. I am floating almost soundlessly over the ground, I am confident that at any moment I am going to stumble upon a snoring deer and return with abundant meat to feed my brood. John the city boy transformed to woodsman. Usually the feeling of proficiency ends abruptly when I trip over a creeper, fall through a rotten log or get tangled in a thorny thicket. But when I see some potential victim and sneak up to get in position, the adrenalin and excitement make me quiver like a jelly. At that moment I understand why people hunt for sport. However, when I retrieve the bloody heap of feathers or fur the emotion is at once replaced by sadness and guilt.

That day I followed the ridge at the top of the hill for a while before the ground dropped to a marshy hollow. So far all I had seen was a bush turkey that flew up and away, and soaked with sweat I was beginning to wonder why I bothered. I paused by a large tree, rested the gun and squatted down to roll a cigarette. A movement made me glance up. There was a wild pig trotting my way, 40 metres off and brisky narrowing the gap. Later I cursed myself for my slowness in responding. The animal could not have scented me and movements on my part would not have alarmed it too much. However I reached with ridiculous slowness for the gun, cocked it and began to raise it to my shoulder. The click made the pig stop 10 metres away, nose up and twitching, and looking straight at me. Oh how slow I was! A smooth raise to the shoulder, bang, and it would have been pork chops for the boys. However the gun was still only halfway to my shoulder when the pig turned without panic and trotted away. A tree hid it from sight for a while and by the time it reappeared it was just out of range.

Mark was passionately interested in firearms and made little attempt to conceal his scorn for our cheap shotgun. This was a single-barrelled 20-gauge of Brazilian manufacture. Robust and uncomplicated, it was a good weapon for jungle conditions in my opinion. But the hammer had to be cocked before each shot, and that was its one defect. That 'click' could sometimes sound deafening when stalking any nervous creature.

Mark gave me lengthy dissertations on the ideal choice of firearm for our situation. They all seemed to be Magnum something or others and to have the ability to blow doors off barns. If you hit some small creature you would be picking fur and feathers out of the trees in a 100-metre radius.

When I returned to camp still cursing my stupidity Mark felt motivated to go on a hunt himself, his first in the jungle. I watched in amusement as he put on his heavy jacket, strapped on the compass, stuffed his pockets with cartridges and set off full of optimism and assurances that I should prepare a hot fire for tonight's roast.

Three-quarters of an hour later he was back, sweaty, scratched, empty-handed and disillusioned.

'How the hell can you hunt in that stuff?' he muttered, and for the rest of the trip he never tried hunting again.

'Of course it's not like shooting kangaroos from the back of a landrover,' I jibed cruelly. In all fairness though, Mark at over 2 metres tall was not built for the jungle. Even at 1.85 metres or so I am too tall. The ideal is the Indian's stature of a little over 1.6 metres.

From now on our progress up the river became more and more difficult. We asked the one or two passing boatmen about the river up ahead and they all mentioned a large rapid called 'Tracaja', which would need a portage and three or four others further on. That would have been all right, but there were dozens of areas of fast water that gave us problems and which the boatmen had not considered worth a mention. With a motor they might not have seemed so noticeable, but to the paddler they were a curse. We had to wade them holding the bow of the canoe, or if the water was too deep to get a secure footing, one of us had to go ahead with the rope while the other swam and guided the boat. The American had told us we would reach Tracaja the next day – but four days later we still had not arrived.

After negotiating a maze of channels with small rapids we emerged into a narrow sluggish river and having no detailed map we were concerned that we might have strayed from the main river. We passed two small rapids and then stopped. No boat had passed us all morning and that was unusual. We sat on some rocks and brewed tea while we considered what to do. We certainly did not want to go several days upstream only to have to return. We decided to retrace our steps, but after going back down one of the rapids we heard a motor and hailed the boatmen.

'Is this the Jari or one of its tributaries?' It must have seemed a dumb question, and the ruffians packed into their canoe regarded us stonily.

'Of course it's the Jari,' answered the *motorista*, cursing us under his breath, because in the process of stopping to speak to us his ancient outboard had died. We thanked him and turned around, but until we rounded the next bend we could see the guy repeatedly tugging at his starter cord, and no doubt insulting our particular parentage and all gringos in general.

We began to catch a few more fish, because rapids are where fish congregate in greatest numbers. My favourite is the tucunare – a beautiful yellow-green fish with a marking like an eye on its flank. It reminds me of the European perch in shape, and by its dorsal fin that becomes erect when the fish is angry or frightened. It is also a fine fighter. When filleted, coated in flour and fried it is delicious. We also caught a brown, scaly fish with pink eyes that I had never seen before. I later learnt it was a trairao, but for a few weeks we scientifically named it 'the bony bastard', and we were to catch many of them.

Amazonia is an angler's paradise, containing over 1,500 species of fish, making it by far the richest freshwater fishing area in the world. The Congo, for example, has a paltry 500 species, and all the rivers of Europe together only 150.

The pirarucu is the largest freshwater fish in the world, growing to more than 3 metres and 150 kilos. It is an unusual fish in other respects, caring for its young for the first four months of life by secreting a milky fluid from pores in its head. While it has gills it also has a lung, and comes up for air every three minutes. Its scales are bony and abrasive, and these make excellent nail files should you be worried about the effect of paddling on your manicure.

There are over 500 members of the catfish family in the Amazon — twenty-five times more than in the Mississippi. The largest is the piraiba, which attains over 2 metres and 100 kilos, and there have been cases of piraiba devouring swimming children. The surubim, pintado, pirarara and cuu-cuu are other catfish, some covered with armoured plates and with bony fins behind their gills that can be used to 'walk' across the jungle floor from one pool to another.

The matrincha is one of the best eating fish, because when it is boiled it gives off a rich, red sauce. The Brazilians say 'it has tomato sauce included.' Some fish have firm, red flesh that is indistinguishable from veal when cooked. Others seem to lack bone structure. They sag in your hands in a repulsive manner, and when opened up seem to have a disproportionate amount of intestines. Yet if the process of cleaning them does not make you throw up, they are good to eat.

Some species of fish — the tambaqui and pacu, for example — live on fruit, and can be seen splashing under trees when a breeze is shaking off the ripe fruit. They even raise the major portion of their bodies out of the water (without jumping) to pluck berries off overhanging branches. The take is instantaneous or not at all. The tambaqui is a large fish of up to 5 or 6 kilos, and fights furiously with its flattened shape catching the current and adding to the strain.

Naturally there are a lot of predators — and it was these that we caught on the spinners — tucunare, trairao, pirapopo, piranha, and others we never learnt the names of. A lot of times, to our surprise, we also caught pacu and tambaqui by this method, showing that they are not purely vegetarian.

That night, after filling up with fish and rice, I went down to the water's edge to rinse my plate and heard a scuttling in front of me in the dark. I stopped in mid-stride and called to Mark to bring a torch. There a metre away was a large tarantula 12 centimetres across, rocking slightly on its hairy legs. It was debating whether to run away, and that made three of us. There is a temptation, a primeval urge almost, to kill any poisonous creature on sight, especially if it is threatening your territory. This we overcame as we were feeling benevolent and in harmony with all God's creatures. Instead we shooed it into the undergrowth with much banging of saucepans and encouragements. Mark in fact used to keep a pet bird-eating spider in his bedroom in England and has an affinity for these creatures. He said it had been entertaining to try the spider-in-the-bath routine when he had a girl visiting him.

Later that night I regretted not killing the tarantula because I kept imagining it was creeping up inside my mosquito net, or at the very least would be in my shoe in the morning. Tarantulas are not particularly venomous, actually, but to have one trot across one's face in the night might banish peaceful slumber for a lifetime.

After two portages and a lot of struggle we finally came to the Tracaja rapid. The river fell at 45 degrees over a drop of about 15 metres, but it was not a very long portage, and there was a well-trodden path around it. We made some coffee before we started, and got talking to a young prospector who was waiting for a canoe down river. After chatting for a while about our trip and plans he asked me a question that made me doubt my Portuguese.

'Has a loved one been ill recently?'

'No,' I answered, wondering what the hell that had to do with a conversation about the Jari and her difficulties.

'Here in Brazil,' he explained, 'when someone is ill and looks as though he might die, people make vows in church to undertake some sort of painful venture as thanks should there be a recovery.'

I laughed, and reassured him that was not the reason we were there.

'Oh, gold then?'

On every trip I have made in Amazonia I have found that the locals, although invariably friendly and hospitable, assume that I am some agent for a multi-national mining company prospecting the big find. However many times I deny this, or even invent other plausible motives such as being a wild-life photographer, I still hear them telling friends that I am a geologist.

This young man kindly helped us get all the gear round the rapid, but it became a race against time because he was drinking steadily all the while. I remember he had his fly buttons undone and no underpants on, but he was totally indifferent to his indecent exposure. At first we trusted him with some sacks that contained fragile objects, but he was swigging with such abandon that by the third trip he could barely get himself over the rocks unladen. That *cachaca* is so potent it can transform you from a sedate, upright human being to a weaving, slurring liability in five good gulps. By the time we carried the canoe he was leaning on it for support rather than actually lifting it. When sober he had assured us that he was helping out of the kindness of his heart and because he had nothing else to do. Later he tried to demand $20 for his services.

Even once we were past Tracaja we could only paddle a few metres before we had to unload the canoe again to negotiate a fast stretch of turbulent water. Then before nightfall we had to carry the gear for over 500 metres and haul the empty canoe through the shallows. It was a pretty tough day, but we ended it with a smile and joke on the lips. A sign that we were getting fitter.

That night we met the Indian who had been boatman for the American. As he seemed knowledgeable about the river we told him of our plans to portage over the Tumucumaque hills. From the maps there seemed to be three possible tributaries which entered the Jari and which would take us to the border of French Guiana or Surinam. The Cuc, the Ximim-Ximim and the Mapaoni. The Indian had worked in 1967 with a team demarcating the boundary region, and knew the Mapaoni and the Cuc. He reckoned the Ximim-Ximim would be too small and difficult, and thought we would have trouble on the Cuc finding a portage point. There used to be a house and trail up there he told us, but they would have disappeared long ago.

He recommended the Mapaoni and told us a good trail had been cut in 1967 by the Surinamese government to the River Litanie. It was in fact marked on two of our maps, and he thought there would be enough Indians regularly using it to keep it open. Great news! The problem was we had planned to avoid Surinam owing to the political situation there. Just before we left England it was announced that Brazil was sending a task force to the border, complaining of Cuban presence in Surinam. We did not want to blunder unauthorised into a tense military area. With our 20-gauge rusting shotgun we would hardly look like crack soldiers of fortune. But to some bored, bush-crazy frontier guard, we might be of interest.

So we favoured the Cuc that connects with rivers in more stable French Guiana, and asked the man no further questions about the Mapaoni. We were to regret that later. However, we did learn that the Cuc only had two major rapids — the rest was calm — and also that after the Ipitinga the Jari was easier. The present stretch was the worst on the whole river.

It had apparently taken his party twenty-eight days to get to the head-waters of the Mapaoni by motorised canoe. He was envious of our trip. 'You'll have a great time,' he said, and listened to our plans without surprise or amusement. I asked him the names of rapids between Monte Dourado and Ipitinga, and it was a long list: Santo Antonio, Itapeara, Escalao, Tracaja, Acaipe, Cumaru, Itace, Veriverina, Sete Pancadas, Caju, Inaja, Aurora, Mar-caranduba and Ipitinga, in addition, no doubt, to a lot of small stuff in between not worth a mention. (A common term for the smaller rapids among the Jari boatmen was 'bubbles'. These 'bubbles' would frequently take us an hour or two of danger, strain and discomfort to ascend.) At least that list did not have the evocative names of some Brazilian rapids: 'Hell', 'Purgatory', 'Disaster', 'Sweet Illusion'.

His assurances that the stretch of the Jari up to the Ipitinga was the worst on the whole river gave us much-needed encouragement over the next couple of weeks. There was never more than ten minutes' quiet paddling at any one time. Either the current became so fast we had to churn the water to a froth just to make headway, or small rapids would make us get out and wade. Luckily it was still a novel experience, so we hopped in and out of the water with good humour and stoicism. We had expected rapids on the Jari and we were gaining experience in the teamwork and technique to get past them.

We evidently had a lot to learn, for on the tenth day out we came near to disaster. We had just stopped at one of the rare houses to inquire about the river up ahead, and the owner told us that we were just below the rapid of Itace which flowed round dozens of islands in channels of varying ferocity. Like all the people hereabouts he had his favourite disaster story. Two rainy seasons previously a canoe with ten people on board had mistaken a channel and overturned. Pieces of canoe and one or two personal effects were found, but not a single body was recovered.

Cheered by this information we followed his advice and set off up the right-hand channel. Half an hour later as we were struggling to get past a small fall we were overtaken by two men in a dug-out and we watched their technique with admiration. The one in the bow stood up and used a punting pole, and the other sat in the stern with a paddle. Reaching the 1-metre-high fall, the poler ran back down the canoe to make the bow rear up, gave a fast jab with the pole, and banged the bow down on the rocky lip of the drop. A few more pushes and they were above it and on their way. Waist deep in water as we unloaded half the gear and then gingerly walked the canoe through the white water we were impressed and envious. Of course our canoe would not have withstood such treatment, and we were fully laden with provisions. You can't have great strength together with lightness. 'Flash buggers,' we muttered, and got on with it our way.

Soon we came across a section of river that did not look very fierce. The water poured down a small chute, and we decided that if we used the rope it would give us few problems. I took up position on a rock 10 metres in front, and Mark stayed at the bow and began to walk the canoe up. We had done this type of operation ten times that day already. Perhaps we were too off-hand. We nearly made it, and then Mark lost his footing in the deep, fast water, and the bow swung sideways and tipped.

'Look out!' I yelled, 'Let go of the canoe, let it go!' As Mark couldn't get a footing he naturally held on to the bow for dear life, but he was pulling it across the current and adding his weight to the rope.

As Mark said later, 'It was fine for you up there on that dry rock to shout "Let go!", I just thought "Up yours" and held on like a bloody limpet.'

Understandable — there was a lot of fast water below this rapid, but the canoe had started to fill. The strain on the rope grew impossible.

'I'm letting go of the rope! Try to straighten her up!'

There was still a chance that if the canoe was put bow-on to the current it would zip straight down the rapid to the calm water below. No luck. She filled, turned on her side, and our stuff spilled out and started to float away.

Leaping into the water I helped Mark throw gear onto the rocks. The canoe meanwhile had ended up broadside to the current, wedged between two rocks with the full force of the water pouring into and over her. It was imperative we did something or her back would break, but to get the canoe off we had to lift her full of water, causing even greater strain, before she floated clear. We hung on, and were swept downstream, with Mark being sucked under before we could get her into a quiet eddy. The canoe was still intact. Full marks to Granta Boats (and our craftsmanship of course).

A lot of gear had disappeared; most important the shotgun and machete. Some bags of provisions were wedged in the bushes on the bank, heavier ones were on the bottom where the canoe had tipped over. We spent the next two hours wading in the fast water, feeling in every crevice with our toes (not now sting-ray, I'm busy!). That way we found the gun, machete and nearly everything else.

It had been a narrow escape, but we had got off very lightly. Everything was soaked, water had penetrated all our treble-wrapped food supplies, and our two cameras were full of water. As mine was a sophisticated model with electronic shutter, absolutely nothing was working. Mark's was a mechanical one that he could dismantle and spread out to dry in the sun, and we were confident his would be all right. Fortunately it was a sunny day for a change, so we laid the tarpaulins on rocks and spread the wet food supplies over them to dry.

A sobering lesson. Having previously always travelled downstream I still had to learn the difficult techniques for negotiating up rapids against the current. When roping downstream you can often get hastily through tricky bits by slackening the rope and letting the canoe buck over. Going upstream you are crawling up through these sections for much longer and it only needs the shipping of a few gallons of water before the canoe becomes too heavy to hold.

We had also learnt that in deep fast water the 'swimmer' is no help at all. He can't get a firm footing, flounders and leans on the canoe for support, thus pushing the bow sideways. Most important, and tedious though it is, it is essential to unload a few bags of gear first. It makes the canoe much easier to handle, and by selecting the bags you unload you can make sure that the important stuff is safely on the rocks should things go wrong.

That night it poured with rain for five hours. After a hard day the Jari likes to put the boot in when you are down. Already a love-hate relationship with the river was developing. She was beautiful but mean, unpredictable and intolerant of mistakes. 'Not for boys,' we would joke as we struggled up yet another fierce section. 'A man's river.' But we were not sure in which category we belonged.

Wild food remained scarce. Often at this time we were only doing 4 or 5 kilometres a day, so we felt impelled to do longer days. Longer days meant less time for hunting and fishing, so on many nights we just delved into our food rations with enormous appetite but no fish or meat supplement. We saw monkeys, but at that stage had imposed a moratorium on them. In the past I had shot them, but only reluctantly. Now surely, we felt, we could find large birds which would cause us less feelings of homicidal guilt?

Each day we had to spend an hour or two reconnoitering the river ahead, finding the easiest channel, and checking that it would not be impassable upstream. We always took the shotgun just in case, but the only animal I encountered was the largest, blackest tapir I have ever seen. I was within 3 metres before I saw it half-hidden in some bushes. We stood and contemplated each other for a minute or two before it caught my scent and crashed away with a thunder of hooves. Just our luck. Here was another animal in our protected category: tapirs weigh up to 250 kilos which is rather too much meat even for two ravenous boys like us.

The tapir is the largest land animal in Amazonia (the manatee being the largest creature). It is solitary, shy, short-sighted and hard of hearing. Its sense of smell, however, is acute. With its short proboscis and great bulk it is reminiscent of a small elephant, and we frequently saw their deeply-punched tracks in the muddy margins of the river — three toes on the forefoot, and four on the hind. The river is the tapir's second home, where it feeds on the water plants and wallows in the water during the heat of the day. When alarmed it can submerge and stay under water for several minutes.

At all events we pushed on. Being rocky, the banks were often difficult to portage over. It was a matter of hopping over huge boulders with the gear and canoe, risking a broken leg or worse accident. Several times we had to return downstream to find another channel and our spirits started to flag for the first time. It was an unmitigated slog with no respite and without even the compensation of good progress. We had no idea where we were. We had been given the names of rapids, but as they were more or less continuous we did not know where one ended and the next began. For example Sete Pancadas is, as you'd expect from the name, seven separate drops over a kilometre or more. Our legs and feet were suffering badly. While walking in the deep, rocky water we would often bang our knees or shins. Soon we were covered in bruises and cuts that we re-opened several times a day. These were not the only perils of spending so much time in the water. Twice we saw snakes swimming nearby — a 1-metre venomous coral, and another of nearly 2 metres.

At least I had been in Amazonia long enough not to be worried about piranha. They were everywhere, and we grew pretty blasé about them. I've never heard of anyone being attacked by piranha, only bitten when taking them off the hook. The locals show little concern. Like sharks they perhaps have mad moments when they might attack, say when cut off in stagnant pools in the dry season with a shortage of food. But we certainly gave them every chance on this trip — wading, swimming, often oozing a bit of blood, and they were a disappointment. Poor piranha, stars of Hollywood movies, lurid travellers' tales and all — a tough reputation to live up to. The only fish that did bite us were the little ones an inch or two long that made us jump by nibbling at the pus of infected cuts.

However we did learn quite a lot about piranha during those days. I had always associated them with slow, sluggish water, but we caught several in rapids. We were also surprised to catch them on a spinner. While they never provided us with first-hand experience of their flesh-stripping ability, they are ghoulish little horrors. We were mystified as to why so many of the tucunare and trairao we caught had bloody, semi-circular chunks taken out of fins and flanks. Then we realised that while they were fighting the hook groups of piranha would take advantage to nip in for a nibble.

Piranha grunt, and these grunts can be heard before you have pulled the fish to the surface, so that you know what is on the end of the line should you not have recognised the feeble tugging fight. I have seen piranha bite through a hook, and if you put a knife blade in their jaws they will snap and snap at it until rendered toothless. They also grew very large on the Jari —

2½ kilos was common — and they are reasonably tasty although hard to scale. It is best just to gut them and pop them on hot coals, let them blacken on both sides, and then peel the skin off before eating.

I do have one piranha story. It was on the river Teles Pires in 1980, when Andrea Bettella and I came across a camp of Sao Paulo businessmen. They had come to spend a week's holiday hunting and fishing in the jungle, and they were a friendly crowd although a conservationist's nightmare. They shot everything in sight, placed gill nets everywhere and caught hundreds of kilos of fish which they dried and salted to take home. We stayed with them for a day without much persuasion; after all they had coolers filled with cold beer, bottles of whisky and all sorts of tasty food such as we had not sampled for a long time.

The day passed in an inebriated haze but I clearly remember the following incident. One of the Brazilians became a bit tiresome and drunker than the rest of us. He began blasting away with his arsenal of weapons and gave me a shock by shooting a can of beer just as I was reaching to pick it up. The job of the afternoon was to bring in the catch from the gill nets, and I estimate we had over 80 kilos of fish which we cleaned on the river bank. All the entrails, heads and muck were tossed into the slow current in front of us. When we had finished, the tiresome fellow announced he was going for a swim. We all did our best to dissuade him, after all we had just dumped 20 kilos of blood and guts right there, and the water must have been swarming with piranha. . . . He paid us no heed so I gave up trying and furtively got out my camera. I was not going to miss this scoop of the century, the first authentic case of a piranha attack. Already I could picture the water boiling and the stripped skeleton of a hand appearing and waving a couple of times before it disappeared. In he went, and I followed him through the viewfinder as we all held our breath. Well, the bastard swam for ten minutes and nothing happened. Nothing. Not even when in my disappointment I suggested he went out further and tried swimming downstream.

4 Slow progress

During the days we spent struggling with Sete Pancadas (or was it Caju or Veriverina?) we were aware of the beauty of the river, but without much time to appreciate it. We paddled past dozens of jungle-clad islands, and large black boulders jutting out from the swirling waters. Steep hillsides rose 40 metres or more on either bank, and we negotiated little channels full of exotic scents, butterflies and flowers, while raucous macaws flew overhead. We enjoyed some beautiful campsites on rocky islets with mica-strewn sandy beaches, because occasionally we would forget the difficulties, tried not to look at all those rapids upstream, and just opened our eyes to the good things around us. If only we had a bit more time for leisure as well. We came to regard getting past the Ipitinga as the beginning of the trip proper. What we were going through now was a hard and unfortunate initiation. Up there we should live better.

After not seeing anybody for five days we happened to be chest-deep in another rapid when a canoe pulled alongside. It was not the most dignified position from which to conduct a conversation, and the occupants of the canoe, gold-prospectors and whores from upstream, must have thought we were crazy. We had begun to share those sentiments. Our fame was apparently spreading. They had heard about us. But we were going very slowly, weren't we? We smiled through clenched teeth, and muttered that naturally we could not go as fast as they could with their motor.

'Muito corajem (very brave),' said the boatman. What he really meant was, 'You gringos are a bit soft in the head; and with all the money those multinational mining corporations have, you'd think they could buy you a motor.'

We learned that we had passed Sete Pancadas, and were now just below Caju rapid. This is one of the fiercest rapids on the river — it only drops once, but down a chute and across submerged rocks that create huge waves. We camped below it in one of the loveliest campsites we'd found to date. There was a huge bay over 500 metres across before the river separated again to depart down seven major channels. Round the bay were numerous sandy beaches that I walked along, occasionally casting the spinner, hoping to catch some supper. It looked a superb fishing spot, with eddies and a current, but to my surprise there was not a bite.

That evening black clouds started to roll in from the east yet again, and we quickly rigged up our tarpaulins and collected enough dry wood to cook both supper and next day's breakfast. All we had was rice again, and a packet of dried soup: not a great meal after a hard day. The trees near our fire proved too flimsy to take our weight, so we hung the hammocks a few metres away, and, since the clear and star-filled sky now seemed to promise no rain, decided to leave the tarpaulin. For a while, annointed with insect repellent, we lounged on the beach, and Mark gave me an hour's tuition on complex star constellations.

The heavens were ablaze. It would have been pleasant to lie smoking, contemplating, chatting and watching the shooting stars for several hours, but we were suffering too much from insect bites through our clothing. For repellent to be 100 per cent effective on the Jari, you have to put it all over the body before getting dressed. Our thick shirts and trousers alone were no match for the insects.

After a mug of rum we settled into the hammocks and went to sleep in a good mood. At midnight it began to pour with rain. It is always the same story — put up the plastic and you are guaranteed a dry night, leave it off and it will rain for sure. As we were blundering around in the dark moving the tarpaulin I felt a searing pain in my ankle that made me cry out. Mark shone the torch and it was a relief not to see a snake slithering away. We never found out what had stung me. A scorpion probably, but although my ankle swelled a bit and I felt feverish that night, I suffered no long-term effects.

The next morning we had some good news to start the day. I had taken to sleeping with the camera batteries inside my trouser pockets to warm them up and dry them out, and when I tried one in the camera at breakfast time, everything seemed to be working all right. I reloaded with film and looked forward to being able to record our progress once more.

We were lucky with the rapid too. On the left bank of the river there was a shallow section that we could wade up, although only 3 metres to our right the water boiled up into back-curling waves higher than our heads. Gingerly we crept along, knowing that after one false move our bodies might not surface for weeks. Best not to look there, best not to even think about it. The roar of the water was so loud that we had to shout to hear each other even though only a metre apart.

Somehow we kept in pretty good spirits over this period. Occasionally we had little tantrums and cyclical depressions, but were generally amazingly cheerful. We sang and joked, or swore and cursed. We took each new difficulty that the Jari threw up as one more challenge to be overcome. We were not going to let that river break us, even if she came near to it several times. After Caju we had five days when we never paddled more than 100 metres at a stretch without having to get out to wade, rope up or portage. It seemed like it was never going to end. A couple of boats passed us, and it made us feel better to see that even with their motors they were having a hard time too. With the engine full throttle the crew still had to leap out and pull on a rope.

The six days we were told we would need to get to Ipitinga had stretched to three weeks. We gave up asking people how many days they thought it would take us. No one had paddled up here for years, and all they did was double the time it took by motorboat — not realistic at all. Finally on the twenty-first day we had a much-deserved stroke of luck. It had been a bad morning of the usual kind and we had nearly had another disaster when the canoe turned broadside and hit a rock. We shipped a lot of water but luckily were able to leap out and bring it under control. We then had a very tiresome kilometre during which we paddled like crazy and saw the jungle crawl by. If we stopped paddling to wipe the sweat out of our eyes we would be swept back to where we had been five minutes before. We had become quite good at 'hedge-hopping', keeping right into the bank using the protection the bushes afforded from the current. We were lashed by branches as we zig-zagged along, but saved a little bit of effort.

Soon the water was so fast we were making no headway by paddling. Yet the water was too deep for us to wade. It was up to my chest, and there are few more frustrating attempts than wading in deep fast water. Lift one foot off the bottom, try to move it forward, and it seems paralysed. Mark's height was a great advantage however — he could struggle up quite deep water — and we often hung on to bushes and pulled ourselves up hand over hand with our legs being swept out horizontally behind us, the canoe being towed by a rope around our chests.

It was while we were in this dispiriting situation that a canoe came up behind us. We waved it over.

'Are we near the Ipitinga?' we asked.

'Oh no,' came the reply. 'It's still a long way.'

Seeing our crestfallen faces they offered us a tow to a place called Carecaru. We transferred all our gear into their large canoe and Mark got in as well. I stayed in ours so I could steer and follow their line. It was a bit hairy but a great feeling to nip along and be making some progress at last.

The boatmen zig-zagged across the river choosing the easiest sections and avoiding rocks, and by ruddering with the paddle I had to keep exactly on his line or risk holing the canoe. Once the motor stalled in a fast section and all the men jumped out to hold on, but the canoes began to slip backwards with me dangling on the rope in the fiercest section, unable to do a damn thing as the canoe bucked and weaved. On other occasions the motor was not powerful enough to get the pair of canoes up, and one of the men would have to get up ahead with the rope. As the current stopped him getting there direct, he would jump overboard, swim to the bank, make his way upstream on land, and then swim out to a rock where the rope would be thrown to him. Not a job I would have relished. But in three or four hours we covered what would have taken us two or three days to paddle and we got to Carecaru at dusk.

The last part of the towing exercise had been misery for me. I felt frozen stiff, and in the breeze of our progress my teeth were chattering and I was covered in goose-pimples. Unfortunately my clothing was in the other canoe, so I had to sit there in only my shorts for an hour trying desperately to concentrate on steering. Had we entered a new climate zone or was it me? I looked at the others. Everyone seemed warm and comfortable. Why then were my fingertips blue? There is really only one plausible reason for people to shiver in a tropical afternoon with the air temperature over 75 degrees F. Malaria. It was a truth I did not want to accept, and once we reached our destination I put on a couple of sweatshirts and put it out of my mind.

Opposite the mouth of the Rio Carecaru are three houses, and there is a gold field two days' journey upstream. A lot of people hang around there waiting for a boat up to Ipitinga, or down to Monte Dourado. Mark and I stayed two days and the people were good to us, letting us cook on their butane stove which seemed unbelievably luxurious after our open-fire cooking, and giving us food, shelter to hang our hammocks, coffee and booze.

We tried to gather as much information as we could about the river up ahead. But now we had dropped the pretence of going no further than the Ipitinga, and told the inhabitants of our project to try and cross to French Guiana. No one had actually travelled personally beyond the Ipitinga, so information was scarce and based only on hearsay. Two people did tell us that there was a FUNAI post (Indian Protection Agency) at a place called Molocopote which stopped everyone from going any further upstream. Where exactly this Molocopote was no one could agree. At the mouth of the Cuc, said one. Forty kilometres beyond the Cuc said another. However the information did reinforce our choice of the Cuc. It seemed we would not get up to the Mapaoni without passing this control.

On our first night in Carecaru two men went out hunting and shot a puma and a paca (a large nocturnal rodent prized for its meat). Seeing only the eyes of the cat in the torch beam they had shot it, but discovering it was a puma, whose coat is considered worthless, and not a jaguar, they cut off one of its paws as a memento and left the rest to rot. Fortunately the number of professional cat hunters (*gateiros*) has declined in recent years. In the early 1960s they were taking an estimated 15,000 jaguars and 80,000 ocelots a year, but that has now dropped to about half. In 1967 the Brazilian government banned the commercial exploitation of all wildlife. The powerful skin exporters complained bitterly that they were left with large quantities of furs already in stock, and the government gave them until 1971 to liquidate these. Naturally the firms had inflated figures of their stocks, so the hunting actually intensified between 1967 and 1971. In 1968, 6,389 jaguar and 81,226 ocelot skins were exported from Brazil to the United States. Even in 1975 the UK imported nearly 50,000 ocelot skins from Brazil.

The hunting obviously still goes on — Amazonia is far too large to be effectively controlled. Yet the consensus of opinion on the rivers I have travelled was that there are too many obstacles placed in the way of the gateiro now to make it worth his while. Most importantly some of the countries which were the main markets for these furs have imposed a ban on their import. One cannot condemn the Brazilian peasant for shooting these cats — he can earn two or three months' pay for each one — and as long as the demand exists he will continue to do so.

An ex-gateiro told me how he went about his business. A *patrao* (boss) would equip a team of three or four men with food and ammunition on the understanding that any furs would be sold to him on their return. They would set off up the remoter tributaries at the beginning of the dry season and hunt for four or five months. Ocelots were generally caught in baited traps with a sliding or weighted door, and the men would construct a hundred or more of these along the river bank. A far crueller method was to tie three large fish hooks together and cover them with a lump of meat. This was suspended about 1½ metres off the ground so that the ocelot would leap for it and impale itself in the mouth. A horrible end, but favoured as it entails less work than trap-making, and the fur is not spoilt.

Jaguars were generally attracted by dragging a monkey carcass along the jungle floor to leave a scent trail, and then shot by a hunter at night from a hammock suspended a safe distance above the ground. Or they could be called by imitating the panting groan of a cat. The instrument used to do this is a hollow tube of wood covered at one end with a stretched hide. A horse-hair cord was passed through a hole in the hide and through the tube, and by wetting the finger and rubbing it down the cord the call is reproduced.

A team of men working intensively like this could account for a large number of kills. If the take fell below two cats a night they considered the area to be poor and would move on. Five or six cats a night was common, and naturally any other animal with a commercially valuable skin was taken into the bargain – giant otters, brocket deer, peccary or alligators.

These days it is habitat destruction that presents the greatest threat to Amazonian wildlife, and while men continue to take animals for the pot and do not pass up the opportunity to shoot commercially-valuable animals, there are few nowadays engaged in the activity full time. Others, like the men at Carecaru, will shoot because it is supposedly manly to confront a jaguar or puma with a 20-gauge shotgun. Probably the fur would be damaged anyhow or improperly cured, but the hunter would have risen in his own esteem and in the eyes of his fellows. Machismo accounts for a good proportion of jaguar deaths in Amazonia.

We grew concerned at Carecaru about our dwindling food stocks. We had eaten much more than we had expected to, owing to our lack of success at hunting and fishing. One of the men was taking sacks of provisions up to the gold fields, and a lucrative business that must be. We bought 15 kilos of manioc flour (farinha) off him, some oil, torch batteries, rice and sugar at prices four times those in Monte Dourado. A bottle of booze that sells for US 50 cents in town can be sold for $10 in gold in these remote camps, while shotguns costing $70 in Manaus would sell for over $200.

Farinha is a gritty manioc flour that hasn't much flavour, but which provides a welcome crunch to a plate of rice. It is prepared by soaking the manioc tubers for a day or two, and then crushing them to remove the poisonous prussic acid before grating and roasting. Surveys done on *coboclos* have revealed that nearly all of them have dangerously high levels of this poison in their bodies owing to years of eating inadequately prepared farinha.

My suspicions of having malaria were reinforced during our stay. Having had it before, I was able to recognise the symptoms — headache, muscular pains, shivers, tender midriff, and weakness. Several people at Carecaru were suffering from the disease and we handed out a few Fansidar tablets to control it for a while. Rural Brazilians have a blind faith in anything pharmaceutical. Rarely able to afford to go to a doctor (or indeed find one in remoter areas) they are prey to the pharmacies which are big business in all South America, and there seems to be one on every corner. On their shelves one sees medications long ago banned in the developed world, but which have been dumped there by unscrupulous drug companies. There are 14,000 types of drug available in Brazil as opposed to 7,000 in Britain.

Brazilians stress the need for vitamins after a malaria attack — and I think there is some justification in that. Malaria does make you anemic. Yet strength could easily be regained by a good diet and taking vitamins orally. Not good enough. A pill is always better than a syrup, and an injection better than a pill. We saw the boss of Carecaru giving his daughter a huge intravenous injection of vitamins taken from an unsterilised bottle — liquid which was probably designed to be taken orally anyway. We did try to mention tactfully that it was not such a great idea, but as he had done it several times and so far got away without killing anybody, he was not to be dissuaded.

The next day we set off early and weary as the Brazilians had been having a party and were drunk and noisy until 3 am. Had I felt better I would probably have joined them.

A couple of kilometres upstream we passed the airstrip belonging to CPRM — the government agency that explores mineral resources. I was beginning to feel very unwell but tried to ignore it as we dipped our paddles against a strong current for the next two hours. Finally I suggested a rest to brew up some coffee, and out of curiosity took my temperature. One hundred and three degrees. This was malaria, no doubt about it.

5 Malaria

In 1980, when I first came down with malaria, I refused to believe it. I was still in that period of naivety when I trusted implicitly in my anti-malaria pills.

'No, it can't be malaria,' I told Brazilians who should recognise it when they see it, 'I take Maloprim once a week.' Anyway I was twelve days from the nearest place where I could get a diagnosis so had to let it run its course.

It started when I was riding on the top of a truck from the Mato Grosso up to Santarem on the Amazon. Baked during the day and frozen at night it did not add to the fun, and the journey took five days instead of the normal two because we were delayed by a bridge that was collapsing.

Several trucks had drawn up on both sides of the creek, no one dared to cross the bridge that was tilting alarmingly. After a consultation, the drivers decided they would shore it up themselves rather than wait two weeks for the authorities to do it. They set to work, cutting medium-sized trees into 3-metre lengths with a chain saw, and carrying them the 200 metres to the bridge. I tried to help but as I'd had bad attacks of fever for the previous three days, I felt too weak and retired to the shade. The two drivers of my truck were fairly sympathetic, having seen that I was ill, but the others weren't at all. I've noticed this in Third World countries — sick people do not receive the pampering and fuss we have come to expect, and a sick gringo is often a source of entertainment. One of the drivers commented that no wonder the British economy was in such a state if everyone lay down instead of working! Another, when I said I'd had fever for three days, spat and said he had once had it for ten days but still drove his truck.

'Very macho,' I snarled sarcastically, pulling the blanket over my head.

At Santarem the delays were not over — there was no boat to Manaus for three days — so I lay in a hotel room and continued to suffer every night from rigours and fever. The problems were compounded by a shortage of money. I had just come off the Teles Pires river, and all I had was $10. Saving some for the boat journey to Manaus (where money was waiting), I had to choose between a hotel and eating. Good job I was not hungry for the idea of lying in the streets in this condition made me choose the former. Even when treated to a meal by another traveller I found I could not eat more than a mouthful anyway. Everything tasted unpleasant, and just looking at it or smelling it made me retch.

So I had not eaten for several days by the time the boat set sail. I slung my hammock and crawled into it, knowing that at least food was provided with the fare if I felt like it, and that within three days I would have money to see a doctor in Manaus.

However, South America always chooses such moments for delays. Twelve hours out from Santarem the propellor broke and another two days passed before we got underway again. By now I had had fever for nine days and each afternoon the attacks seemed more severe. Trying to fight the violent shivers left me totally exhausted, and then I poured with sweat until my shirt and trousers did not have a dry patch on them. After a few hours, feeling marginally better, I'd had to get up for a pee and to drink some water. By this time it was usually midnight and everyone was asleep.

The deck was completely obstructed by hammocks and the only way for someone of my size to get to the toilets at the far end was to crawl along the floor, over the luggage and under the low-slung hammocks. After risking other diseases by gulping a litre or two of untreated river water I returned the same way. Before retiring to my sodden hammock I dug out some aspirin from my back pack – although they did little to relieve the appalling headaches.

Perhaps it was paranoia, but the passengers on the boat seemed hostile and unfriendly – two very rare characteristics in Brazil. Perhaps it was partly explained by my lack of attempt to chat to my neighbours. I was not in the mood, and made no effort to pick up the conversational openers thrown in my direction. I wanted to lie there and suffer in peace and privacy.

On the second night of the renewed boat journey I crawled to the far end for the usual reasons, and found several men still up and playing cards. Finding the water container empty, I asked one of them if he would mind filling it for me. That meant hanging over the side of the lower deck and scooping it from the river, and I did not trust my strength and feared I would fall overboard.

'Fill it yourself, gringo,' he replied, not looking up from his cards.

I must have looked ill; hair plastered to my head with sweat, clothes sodden, swaying on rubbery legs, but I explained I was sick and was afraid of falling overboard.

One of them got up reluctantly to fill the jug, but another commented that a fall into the river was the best thing that could happen to me. I burst into tears. I felt so bloody ill, miserable and weak, that this was the last straw.

That night the nightmares started; gold was hidden on me and everyone on board was out to kill me. My illness was their chance to get the gold and toss me overboard. The next morning I could barely distinguish between dream and reality, and with a temperature of 104 degrees those delusions continued all day. Everyone passing near my hammock was a potential assailant, and anyone regarding me with mild curiosity was a jackal waiting for my end. That end did not seem far away: my clothing after several pints of sweat poured over it had the sickly sweet odour of death. I imagined my body was beginning to rot already.

In the late afternoon when I started to shake, rattle and roll in another attack, I became aware of a commotion around my hammock. Summoning reserves of strength I listened to the shouting voices.

'Every night I see him crawling around under the hammocks opening suitcases,' said one.

'Let's search his pack to see if he's hidden it in there,' suggested another.

People then grabbed my pack and began to pull out the contents. When they found my camera they let out a cry of delight.

'If we don't find the money, this must be worth something.'

I sat up, shivering violently, asked what the hell was going on.

Someone had a large sum of money stolen from his suitcase, I was told, and I was the prime suspect. A large crowd had gathered – everyone shouting excitedly, so I asked who it was that was accusing me. Two men came sheepishly forward and I tried to conduct my defence through chattering teeth. I said they were welcome to look through my pack, and if it were really necessary I would even get up and let them search my clothing and body too.

'Why do you open people's suitcases at night?' one asked me. So I explained that I was ill (they did not seem very perceptive, this lot), and that the only baggage I opened at night was my own to get aspirin.

Without even finishing the search of my luggage, the men departed and the passengers collected in little groups discussing the case out of earshot. I realised I was crying again, and I suppose I had been sobbing when replying to my accusers.

Later the captain himself came over, and said that I was cleared of suspicion, that they'd decided the thief must have got off at the previous stop.

'You've got malaria,' he told me.

'Oh no, it can't be. I take a pill called Maloprim,' I replied and even refused some chloroquine that he offered me.

We got to Manaus the next day, and after collecting my money from the bank (and fainting twice in the street on the 1-kilometre walk there), I got a taxi to the hospital where they diagnosed Falciparum malaria.

Now, when I think back on that boat trip, one thing bothers me. Did the incident of the stolen money ever happen? There is no doubt that I believed it at the time – and probably even sat up sobbing a defence. But did I imagine the rest? Three days after arriving in Manaus, when I felt stronger after some treatment, I spent half an hour searching my possessions for that gold. The nightmare had taken hold. Had it been stolen, or had it never existed? I still don't know.

* * *

Well, here on the Jari three years later, malaria was back. This time I had been expecting it despite taking the preventive pills. That naivety and blind faith in their effectiveness had gone. Fortunately we had plenty of drugs to cure or control the disease; enough quinine for six treatments if the malaria was Falciparum (the most dangerous strain), and plenty of chloroquine for Vivax. Obviously without a blood test we could not be sure which type I

had at the time, but attacked the possibility of Falciparum first. I felt terribly
weak. Two days previously I had been able to paddle, portage and toil all day
without feeling particularly tired. Now a walk to the river to fetch water
would have me leaning on trees for support, my heart thumping wildly. This
is the most dangerous aspect of malaria for the jungle traveller. He becomes
too weak to fish, hunt or feed himself, nor can he get in his canoe and paddle
to the nearest help.

Quinine is still the most effective treatment for Falciparum malaria after
its widespread use for over 300 years. Malaria has killed many millions of
people throughout the world since ancient times, and was rife in Europe until
quite recently. Alexander the Great and Oliver Cromwell are thought to have
been among its victims. In 1633, Father Calancha, a Jesuit priest, learned of
the healing powers of the bark of the Cinchona tree while living in Peru, and
Jesuits brought the first samples to Europe. It became known as 'Jesuits'
Powder', and for many years was shunned by the medical profession which is
so often slow to accept herbal or folk remedies. In any case it threatened to
impinge on their existing lucrative malaria 'treatments'. In parts of Europe, I
have heard, it was regarded as a Papist plot to exterminate Protestants.

The Cinchona tree grows in the wettest parts of the Andean rain-forest in
Ecuador, Bolivia, Colombia and Peru, and it was 200 years before a proper
study was made of it. Attempts were made however — the most tragic being
that of the Frenchman Jussieu who spent thirty years living among the
Indians, collecting and studying the different species of bark tree that he
found, only to have all his papers and specimens stolen by a servant the day
before he was due to sail triumphantly back to Europe in 1761. Poor Jussieu
never recovered from the shock and ended his life in an asylum.

Von Humbolt and the French botanist Aimé Bonpland were the first to
publish a serious study of different species of Cinchona in the early 19th
century. Soon afterwards two French doctors, Joseph Pelletier and Joseph
Caventon, discovered the alkaloid that made the bark effective against malaria,
and called it quinine after the Indian name quinaquina, meaning bark of barks.

Meanwhile in South America the Spanish and Portuguese had imposed a
ban on the export of seeds or seedlings so as to maintain their monopoly of
this increasingly important commodity, and collectors were beginning to ruin
the trees by over-collecting and carelessness. The British and Dutch, both
with malaria-ridden colonies, sent expeditions to the Andes and managed to
get seeds out. The Dutch planted 2 million trees in Java but none contained
useful amounts of quinine. Richard Spruce collected hundreds of thousands
of seeds of different species, but when they were planted in India and Ceylon
these too proved worthless.

It was a Bolivian Indian, Manuel Incra Mamari, who eventually passed on
seeds from the best trees to Charles Ledger in the 1870s, and he was executed
for treason in consequence. Ledger offered them to the British Government,
which refused them, and in desperation, knowing that the seeds would soon
die, he turned to the Dutch who reluctantly bought one pound. He peddled

the rest to a planter who was home on leave in London. These seeds were to prove the most potent type of Cinchona ever found, yielding up to 13 per cent quinine, but the Indian plantation manager failed to grow any of Ledger's 1 million seeds to maturity. Fortunately the Dutch were more successful with their 1 pound of seeds. These grew to 12,000 trees in Java and gave the Dutch a European monopoly for more than a century.

In 1942 this monopoly was interrupted when the Japanese invaded Java. Moreover, in 1940 the Germans had taken Amsterdam and all the quinine reserves in Europe. This was a time of crisis for the Allied troops. The Allied war effort in the Far East was threatened by the number of servicemen who were incapacitated through malaria. Fortunately the US Government sent a team of botanists to Colombia, where they collected 12½ million pounds of dried bark which kept the Allies supplied during the war.

In 1944 William Doering and Robert Woodward synthesised quinine, but although it seemed for a while that malaria was on the wane, the disease began to increase in the 1970s, and is now estimated to kill 1½ million people a year worldwide. In India in 1952 there were 100 million cases. This dropped radically to 60,000 in 1962, but rose again to 6 million cases in 1976.

Natural quinine is now back in demand throughout the world, having superior properties to its synthesised counterpart, and in the 1970s abandoned plantations were reopened in Zaïre, Guatemala and Java. The story of quinine should teach us some valuable lessons about the natural remedies of the rain-forest, and the Indians' knowledge of them. Yet it seems probable that we shall destroy both.

* * *

On the second day of this enforced rest, while I struggled to overcome the malaria, Mark almost trod on a bushmaster – the most poisonous snake of Amazonia. He went down to the river for water and spotted the snake on the path, its brown skin almost invisible on the carpet of leaves and sticks. We usually had a live-and-let-live policy towards snakes, but this one was too dangerous to have around the camp. We shot it and added it to a stew we were cooking at the time. We had no snake-bite serum with us. Doctors had advised against it, saying the serum was frequently more dangerous than the bite itself. Other arguments were that over 60 per cent of people bitten by snakes recover anyway, that the snake often fails to inject a lethal quantity of venom, or that its toxicity is affected by factors like how recently the snake has eaten. They also told us not to suck or cut the wound, or apply tourniquets. What should we do? Oh, relax, they said: relax and rest. Relax? Pick up a novel, and sit down with a cup of tea? That would be a hard test indeed. Running around the jungle yelling 'God, I'm going to die! Why me?' would be a more likely response.

I have also on previous trips received much and varied advice from ca-boclos on what to do after being bitten by a snake. Drink a litre of kero-

sene say some. Cut across the bite marks, empty the gunpowder of two
cartridges into the wound and set fire to it say others. Run away from caboclos, I say!

* * *

Late one afternoon on the Rio Teles Pires in 1981 Andrea Bettella and I saw
a house in the distance, and quickened the pace of our paddling. It is cus-
tomary in Amazonia to ask to spend the night at any house rather than sleep
in the jungle, and you are unlikely to be refused.

There was a man taking his evening wash on the rough wooden jetty where
two other canoes were moored, and with the self-control showed by all the
Brazilian caboclos kept his face impassive and refrained from staring as we
approached out of nowhere and so obviously alien. He returned our greeting,
and consented to us staying the night, asking us a few friendly questions
about our trip and where we were from. He was missing his right hand, the
forearm ending in an ugly stump.

We took what we needed from the canoe and followed him up the bank
where some neat steps had been cut. We emerged into a big clearing with a
large thatched hut at the far end, and headed towards it. The tinkling of a
cow bell made us look round to see it attached to the neck of a playful,
well-fed dog that leapt and frollicked around its master.

'It stops the jaguars eating him,' he explained, pretending to be stern with
the creature. 'Dogs are their favourite food.'

On the way across the clearing we passed a strange sight. A large plastic
tarpaulin had been rigged up into a peculiar igloo-like construction that one
would have to enter on hands and knees. Outside it, cooking his supper, was
a rather scruffy man who barely looked up as we passed and returned our
greetings with a grunt.

We entered the large hut and were very impressed with the cleanliness and
order of the interior. A swept earth floor, sacks of provisions placed on
trestles, possessions hanging from the rafters, and a gleaming collection of
pots, pans and utensils around an earthenware oven. The place reinforced the
impression we'd had of the man as being a very capable individual, well-
versed in jungle life and able to make himself comfortable in it. Little things
like the jetty, the steps in the bank, the well-fed dog (most Amazonian dogs
are mangy, scrap-fed curs) and his clean clothes and neat appearance, were all
unusual in remote dwellings where men lived alone. We began to feel ashamed
of our wild beards, tattered shorts and grimy fingernails.

Jorge insisted that there was plenty of food already cooking for all, and
soon we were tucking into a good curassow stew with rice and beans. I went
to get our plastic container of booze from the canoe, and on the way back
asked the other man if he'd like to join us for a drink. 'No,' he replied, 'thank
you' coming as an afterthought, so I shrugged and left him staring glumly into
the centre of his fire.

We spent a pleasant evening with our host, getting a bit drunk and chatting about our respective lives. He was employed by a Sao Paulo businessman to clear a *fazenda*. A few hundred metres away there was an airstrip, and every month or so the owner would fly in, bring pay and provisions, spend a day fishing and depart.

All the time we were talking I couldn't help but stare at the stump and wonder at the missing right hand. It had obviously occurred a few years before because he had become so adept at life without it. For example he rolled cigarettes one-handed with ease. I vowed to ask him about it after another drink or two. Meanwhile I broached the subject of his strange companion. His face clouded for a moment, and I was concerned that I had offended him. However he shrugged, grinned ruefully and began to talk.

'Yes, it must seem strange to you I suppose. Here are two men living a long way from any company, and yet I live here, and he lives over there in that ... construction' he said ironically, gesturing towards the glow with his stump.

'A few months ago I was feeling a bit lonely so I asked the boss if he could find me another man to help. In fact I asked him to get me a woman, but he couldn't find one who wanted to leave the city and live out here!' He laughed pleasantly.

'It's difficult to believe now, but I was very, very pleased to see him. I'd been here by myself for over a year, and to have company at last was like a dream. He moved in here, I cooked and cleaned for him, and we talked and talked; or rather I talked and talked.'

He sighed. 'And yet slowly, my eyes cleared, and I saw him for what he is. A dirty, slovenly and lazy man. Not at work, mind you, I've no complaints on that score, but in personal habits and hygiene. He never washes, his clothes and hammock stink, he spits fish-bones on the floor so every insect around began to invade the place. So after a time things began to get cold between us, and in the end I gave him a plastic sheet and told him to build himself another hut in the clearing. I was going to help him build it, but he refused, and he rigged up that strange place that he has to enter like an animal. Now it's the dry season but when the rains come he'll be floundering in the mud.'

'Do you talk at all now?' I asked.

'Only about matters of work,' he replied, 'and then only the necessary.'

'In a way it must make you feel more lonely,' I ventured, the booze making me less concerned about asking too personal a question.

'Yes it does,' he answered willingly enough. 'Sometimes at night I look across from here at him sitting over there, and feel like calling him over. But I don't.'

A bit later, after a discussion of the animals of the region, we finally got around to the subject of his hand. It emerged quite naturally in fact. He looked up as I was watching the dexterity (not the choice word in this context perhaps!) with which he rolled a cigarette, and he grinned. 'Now it's easy to do, but at first it would all end up on the floor!'

'It happened seven years ago when I was working in Mato Grosso do Sul, doing the same sort of work, but for another boss. I was out hunting one day a kilometre or two from my hut when I came to a place where a big tree had fallen across my path. It seemed easier to climb over it than to go round so I reached up over the trunk to pull myself over, and got bitten at the base of the thumb by a *surucucu*.'

We winced. Of all the snakes in the jungle, this is the one we feared most. The bushmaster. I could remember some facts I'd read about it. Growing to 4 metres long, it is a fairly slender snake with a rough skin of pale, reddish-brown which has dark brown or black diamond-shaped patches. It can vibrate its tail like a rattler, but having no rattle it only produces a warning buzz when in dry vegetation. It has fangs over 3 centimetres long, capable of penetrating clothing that would protect you against most other species, and injects a considerable amount of venom.

Once bitten, and a large amount of venom injected, you don't stand much chance. The bitten limb will start to swell, and blisters to appear. Sometimes the skin will become tight and shiny from the internal tension and even split open. You'd become faint and experience profuse cold sweat, the pulse would become rapid, feeble or frail. Bleeding would occur in lungs, heart, kidneys and brain, and you'd soon enter a coma or convulsions and die.

'I knew I didn't stand much chance,' Jorge went on, 'it had bitten me too deeply and I could tell from the burning pain that the venom was in there.' He drew on his cigarette. 'So I decided to cut my hand off, thinking that so long as I did it in the first thirty seconds after the bite most of the poison would come off with it.'

We gasped, and he grinned. 'Yes, it was a tough thing to do. I thought that if I spent too long thinking about it I'd never do it, so I rested it against the tree trunk, put the machete in my left hand and chopped. Unfortunately, you know, I was right-handed and couldn't do much with my left, and also the machete wasn't as sharp as I would have liked. The first cut only half did it, I had to chop again, screaming with pain and thinking I was going to pass out before the job was done.' He paused, staring into the fire.

'But my troubles weren't over. I was still 2 kilometres from home, and at home there was no one to help. I tied my shirt around my arm up here until the blood stopped pumping and started to walk home. But I'd only got a few paces when I looked back and saw my hand lying there on the jungle floor, and it didn't seem right to leave it there. So I picked it up and walked home – hand in hand, so to speak.' He laughed, and we joined in, relieved at a touch of black comedy.

'The pain was awful, but I made it home, and I knew I couldn't leave the shirt tied around my arm much longer or the whole arm would die. So I had to do something that now I remember was worse than cutting it off. I heated a sheet of metal over the fire until it was red-hot, and then plunged the stump down on it and sizzled it closed.' He sighed, 'And that hurt, my God, how that hurt. And all the time the metal was heating I sat there staring at it, gulping rum, and knowing how much it was going to hurt.'

'I then got into the canoe, which fortunately had an outboard motor, and travelled for three hours to the road, where a truck took me to the hospital, and I still had the severed hand wrapped in a shirt. I think they took it off me and buried it.'

Well, we'd got the story of the missing hand, and pretty soon we turned in for the night. You couldn't really switch the conversation back to trivia after a tale like that, and we lay there for a long time in the darkness thinking about it. One thing was for sure — our admiration for Jorge was verging on awe.

The next morning we had breakfast with him and decided to be on our way. We thanked him gratefully, shook hands (left-handed) and departed.

As we paddled along Andrea and I had our first chance to discuss the tale, and he summed up our feelings neatly. 'That man has a bloody big pair of bollocks,' he said, 'Jesus Christ, what a big pair of bollocks!'

We'd gone about a kilometre when we came across the scruffy man out fishing in his canoe. As we hadn't been impressed with his cordiality the night before we planned to say goodbye and paddle on past, but he smiled pleasantly and called us over.

He seemed a different person asking us a lot of questions about our trip and showing us three big catfish he'd caught.

We chatted for half an hour, exchanging tobacco, and just before we left I made some comment about the terrible thing that had happened to Jorge's hand.

'Yes,' the man replied, 'so many men who operate circular saws have accidents.' I stared in amazement into his eyes expecting to see malice or deceit. They shone back at me clear and innocent, tinged with a bit of sadness at the cruelty of modern machinery.

6 Burnt Foot Camp

When I at last felt strong enough to move on we finally reached the mouth of the Ipitinga, its muddy waters spreading a stain into the clear Jari. As we paused to fish at the confluence a canoe came down the Ipitinga paddled by two villainous-looking characters. They had a sick companion lying under the shade of some banana leaves. They confirmed that this was indeed the Ipitinga, and told us they were going down to Carecaru so that their friend could be flown to hospital. He had been stabbed in the back. As we talked their eyes were flitting interestedly over the contents of our canoe. We began to feel uneasy.

When I first visited gold camps in Amazonia I was expecting to find a bunch of psychopaths and homicidal maniacs. But they turned out to be a perfectly reasonable bunch of men really. Codes of honour exist: the fortunate would help out the less fortunate, after a lucky strike the fortunate ones would treat the whole camp to food or drink, or arrange to have girls flown in from a nearby town. Murder was uncommon, or unheard of, especially in the remoter camps where there were no women to fight over. Maybe I'd just been lucky in the choice of the five *garimpos* I'd visited. I am told that some camps are full of men on the run, *pistoleiros* and the scum of the cities.

We did not know what the garimpo of Flechao further up the Ipitinga was like, but judging from these two characters it could be a rough one. One had a scar running from the corner of his eye to the edge of his jaw, and the other had a dead eye that had turned as white as that of a fish after cooking. They set the warning bells ringing.

Mark and I said a hurried goodbye and set off upstream, having to stop and wade through a rapid.

'Shit, they were a mean-looking couple of cut-throats, weren't they?' said Mark, and we glanced back to see the men still had not moved. They just sat in their canoe and continued to watch us.

'I don't like this at all,' I said. 'Did you see the way they were checking out our gear? I think we'd better push on until late and put some distance between us. They couldn't follow us up these rapids with their heavy canoe, but it would be easy for them to walk up and see our fire.'

'Let's face it, we're the easiest couple of guys in the world to bump off and get away with it,' contributed Mark cheerfully. 'Look, they're still there, the bastards.'

We rounded a bend and travelled hard for two hours until we felt we'd covered enough ground to be safe. For once we were grateful that the river had so many channels. Much more difficult for them to find us.

Martin and Tanis, when we separated at Obidos, had given us five of their dried dinners — beef and chicken curries — and we had allotted our first one to celebrate the passing of the Ipitinga at last. We poured a stiff shot of rum and toasted our venture.

'From what they tell us, we're over the worst,' I said. 'Here's to more wildlife, less rapids . . . '

' . . . easier going and easier living . . . ' contributed Mark.

' . . . fat juicy pigs, giant fish . . . '

' . . . and no more fucking mosquitoes.'

While Mark prepared the feast I took the canoe out and fished the channels of the rapids. I caught a sleek, torpedo-shaped predator of about 4 kilos, but what an incredible fight it gave, like a small freshwater marlin. It performed huge head-wagging leaps, stripping line off the reel with long dashes, and then doubling back and nipping under the canoe. The confrontation was made even more exciting by the fact that the canoe was drifting steadily towards some small falls, and it was touch and go whether I'd get the fish on board before I went over the edge. Mark said all he could hear was SPLASH. 'Jesus Christ!' Zing from the reel. 'Bloody hell!' SPLASH. Just in time I managed to scoop the fish out by the gills, throw it aboard and grab a paddle.

We had a marvellous meal. Meanwhile it had poured with rain yet again, so during a lull I decided to go and bail out the canoe. The batteries in my torch were getting low, and I directed the feeble glow a metre ahead of my feet. Indians say a snake is more likely to bite after rain, and I figure they should know. I reached the steep bank and shone the torch down on the water. 'Strange,' I thought, 'wasn't this were we left the canoe? Must be further along here.'

I walked to the left, and then to the right. There was no canoe to be seen.

'Mark!' I yelled. 'Come here!'

'What is it?' he called.

'I think the canoe's gone!'

While I was waiting for him, I considered the possibilities. None of them was pleasant. The weight of the rain water might have sunk the canoe in which case the bulk of our possessions would have been swept away. Perhaps we had not tied her up securely, and she had drifted away to be wrecked in the rapids? Or most likely those garimpeiros had followed us and stolen our canoe.

Mark came running up.

'I reckon the garimpeiros have stolen it,' I told him, trying to control my panic.

'No way,' said Mark calmly, flashing his bright torch about.

'What makes you so sure? Where the hell is it then?'

'Well, it's not here.'

He was getting exasperating.

'Jesus, Mark, I know it's not bloody well here. Have you got any idea where it might be perhaps?'

'It's not here because we didn't leave it here.'
'What?'
'We're on an island, and the canoe is on the other side.'
He was right.

* * *

The incident reminded me of my first-ever canoe trip in Amazonia. Patricio, a
Chilean, and I paddled most of the way from Boa Vista to Manaus down the
Rio Branco. It was a very incompetent, ill-equipped and uncomfortable
initiation — made worse by the rainy season that was at its peak. It rained
every day and every night, and once it rained torrentially for thirty-six hours
without a pause, without the tiniest break in the greyness.

One morning we packed up our camp and carried out gear down to the
river bank to load the canoe. We reached the spot, and stopped dead. The
place was empty. The canoe had gone.

We dropped the stuff and ran to and fro along the bank in a panic. No
canoe.

'You tied it up last night,' said Patricio accusingly. 'Did you do a good
job?'

'Yes. Yes, I did,' I answered, but I was doubting it then.

'You can't have, can you?'

We slumped to the ground and watched the muddy river flow by.

'What shall we do now?' I asked.

'We'll have to walk downstream until we find a house. There must be one
within a couple of days' walk.'

What a mess. What a pair of incompetents.

I stared gloomily down at the water, and suddenly let out a cry of excitement. I'd seen the canoe's rope — it was still tied to a tree to the left, and it
was pointed straight down to the depths. We pulled on it, and the great
weight confirmed that the canoe was still attached to the end.

We sat down and laughed hysterically. The canoe had always leaked pro-
fusely, and the rain-water had obviously helped push it under.

* * *

Despite reaching a bit of a landmark in getting past the Ipitinga, our spell of
optimism was doomed to be short-lived. For one thing, the rain was relent-
less. What sort of dry season was this supposed to be? We felt a nice sunny
spell would reduce the numbers of mosquitoes which were plaguing us. They
arrived at dusk and stayed until dawn; it was impossible to avoid getting
bitten despite a good insect repellent. They attacked through our thick shirts
and trousers, and bit through the bottom of our hammocks. It would have
been bad enough if they were merely a nuisance, but with the risk of malaria
as well, they were much more.

We found that insect bites have a cumulative action. Our skin did not react
visibly at the time of the bite, but every three or four nights all the old bites

would suddenly start to itch in unison, and we would be reduced to a scratching, cursing frenzy.

The river did seem to be easier, though, and for two days we had long stretches of calm water, a rare treat indeed. Even the small rapids seemed easier. With a little walking or portage we traversed them quickly.

One evening we camped below a small falls and put out night lines baited with large pieces of piranha. We used nylon cord and large hooks for these. Often, however, we had found them broken or the hook straightened by morning. As we were having supper that night a splashing and commotion announced a catch. It was a pirarara of about 10 kilos, a catfish with an armoured plate over the neck. We got him beached with difficulty, giving Mark a bit of amusement as I got my hand trapped between the line and the torch I was holding as the fish tugged with all its considerable strength.

The question was how to kill a fish like this? We could leave it out of the water — but ten hours later it would still be alive and gasping, and probably with a column of ants entering its mouth and attacking its intestines. Any blow with the machete to the head bounces off the armour. The only way seems to be to roll the fish over and disembowel it.

We baited up the line again and cast out before we turned in. An hour or two later further splashing came from the river. Getting up with the torch I told Mark to stay put — that I would call him if I needed any help. He misunderstood, and got up in the dark to give me a hand.

We had left a pot of beans to simmer overnight on the remains of the fire. Disaster struck. Mark tripped and upset the contents over his foot. He was wearing thick socks at the time as protection against mosquitoes, and the wool naturally soaked up the boiling water. He ran down to the river to plunge it into cold water, but when he removed his sock a lot of skin came off with it. It was a very nasty scald indeed and he was in a great deal of pain. Sitting on the edge of the canoe in the dark with the mosquitoes making the most of our vulnerability we bathed the foot and gave him an injection of Fortral — the strongest pain-killer we carried.

Obviously we were going to have to stay put for a week or more to give the foot time to heal. Mark started a course of penicillin to combat possible infection, but any healing is a slow process in the jungle. What had been an overnight stop, became Burnt Foot Camp, and it was to be the scene of a lot of inactivity, frustration, hostility and important decisions.

There are bound to be mixed feelings in a situation like this. I felt sympathy for Mark, but it was so frustrating to be held up just when we'd started feeling optimistic. I felt exasperated, impatient, and guilty, too, because of all my uncharitable reactions. When travelling, only one thing is worse than being ill. Someone else being ill. One very good reason for travelling with only one companion is that such delays as this are less frequent. In a large group someone always seems to be laid up.

The fish that caused all the trouble was a small surubin of 2 kilos which we had for breakfast the next morning. I gutted and cleaned the large one into fillets which I then salted and took across to some rocks in mid-river to dry in the sun. Half an hour later I glanced across to see the rock black with vultures contentedly belching, having eaten the lot. I should have known better. However it looked to us a good place for fishing and we felt sure we would catch a lot more, and be able to continue on our way with a large supply of dried fish. In fact over the next eight days we only caught one more large pirarara, but lots of giant piranha.

This period was hard on both of us. I could pass some of the time hunting and fishing, but Mark had to stay and rest up in his hammock all day. Once the mosquitoes discovered us they began to work day-shifts, and we were only able to relax under the nets. The terrain was very tough for hunting — steep hillsides covered with fallen trees and thick tangles of bamboo. I would return after sorties of two or three hours, soaked in sweat and usually empty-handed. One monkey and one curassow was the sum total of those days of hunting. The curassow or 'mutum' is the largest of the jungle fowl. A rather foolish bird, a bit larger than a chicken and black except for its yellow face and a few white feathers on its rump, is the ideal size for feeding two hungry people. On other trips I had eaten plenty of curassow, but this was the first time I had seen them on the Jari. It is also a good bird for bad hunters. It feeds on the ground, and when scared flies up to the lower branches and, thinking itself safe, makes a sort of clucking tweet alarm call. They often go around in groups of four or six, so it is sometimes possible to shoot more than one at a time.

The monkey I shot was a squirrel monkey — one of the smallest monkeys in these forests. By the time it was skinned and gutted there was a pitiful amount of meat left and we ruled out these species for further consumption. Even in populated areas they are numerous because their small size has proved their salvation. Brazilian hunters need a large creature to justify the expense of their shotgun cartridges. Squirrel monkeys have golden-green coloured fur and a black muzzle, and are the only species of primate where the male becomes spermatogenic, being unable to breed for most of the year. Just prior to the breeding season, they take on 20 per cent in body weight, all of which they later lose in their campaign of competition to receptive females. The mortality rate is high among males, and the sex ratio among adults is four females to one male.

Other monkeys we were to see over the next months would be the tufted capuchin — one of the commonest in Amazonia, and one of the most intelligent. It has a golden-brown coat with darker back and head. The larger, gangly, spider monkey is one of the most endearing, being marvellously agile, curious and having a wide range of facial expressions. We also heard howler monkeys nearly every night, but hardly ever saw those, the largest of the New World primates.

We were less likely to see the attractive woolly monkey, as we were on the fringes of its habitat, or the rare sakis or uakaris. The latter has a very unappealing appearance, with long fur and a bald red face that grows redder

Above: passenger and cargo boats in the port of Manaus on the Rio Negro. There's not much to do on these river boats except swing in one's hammock and wait for the next meal.

Below: opera house, Manaus

*Right: assembling the canoe.
Below: our young assistants in
front of the assembled canoe
and (foot) proving that it could
indeed float!*

with excitement. The Brazilians call it the *macaco ingles* (the English monkey), and it does remind one of an apoplectic squire after a heavy luncheon.

We had finally lifted our moratorium on monkeys — we needed to eke out our food supplies by living off the land, and so far we had been very unsuccessful. We could no longer afford to let sentiment interfere with practicalities. Monkeys are easier to kill than most Amazonian creatures for several reasons: they are numerous, their commotion in the treetops betrays their presence from far away, and they are just too curious and trusting for their own good. It is unpleasant and shameful to kill such endearing creatures, and we hoped to find enough large birds to shoot instead. Hunting monkeys was always upsetting because they had such human responses to danger. They shook the branches in outrage, screeched defiance, pelted us with fruit and sticks, and often stayed loyally by a wounded companion. You could always see the conflict in them between the instinct to flee and the overwhelming desire for just one more peep. When they ended up in our stews, their meat was much appreciated. It is rather gamey and lean, somewhat akin to wild rabbit in flavour.

Hanging around for so long was bound to bring despondency, and we had plenty of time to assess our situation. Certainly we were short of some items of food. The canoe, although scraped and battered along the external joints seemed to be holding up okay. However we were still only just beginning the trip, with up to four months ahead of us and no chance of getting more supplies. Did we really want to face being 100 per cent dependent on living off the land? Was it wise to continue with no polyester resin for emergency repairs to the canoe? In addition to all these doubts, Mark's foot was healing very slowly and we were running out of dressings for it, or for any future injuries. There were also quite a few other important items that had run short, or we had realised too late that we needed — spinners, wire for fishing traces and repairs, a larger plastic sheet if it was going to continue raining so much, and new shoes as we had worn through two pairs each already.

We discussed the situation, and Mark viewed it with more realism (I'd say pessimism) than I did.

'We're in trouble,' he said. 'We're short of food, medical supplies, and materials for mending the canoe. All fairly important items, I'm sure even you will agree. Adventure is one thing, and bloody recklessness is another. I love adventure, but I like to keep the odds on my side.' He paused, and stared glumly at the grimy bandage that covered his foot.

'Nothing has gone right on this bloody trip since we started. Hundreds of rapids, no hunting, lousy fishing, malaria, a burnt foot, too much rain, and slow progress. I expected it to be hard, but not like this. I expected the going to be hard, but the living to be easy, know what I mean? Lots of meat, a beautiful jungle. That's what you said it would be like.'

'That's how I thought it would be,' I interrupted angrily. 'We haven't had much luck with hunting or fishing because the stretch to Ipitinga was too travelled. Also there were so many rapids to get through that we haven't had time for serious living off the land. It'll be easier from now on, you wait and see.'

Mark wasn't convinced. 'The Jari easy! I don't believe this bloody river would ever be easy! We've eaten over half our food supplies already. Within six weeks we could be completely out. I don't want to get to the stage when we're scavenging for all our food. Hell, we've got at least four or five months' travelling ahead of us! What about canoe repairs? We've got no fibreglass to repair her if she gets damaged, and she's sure to get bumped and scraped all the time. It's crazy to go on without these things.'

I knew he was right, but I wanted to carry on and risk it. Reckless perhaps, but preferable to turning back. Personally I've always had tremendous confidence in my ability to muddle through difficult situations. This isn't a mood that you can infect others with, however, and Mark did not share my optimism. It seemed to me that he was clutching at pretexts to have any excuse for pulling out. He wasn't really assessing the problems and thinking of ways to overcome them, but using each as a prop for his defeatism. I, on the other hand, was shrugging off the risks and ignoring common sense.

'The trip has been disappointing,' he continued, 'and it all seems pretty meaningless. We might get through, and succeed in crossing the Tuucumaque hills. But what's the point?'

Such heresy and mutiny in the ranks! How could we quit after only five weeks with almost nothing achieved? So much planning and money had gone into it. Of course I didn't have a burnt foot, so my mood was more buoyant, but Mark's defeatism aggravated my normal stubbornness.

'You'll feel better about continuing after we've had a rest and your foot has healed,' I tried to reassure him, but I knew all too well that once the enthusiasm has gone on a jungle expedition, it's gone for good. Our relationship had begun to sour at this point, which was a shame because we had got on well up to then. He had proved to be a cheerful and resourceful companion. Yet in England I'd warned him repeatedly that I was looking for someone who had the determination to stick things out when the going was hard. That did not mean I would carry on in the face of disaster, I'd explained reassuringly. There would have to be a good reason for quitting. Now he could see that we each had different ideas of what the good reasons would be.

'A burnt foot, malaria, no canoe repairs, a shortage of food and medical dressings: all that's not good enough motive for you, is it?' he muttered, avoiding my eyes. 'What is, then? Death?'

We spent long hours in tense silence after that, and Burnt Foot Camp became a miserable place. I went on long exhausting hunts to purge my frustration and worry, and Mark swung in his hammock, his face closed to scrutiny behind the mosquito net. After we completed this trip he planned to go to the USA before he returned to Australia. Now he spent hours poring ostentatiously over maps of that country and consulting youth hostel guides. It was a tough psychological tactic.

'What's Colorado like?' he would ask, out of the blue.

'Why are you asking me that?'

'You've been there, haven't you?'

'Yeah, but why ask me that now?'

'It gives me something to think about.'

'Are you giving up this trip then?'

'I don't know yet.'

This used to infuriate me so much that I'd have to go on an extra-long hunt to calm down.

We spent three days without exchanging a word, and this seemed to get on his nerves less than on mine. He held the trumps. He knew I couldn't carry on without him. There was no danger of me deserting him. If he pulled out I would have to call it off too. There were far too many portages involved for me to contemplate continuing alone. I was at his mercy and I hated him for it.

We had each kept a lengthy diary during the past weeks, and I became obsessed with the idea that if I could get a peek at his recent efforts I would find out what was going on in his mind. No doubt he had the same idea and more opportunity. He only left the camp to defecate but I was out of camp for hours at a time. So I began to write expressly for his eyes, indicating disappointment and criticism, or challenges to his pride and masculinity. From what I had learnt of his character, he was into machismo. So I wrote, 'Mark's tough, and he's keen to join a tough elite – the Australian army. I don't take him for a quitter; I reckon it would take a really rough run of luck to make him give up. If he proves to be a quitter, I've judged him wrong. I doubt whether the Australian army selection panel will be so easily fooled.' A couple of pages every day in that vein, then I'd slam the diary closed to attract his attention, rise, pick up the shotgun and depart.

Hell, not even a saint could have resisted the temptation for a peek in those circumstances. I had always chosen somewhere very conspicuous to write the diary too, and every time he looked my way I'd be chewing thoughtfully on my pen as I regarded him. When I finally got a look at his diary, I found it contained no real surprises. He was concerned at my recklessness, and he was demoralised. It offered no glimpses of hope.

'John's only keen for me to go on because he needs me,' said one entry. 'Without me he'd be stuck.' He understood the situation, sure enough.

I began to analyse my apparent obsession for carrying on. Objectively we had stacks of reasons for calling it a day, and Mark had a point when he said the whole thing was a bit meaningless. Why was it so important to me to continue? Could I really pretend I had enjoyed the past five weeks? Was my obsession rational? It didn't seem so, particularly as I would have kept going despite the risks and shortages. I think (of course I don't know), but I think I would have kept that determination even if it had been my foot that had got cooked.

I suppose on a trip like this it is only obsession that reinforces the will-power to keep going in times of hardship. We had the concrete goal of crossing

the Tumucumaque into French Guiana, and objectively it was a meaningless
and faintly ridiculous plan. Yet it provided a focus and target for the trip and
I clutched hold of it obsessively. Mark viewed it differently and more objectively. We might get over the hills, but so what? So what indeed, but you
can't have motivation without a goal.

After days of sulks, silence, bad temper, gloom and despondency, we
finally sat down and thrashed it out. I admitted grudgingly that it would be
more sensible to re-equip the expedition, and that we should return downstream to get more supplies. Yet at Carecaru we would not find a lot of the
items we needed. Crucial things like spinners, and polyester resin would of
course be out of the question. Perhaps it would be better to leave the canoe
there and journey down to Belem — do the thing properly, and get everything
we needed at a reasonable price.

'I really can't afford all that expense,' countered Mark, and I reassured him
that I would mail home for some more money and pay for it all. I knew that
if I returned home I'd want to return to the Jari the following year, and that
after all would cost a good deal more. I later learnt that Mark had more
savings at home than I did, but having found a compromise solution, we
shook hands and the camp became a more cheerful place. Two days later we
set off downstream, after sorting out a lot of equipment to leave behind for
our return. We placed this in a string hammock to keep it off the ground and
positioned it out of sight just in case anyone passed by. That left the canoe
really light for our journey down to Carecaru. We set off at dawn and paddled
long and hard. After weeks of toiling against the current we seemed to fly
along. Since Mark must not get his foot wet, we paddled through all the
rapids. I would go for a reccy and return with complicated instructions about
the stretch below us.

'When we get past that rock over there there's a large eddy and we have to
head quickly over to the left to avoid a submerged rock in the middle. Then
we should bear right and take a channel near the far bank. Be careful, as there
are two rocks we should pass downstream of', etc. Of course such a description is meaningless unless you can see it for yourself — and anyway it always
looks different once you've started to paddle down — so I couldn't even
follow my own instructions. We took a few risks and bounced off some
rocks, but despite expectations reached Carecaru by four that afternoon.

At the airstrip we met a couple from the trading post, who told us that
there was a plane due and the pilot might take us free because of Mark's foot
and my malaria. We spoke to the pilot, and sure enough he agreed. This was a
marvellous bit of luck. We had expected to have to wait several days for a
canoe downstream. In fact the pilot was in a hurry and gave us very little
time to grab some of the gear from the canoe and to arrange hastily for the
couple we had just met to look after everything until we returned in two or
three weeks.

We climbed on board, bounced down the airstrip, and twenty-five minutes
later arrived culture-shocked at Monte Dourado airstrip. Expecting several

days at Carecaru with time to wash clothes and get presentable, we had arrived wild and hairy, sunburnt, clothing in tatters, and stinking of sweat and wood-smoke. When we tried to get a taxi to the town centre the driver asked to see the colour of our money first.

We were a couple of hobbling wrecks. Mark had his foot swathed in grimy bandages, and I had developed very painful sores on the soles of my feet that made walking agony. On the way to town the driver told us that the cheapest hotel in Monte Dourado would cost us US $8 a night, and that if we wanted something more basic we would have to cross over the river to Beiradao. This boardwalk settlement developed during Ludwig's time, and there was an enormous contrast between Monte Dourado with its streets of identical American suburban bungalows, its tennis and social club, and Beiradao with its noise, bars, clubs, slums and smells.

However the town of Beiradao looked more fun, and we found a hotel for $1.50 and had a huge supper of steak, fried eggs, rice and beans. We tried to turn in early, but our room was right next to the bar with its blaring TV, and through the open window came the music and drunken yells from six or seven clubs that went on till three in the morning. Ah, civilisation at last! Like it or not the peace and quiet of the jungle permeate your soul, and the first contact with town life is always an affront: noise, smells, crowds, lack of privacy. Even the longed-for cold beers are a disappointment, and only the women come up to expectation.

While having supper we talked to a cargo boat captain who said he would take us down to Belem for nothing in the next day or two. Even if he failed us there promised to be a passenger boat.

The next morning, we went over to the hospital established by Ludwig in Beiradao. As gringos, we got prompt treatment and they cleaned and dressed Mark's foot. It had not become infected; it just had not healed. Then I phoned home for some more money to be cabled to Belem.

That afternoon Mark's temperature soared to 105 degrees, so after sponging him down for a while in the hotel, I took him over to the hospital again. They diagnosed Falciparum malaria, and started him on a course of quinine. Poor Mark, he wasn't having much of a holiday. Also he discovered that sometime on the river (probably when the canoe overturned), his passport had been ruined by water and would have to be replaced before we could cross the border into French Guiana.

By the next day we still had not heard from that boat captain, and had discovered there were no passenger boats to Belem for five days. So long in Beiradao was not a cheerful prospect. As we were swinging our hammocks in the hotel room, a street vendor knocked on the door and told me that Senhor Araujo would like to see us. I said that if Araujo wanted to see us, who-ever he was, why didn't he come in person? A pained look came over his face.

'Senhor Araujo would not come to a place like this,' he replied, glancing around at the grimy walls and the nude pictures that adorned them.

Having nothing better to do and being curious to meet this character I followed him to a supermarket and was shown into the office. Senhor Araujo was about my age, a lot richer and a lot less pleasant. He made no move to shake hands, to get up or to hide his contempt. His lovely secretary unfortunately seemed to share his low opinion of me. But he wanted my dollars and gave me a reasonable price for them. I learnt later that Senhor Araujo is known as the 'Sheikh of Beiradao', with his finger in gold-buying, skins, supermarkets, money-changing and no doubt lots besides.

On the way back to the hotel I bumped into the cargo boat captain who told me he was leaving for Belem in fifteen minutes, so I ran back, dragged Mark out of his sick bed and we got on board. Jorge had travelled a great deal and spoke good English which made it easier for Mark. He had an enormous appetite for marijuana and never seemed to be without a joint on the go — but seemed to be totally unaffected by it. The cargo that he carried between Belem and Beiradao was a more orthodox stimulant — beer — and he told us that in Beiradao alone, 30,000 bottles are drunk a week. Knowing Beiradao I'm not at all surprised.

The other crew members were Jucelino, the mechanic, and Oscar the pilot. It was a friendly ship, but not a very efficient one. Oscar's memory of the deep channels seemed to have become a bit hazy — we ran aground half an hour after leaving Beiradao and had to wait six hours for the tide to float us off. Mark and I did not care. We tucked into a huge supper of steak, eggs and potatoes and turned in. At midnight we set off again, but at dawn Oscar made another miscalculation and we ran aground again, and this time had to wait all day for the tide. Even then it was touch and go as to whether we'd get off. We had run aground at almost full tide, and as there was a full moon it was one of the highest of the month. It seemed ironic to be stranded there all day in that little boat while several ocean-going ships passed us on their way up to the pulp mill. We drove a stick into the mud and attached a rope to it, and by heaving on it and running the engines full astern we managed to free her.

At night Jorge asked me to sit with Oscar from midnight to 5 am to chat and help keep him awake. It was a real graveyard shift and we both had to fight to keep awake, but we managed to chat about this and that, and Oscar had a large supply of cloves that we sucked to let nausea keep sleep at bay. He dozed off quite frequently (he only slept an hour or two each day of the trip), and when he did so he would slump over the wheel and push it round so that the boat would have circled around all night across the busy shipping lanes. Tactfully and discreetly I would tap him with my foot so that he started guiltily awake and glanced shamefacedly in my direction. Being a gent, I'd always be gazing out of the porthole or lighting a cigarette at the time.

On the second night we had exhausted the conversational topics of football, family, travelling, sex, food, Amazonia and Ludwig, and it was barely two o'clock. I searched for a new theme.

'These boats seem really top-heavy. Don't they become unstable in bad weather?' I asked Oscar, whose head was beginning that gentle descent to the wheel.

'What?' he muttered, rubbing his face.

'Aren't there a lot of disasters on these rivers?' I seem to have hit one of his specialised subjects. His sleepiness fell away and he became animated.

'Oh, yes. Every year two or three big ones, and there must be many more small ones we never hear about. There were two catastrophes in 1981 — one near Obidos and one near the mouth of the Jari. Many people from Beiradao died in that last one.'

'Tell me about it,' I urged.

'It was on the night of January 6th 1981,' he started, sitting on the bunk next to me and putting the boat on automatic pilot. That meant keeping one of his bare big toes on the spokes of the wheel. 'As you know January 6th is a public holiday here in Brazil and a lot of people from Beiradao went down to Cacapa for the big *festa*. At midnight they piled on a boat for the journey home, and although the boat only had a maximum load of four hundred passengers, eight hundred got on.'

'Don't they have controls?' I interrupted.

'Oh, sure, but captains are greedy, and the authorities are even greedier. The controls are broken and ninety-nine times out of a hundred they get away with it. This was one of the exceptions.' He sighed. 'It was a stormy night, but in the channels between the islands the river was calm. However when the boat emerged into a large bay it met a fierce side wind and swell, and it turned turtle. People were trapped behind the tarpaulins that had been lowered to keep out the wind, others who got free became disorientated in the dark and choppy water and swam away from a nearby island. Many were probably too drunk to swim anyway. Five hundred people drowned. Almost everyone in Beiradao lost relatives. One woman lost eight children, and many children were orphaned.'

'Did the captain survive?'

'Oh, yes. The guilty usually do, don't they? It's the innocent who get killed. He's still free and has another boat now, but he stays away from the Jari — there are too many people who want his blood. I was in Macapa when the news of the disaster came through on the radio, and every boat went out to look for survivors and to collect the corpses. There were bodies everywhere — floating, caught up in the bushes, lying on sandbanks, covered with urubus pecking out their eyes. It was horrible. I collected fifty-six in my small boat and I hope I never have a cargo like that again. Within twenty-four hours they were all swollen like balloons and the gas started to escape, and in the small space on the deck we were forced to walk over them. For several weeks afterwards other bodies would turn up, caught in fishermen's nets, and let me tell you, there's no corpse worse than a drowned one that's been nibbled by crabs and piranha.'

It was a cheery conversation for those dead hours before dawn, but it did have undeniable qualities for keeping us awake.

These small cargo boats are not supposed to take passengers, and if caught, Jorge faced a fine of twice the minimum salary for each passenger found on board. Twice we had to hide in a locked cupboard when a patrol boat approached. I found the journey enjoyable. Jorge was good company and gave us beers and fresh fish that he bought from the homesteaders who would paddle out to sell. Mark, however, was increasingly morose, and each time I sat down beside him or joined him on the roof for a sunbathe he would get up and move elsewhere. I knew he must still be feeling rotten from the malaria – but he began getting those damn maps of the States out again, and I was in agonies of uncertainty. Meanwhile I paid for him and watched his moods in angry anxiety.

Although I had agreed to pay for transport to Belem and back for re-equipping the expedition, I had assumed he would change a bit of money to pay for his own hotels and food. So far he had made no move to do so, and reading his diary (yes, I was still at it!) I found him complaining that he could only eat or drink beers when I felt like it because I had the money.

My dependence on him was making me take a lot of stick. Normally outspoken, I was pussy-footing around, anxious not to upset him in case it was the last straw to make him drop out. My confidence in him had already gone, so I wondered why I bothered.

On the third night we ran aground again, and I commented to Mark that Oscar was not producing an academy award performance, which I at least found funny. This time the stranding seemed more serious because the boat was stuck on the edge of a shelf, with very shallow water on one side and deep water on the other. Jorge was worried that at low tide the boat would roll down the slope. To avoid being trapped in it, we slept on the roof clutching our money and passports. The boat gave one lurch in the middle of the night that had us awake, hearts hammering, but then settled again at a rather alarming tilt until it refloated on the ebb.

We travelled all the next day and had to cross a huge bay where there was a very strong swell. Oscar somehow got the boat sideways onto the waves which caused empty beer crates to hurtle all over the boat. I got the impression that Oscar was going to be down at the employment office by the end of this trip, perhaps joined by Jucelino because as we struggled into Belem against a fierce rip-tide, he was preening himself in the toilet for the girls of the big city and had forgotten to top up the fuel tank. The motor died, the generator with it, and we drifted unlit and sideways back up the busy waterways of the port for ten minutes while the fuel lines had to be bled and the motor restarted.

We moored up a small creek near a brick-works, and the next day I accompanied Mark to the hospital to have his foot checked. His malaria seemed to be well under control, and he was more cheerful.

I wanted to take Jorge out for a meal to thank him, and as Mark still had not got round to changing any money, I paid for him as well. A few hours earlier he had phoned his parents in Australia, but it was not until next day he told me he had asked them to send money to Miami.

'I'm not going back to the Jari,' he said, as soon as I woke up. 'I'm sorry, but I've got no enthusiasm for that trip any longer.'

'When did you decide this?' I asked, as the news slowly sank into my sleep-sodden brain.

'I've been thinking about it for the last week, but I finally decided yesterday.'

'Why didn't you tell me then?'

'I didn't want to spoil our evening out with Jorge.'

'You didn't want to lose out on the meal, more like. Wanted to get one last good spread out of sucker John, didn't you? How could you just sit there and stuff your face at my expense, knowing that you were going to tell me this morning?'

It felt good to shout at him. I had nearly forgotten how to be sarcastic and unpleasant. My disappointment in his decision was tempered by the relief that I could be myself at last.

'You'd made this decision even before we left Burnt Foot Camp, hadn't you? We plan a trip of six months and after five bloody weeks you've had enough. All that macho talk, all that tough guy stuff – it's all bullshit. You've wasted my time and money, and talking of money I reckon you owe me about £75, which I want this morning.'

I got up out of the hammock and stood up. My anger turned to depression as I paused to consider my situation.

'Shit, you've really loused things up, you bastard. What the hell am I supposed to do now? Go home with bugger-all achieved? I warned you and warned you that this trip was going to be tough and you assured me that you were up to it. Well, we've both seen you for what you are now, haven't we? A bloody windbag.'

7 Back to the beginning

'Don't you realise that it probably needed more courage for Mark to tell you he was quitting, than to have carried on upstream?' said a friend to me several months later. 'God, the poor bastard! If I'd just spent weeks up some pestilential creek with you, you miserable, cantankerous old sod, I'd have packed it in too!'

Now that time has passed, I can understand Mark and forgive him. Five weeks of hardship, a burnt foot and a dose of Falciparum malaria were quite enough excitement for a first jungle trip. That morning in Belem, however, I felt differently. 'Gutless wimp,' I thought. 'All that macho military talk, and what happens? A little temperature comes along and kicks the stuffing out of the windbag.'

The trouble was I hated leaving the Jari with nothing achieved. The whole trip had been a washout, a feeble anti-climax after so much dreaming and preparing. How could I return to England with this feeling of disappointment and frustration? I wandered the streets of Belem in a foul temper. I answered people's smiles with scowls, and snapped at the slow waiters. What to do? I could return the following dry season, but it would mean starting again from scratch. Hell, I had gear seemingly scattered all over the jungle – the canoe at Carecaru, the hammock-full at Burnt Foot Camp. I couldn't rely on any of it still being there next year.

The money had arrived from home in record time. I didn't need it by then, but instead of sending it home I had it transferred to the bank in Manaus in case I had problems there. I then went down to the port and found there was a boat leaving for Manaus that night, so bought a ticket. Later I met Mark in the street, and discovered he had done the same. Oh, terrific.

The passenger boat was a giant steel catamaran – mounted on two floats, and it was one of the biggest on the Amazon. I thought I'd be travelling in style until I got on board and found conditions were more basic than on the little chuggers I had mostly travelled on. Over 700 passengers spent the first hours of the journey fighting for places to hang their hammocks. The lower deck was divided into mesh cages according to marital status and sex: 'Single men', 'Single women', 'Couples with children', 'Couples without children', 'Unaccompanied women with children'. Single men predominated and in our cages the hammocks were slung under, over and across one another. Some touched the floor, others were so high that their occupants had to shin up pipes to get into them. It was claustrophobic down there, and we spent most of the journey up on the only bit of deck open to the lowly masses.

The food was appalling: tiny portions served up on little airline trays with hollows for a piece of meat, a bit of farinha, a dollop of rice or beans. I commented to a Brazilian in front of me in the queue that in a country where people eat such enormous meals the food on this trip was downright stingy. He smiled.

'You've been in Brazil long enough to know how things work. If you want more food, or better food, all you have to do is visit the kitchen on the first day and give the staff a couple of dollars. Then you eat different food, more of it, and no queueing.' He was right, I should have learnt that lesson by now.

There were more than twenty gringos on board — the majority of us backpackers, but also a party of wealthy Americans, and we got to know each other over the next five days. When I heard Mark impressing the ladies with his Amazonian experiences I managed to control my tongue and kept away from him as much as possible.

On the second day I was ill again, and spent the rest of the trip lying in my hammock with a fever. In my more lucid moments I discovered that two of the travellers were interested in taking Mark's place. It was a stroke of luck; but I was viewing life with a very jaded eye right then. I grunted a non-commital reply to their applications and watched them closely. After all, wouldn't they quit too in five weeks? 'Boys and wimps, the lot of them,' I muttered petulantly into my sweat-soaked blanket. In fact I was slightly awed by their vigour and youth. I felt I had neither.

Lutz was on the run from some trouble in Germany although I never found out what. Frankly I wouldn't have cared if he'd chopped up his granny, just as long as he showed the qualities necessary for a river trip. However, as he had been out of Germany for several months he was running short of cash and needed to combine pleasure with a bit of profit on the Jari. I couldn't see how this could be done without changing the trip in a way that I would find unacceptable.

Peter, a Swiss, seemed the better bet. His motives were pure, and he lacked Lutz's aggressiveness (Lutz and I would have been duelling with machetes after three weeks). Peter had round gold-rimmed glasses, brown shoulder-length hair, and was quiet and introspective. He gave an impression of relaxed strength and competence. I had ignored my instincts when recruiting companions in the past, this time they told me that Peter would be all right. If I went back up the Jari myself that is.

When we got to Manaus I had a blood test and was told I had Falciparum malaria. For several days I felt very low, and I longed to go home. Sometimes I felt stronger and more like going back to the jungle. Peter had to live with this uncertainty for over a week.

One evening as I was lying feverish in the squalor of Manaus' cheapest hotel, Mark ran up the stairs two at a time, brimming with health and enthusiasm. His burnt foot had healed, his malaria was cured, and he was soon to leave for the USA. He was infuriatingly cheerful.

He barged in through the door, and snapped on the single bare electric light-bulb.

'Hey,' he said, 'I've just met two fantastic English chicks. They're really gorgeous, and they're downstairs in the bar.'

I grunted unenthusiastically from under the cover of three blankets. I was shivery and miserable, and I wanted him to go.

'Man, they couldn't keep their hands off me. Practically ripped my trousers off. They're dying for it!'

'They must be blind and stupid,' I muttered sarcastically. Mark didn't hear.

'Why don't I bring 'em up here, and we can have one each? It'll do you the world of good!'

His memory of the effect of malaria on the libido had obviously grown hazy.

'No,' I answered. 'I feel lousy.'

'Ah, go on!' He insisted. 'Meet them at least. When you see the little darlings, you'll forget all your troubles.'

Isn't male pride a ridiculous thing? With a temperature of 103 degrees, the idea of flirtation and sex was absurd. Yet I was slightly curious, I had been in the jungle for six weeks and I was being mildly challenged.

'Are they nurses?' I asked.

'Nurses? I don't know.' Mark frowned, and then beamed. 'Ah, you like nurses! Yeah, so do I. They could be. I'll go and get 'em.'

'No, I just fancy the cool hand on my fevered brow,' I answered, but he'd gone, clattering down the stairs in his flip-flops.

I lay back, closed my eyes and waited. There were two thoughts in my mind: that if they fancied Mark, I would not fancy them, and how typical of Mark that he only got excited about English, American or Australian girls. The fabulous Brazilian girls left him cold.

There was a knock on the door, I groaned inwardly, and in walked a blonde. As my contact lenses were out at the time that was all that registered. Slight disappointment too because I do prefer brunettes. Then I gave a gasp of astonishment. It was Tanis Jordan! Behind her came Martin and a grinning Mark. We had a noisy and emotional reunion. It was lovely to see them again. They looked thinner, but in pretty good shape and we babbled and laughed through the recounting of our adventures. They had had a rough time on the Mapuera — it was rapids all the way, and they had decided early on that their proposed route was out of the question. In many respects their journey seemed similar to ours on the Jari, but with two important differences. They had almost no rain and no mosquitoes. To Mark and me that sounded like paradise indeed. They had escaped malaria too.

We went downstairs to the restaurant, and carried on our chat. One of their stories made us laugh. One day on a rapid they had met a canoe-load of Indians travelling downstream. Tanis, naked, was scrubbing some pots at the time and hadn't seen them approaching.

'Tanis, there's a canoe full of Indians coming!' yelled Martin.

'Oh, pull the other one,' replied Tanis while the Indians' canoe went sideways down the rapid as they concentrated on her, and then pulled into the shore at the tail of the rapid.

It emerged they were from a tribe that crossed frequently into Guyana, and consequently one of them spoke a little English. Martin asked them about FUNAI — the Indian Protection Agency, as this was the body empowered to stop people entering Indian territory without authorisation.

'How many people live in your village?' asked Martin.

'Sixty-three,' replied the Indian confidently.

'Are there any FUNAI men living with you?'

'Oh yes.'

'How many?'

'One thousand, two hundred and twelve.' Martin and Tanis could not help laughing.

All our tales of rivers and adventure convinced me to go back to the Jari. Once I regained my strength Peter and I began to make our preparations. We bought some polyester resin, fibreglass tape, spinners, fishing line and a large tarpaulin. Martin and Tanis kindly donated a lot of their medical kit, their shotgun, mosquito nets and snake-bite serum. In the evenings we sought out good restaurants and gorged ourselves on meals that tasted extraordinarily good after our bland regimen of the jungle.

Manaus oozes sensuality. It is one of Brazil's sexiest cities, the Brazilians assure you. Certainly it has an abundance of red-light districts and prostitutes. Any walk at night is punctuated by whispered promises from doorways and enticing calls. The more daring girls block the path and try to encourage you with fumbling and squeezes. Faced with the prospect soon of several months enforced celibacy in the jungle I felt that I should be storing up some memories for lonely nights in my hammock. So often after supper I would go with one or two other travellers in search of sexual fulfilment. We would generally end up drunk at a club called inappropriately 'The Cathedral'. By Manaus standards this club was sophisticated, with dim lighting, modern decor and elegantly-dressed cocktail waitresses. Ravishing girls did poorly-choreographed strip-tease on a small stage, and then put on the bare minimum of clothing before coming to sprawl on our laps. Gringos were courted with zeal. We were supposedly wealthy, and we were different. Also I gather that every Brazilian prostitute hopes that a gringo will one day fall in love and marry her. I have met many foreigners in Brazil whose wives have the un-mistakable aura of fallen angels. No Brazilian would dream of marrying a prostitute, so gringos are their only hope.

Ah, how convincing these girls seemed! How affectionate, how passionate, how sincere. 'I love you,' they whispered after five minutes' acquaintance, nibbling our ear lobes, and we, lonely, bush-crazy, far from home and drunk, almost believed it. Yet we were fickle and inconstant. No sooner had we promised to go home with one, than we saw another who seemed even more beautiful, and we changed allegiance. This caused the real personality of the girls to come to the fore. They swore obscenely, spat, slapped our faces and fought each other. The aura of eroticism and excitement evaporated, and the atmosphere became recognisably squalid and sad.

Anyway, I was still weak and sweaty from malaria and not really in the mood for sex. Undeniably the knowledge of nasty sexually-transmitted souvenirs weighed on the mind: penicillin-resistant strains of syphilis and gonorrhoea, herpes, and one or two new horrors rumoured to be present in Manaus. There reached a stage in every drunken carousel when I would look searchingly at the peachy-skinned girl on my arm and wonder whether she was worth the gamble. If I had been feeling better I would perhaps have decided in her favour. Maybe malaria has its advantages after all.

On my last night in Manaus I was sitting on a park bench when a girl approached and we got talking. She had none of the mannerisms or dress of a prostitute. She was attractive, warm and witty — just the company I needed before I set off back to the Jari. We had a lovely evening, a few beers, a meal, caught a bus to a fun fair outside town, and kissed as we went round on the big wheel. At 3 am we found a cheap pension where they were unconcerned about couples arriving with no luggage, and made love.

In what the Americans tackily call 'the afterglow', I lay back on the pillows, smoking a cigarette. During our conversation earlier she had mentioned that she knew some English, so I prompted her to speak a few of the sentences she had learnt. I expected 'Hello, my name is Helena, I'm Brazilian' etc. I was in for a surprise.

'Hello, meester, what shipya from?'

'What?' I squawked, sitting up in bed.

'Hey, I like you, you like me. Wanna jigajig?'

'Holy shit!' I cried, getting out of bed. Where was the shower? The carbolic soap?

* * *

Peter and I flew to Santarem the next morning; we wanted to get to the river as soon as possible. I was concerned at how quickly the water level was dropping on the Jari. Despite all the rain that had fallen I had already seen it drop nearly 25 centimetres in the nine days we were at Burnt Foot Camp. I was not certain whether less water would make it easier or harder for us on the lower reaches, but there was no doubt that near the headwaters too little water would make progress extremely difficult.

In Santarem we purchased all the new food supplies, and this time we allowed much more: 20 litres of oil, 15 kilos of oats, 30 kilos of rice, 15 of beans, 10 of sugar, 10 of salt, 20 of wheatflour, 4 of powdered milk, 15 of spaghetti, 3 of coffee. Added to the food we had left at Burnt Foot Camp that should be plenty.

We also needed to replenish our fishing equipment. My original choice of spinners to bring out from England had been too flimsy and small. After being chomped by piranha several times they were bent, hookless and worthless. This time we bought two dozen more robust ones.

We tried to buy more quinine but in the chemist it was incredibly expensive: over £1 for each 250 mg tablet. As you need fifty for each cure we tried to get some from the hospital, but they refused to sell it. So after getting one course from Martin and Tanis, we returned to the Jari with only enough for four more bouts of malaria. As an additional precaution we bought a lot of Fansidar which we had been told would control the disease, if not cure it. Had we known then what would happen three months later we would have spent every last penny on quinine.

We travelled on the boat to Monte Dourado, and there inquired about canoes up to Carecaru. We discovered they left from a point 50 kilometres upstream at the end of a road that by-passed Santo Antonio falls and several other rapids. I had to laugh when I learnt this. Mark and I had been in such a hurry to get out of town and avoid officialdom we had missed some vital information. That 2-mile portage round Santo Antonio had been unnecessary. We could have saved six or seven days of toil.

We stayed one night at the same hotel in Beiradao Mark and I had used three weeks previously. The girls who worked there were thrilled to see gringos again, and Peter and I could, no doubt, have spent the night accompanied. However, we were so concerned with our last blow-out meal and drinking our last beers that when our thoughts finally turned to sex our seeming indifference had offended all the girls. So we spent our last night in civilisation alone. (In any case I was worried enough about what horrible things I might have caught on my last night in Manaus. Was our medical kit adequate for treating virulent clap?)

It was Sunday and everyone in Beiradao seemed to be drunk. Some lay sprawled across the broadwalk, and others bounced off the walls or stood swaying and trying to focus on the two gringos — none too steady themselves but kept sober by the threat of violence. We went from bar to bar. A few people were aggressive and provocative, but most were just woozily friendly. Deafening music issued from every doorway. Naked kids crawled between the houses. Beiradao was in urgent need of a rainy season to wash away the garbage piled deep under the stilts of the town. As often happens in Brazil I found myself having long conversations about football and Liverpool FC, although I know absolutely nothing about either. Another bar was full of vociferous Argentina-haters telling us how they had enjoyed the Falklands war. In a third we met two prostitutes who could not have been more than thirteen and who brought out our paternal instincts by the fragile vulnerability which was so badly concealed by their tough talk and posturing.

Early next morning after a breakfast of fried eggs we took a taxi to the boat departure point. A dozen prospectors were already there. Some had been waiting a week. Peter and I were impatient to get moving, the biting pium flies were bad and it was hot and boring, so when after six hours' waiting a boat finally came we ran over eagerly. I had met the motorista before at Carecaru. He told me he was only going as far as the Tracaja rapid, but we asked to go with him.

It was not perhaps a very wise move because there was a chance any canoes going all the way to Carecaru would arrive at Tracaja already full. But we were keen to leave and were not put off even by the prospector who told us the motorista was an incompetent. The week before he had overturned and the prospector had lost his revolver, shotgun and spare clothing in a rapid.

'He's got no idea at all. I'd rather stay here two weeks than go with that bastard again!' he shouted.

We reached Tracaja in a few hours, although the motorista certainly gave us some alarming moments. He took dubious routes in fast waters that had us all leaping out to pull the canoe, and his motor was badly in need of a service — it tended to stall in the most awkward spots.

We camped two nights at Tracaja and it was a disappointing place. As there was a gold field three hours' walk away, Tracaja was the arrival point for men and supplies, and there was a sprawling encampment of men waiting for canoes to Monte Dourado. We watched our mountain of provisions carefully as one by one the garimpeiros came over to check us out. We talked to one emaciated prostitute who told us she had suffered malaria thirty-one times. She also had a fresh bullet wound in her thigh from a bar brawl.

'It interferes with my trade,' she confided laughingly, with her hand on my leg. 'I'll have to take a vacation, but I guess I can afford to. I've got one and a half kilos of gold stashed away.'

'Why don't you return home to Rio, and leave this jungle before it kills you?' I asked.

'Well, that's not enough money to retire on, and in Rio I'd not earn much. How would I compete with those beautiful mulattas? I only got rich up here because I'm all there is, there are no other girls. The garimpeiros either go with me, or use their hand. I have a monopoly.' She laughed, and revealed her solitary tooth sticking up discoloured in an expanse of gum. If she had grown rich, I couldn't help but ponder, the garimpeiros must be extremely frustrated.

One man strutted around with two revolvers stuck in the waistband of his shorts. He obviously considered himself to be one mean son of a bitch so Peter and I called him over for a bit of gentle mockery. He was a gold buyer and carried a pair of jeweller's scales in a box. Out of curiosity I asked to see some gold dust, and after cocking one revolver and placing it on the ground close to his hand, he unwrapped a sheet of newspaper and showed us a few grammes — about £50 worth I suppose.

Peter and I sucked in our breath. 'What a lot of gold! Are you going to retire with that?'

'Good job you've got two revolvers: one wouldn't be sufficient if word got round that you were carrying so much gold!'

It was a dangerous game and he grew nasty and left. His place was taken by another character who began to help himself liberally to our stock of rum. Out of hospitality we let him get away with it until he passed the ½-litre mark and then the bar closed. I lost my temper with his pleadings, told him he was

Amazonia is a fisherman's dream. Above are two of the tastier species — a payara (the teeth protrude through the upper jaw when the mouth is closed) and a pirarara catfish caught at Burnt Foot Camp. Below: Homesteaders skinning a caiman near Monte Dourado. The trade in their skins has declined in recent years, but their meat is still appreciated.

Late afternoon was our favourite time of day . . . when we'd tie up the canoe and put the tootsies up . . .

. . . but all too soon we were driven under the mosquito nets.

abusing our hospitality and suggested he bugger off.

So it went on – a continual stream of visitors, some interesting, most not. Peter repaired Mark's old mosquito net that had so many tears and rips it had been more symbolic than effective. He also got into a hammock for the first time at Tracaja, or, as frequently happens to novices, he got in on one side and was catapulted out the other. The garimpeiros loved that. You could see them describing it to every new arrival. Peter did however find a method of tucking the bottom of the net in such a way that it was completely closed to mosquitoes. I'd never thought of it, and it looked as though Peter was going to bring some Swiss resourcefulness into the venture.

On the morning of the first day, two garimpeiros told us that we were wanted for questioning by the police in Monte Dourado. They had left Tracaja a few hours after us. It seemed we had got away just in time. Taxi drivers had been instructed to run us back into town to see the police.

'Why do they want to see us, do you know?' I asked.

'Well, they say that they've now seen you twice leaving Monte Dourado with a lot of provisions. Weren't you here a few months ago?'

'Yes I was – but we're not doing anything wrong.'

'Maybe not – but do you have authorisation?'

'No.'

'Well, I guess that's what the police would want.'

Why does officialdom always get in the way? I wouldn't normally have been too worried – after all we were already 70 kilometres from Monte Dourado – but we learnt that every Tuesday a policeman would travel up to the gold fields at Tracaja if there had been any trouble. It was now Tuesday morning, and in a gold camp one could imagine that there would be trouble every week. If he made us go back with him to Monte Dourado and apply to Macapa for travel authorisation we would never get our trip off the ground. How we wished we had our own canoe so that we could disappear.

Luckily for us the next canoe contained not a cop but a pleasant motorista who was willing to take us to Carecaru. But he was infuriatingly relaxed and unhurried about everything he did. We portaged his 8-metre canoe – using log rollers – over the rocks, carried sacks of provisions around, had lunch and a little sleep, caulked the canoe, and it was by then so late departure had to be postponed until the next morning. Our impatience seemed ill-mannered and typically gringo – but we were afraid another canoe would bring the police before we could get away. It turned out that this one canoe was to transport seventeen people, three dozen 50-kilo sacks and everyone's luggage to Carecaru. The only way to do it was in relays – three or four trips a day backwards and forwards – and that meant agonizingly slow progress. We travelled for one or two hours, and then had to camp and hang around the rest of the day while the canoe brought the rest of the passengers.

To add to my enjoyment I got 'flu during this period. I was getting really tired of being ill, but for those three days was thankful I could spend most of the time in my hammock. The way these boats operated is as follows: the garimpeiros pay nothing for a passage upstream to the gold fields; they have little or no money then, and anyway all hands are needed to portage the sacks of provisions and to drag the canoe up the rapids. On the way downstream however they pay two grammes of gold because the canoe has no cargo, and presumably the men are richer when they travel back from the gold fields. It seemed a fair system. We had to pay $30 however because we had a lot of sacks.

It took us nine days to get back to Carecaru. It was interesting to retrace the route Mark and I had covered so burdensomely a few weeks before, but there were many places I could not recognise. We must have followed different channels. Peter was impressed.

'Mark said the Jari was difficult,' he said, 'but I never expected her to be like this. You did good to get as far as you did.'

I glanced anxiously at him. Was he overawed by his first glimpse of a tough Amazonian river? Would he let me down too? Once again I was embarking on a trip with a total novice. He had never paddled a canoe before or set foot in a rain-forest. At that stage I knew next to nothing about him. All I had to go on was a gut feeling that he would prove to be all right. For the present I could merely observe his reactions and pray he would justify my untested confidence.

Our companions in this canoe were a friendly bunch. Seven were full-time crew, and it was a pleasure to watch their skill in manoeuvring the canoe past each obstacle. They hopped barefoot from rock to rock with the rope and leant on punting poles to aid the struggling engine through the faster water. The outboard was obviously in need of servicing. It was soon a standing joke that the engine would stall whenever its services were needed most, making us leap out into the turbulent water to stop the canoe from drifting backwards.

One day I got the camera out to record these scenes, and the men were so chuffed at appearing on film they returned downstream a little so that I could photograph them in the most dramatic setting possible. In Manaus the camera had recovered from its soaking when the canoe capsized. All it had needed was a fresh battery, and I had tested it with a roll of film to check the results – perfect.

The men leaned on the rope, tensed their muscles, and grinned widely at the camera. Even though the only full set of teeth belonged in Peter's smile, they looked a handsome team, and it was going to make a fine shot.

'Hold it!' and I pressed the shutter.

'Oh fucking hell!' I yelled.

'What's the matter?' called Peter, relaxing his posture at the rope.

'This sophisticated piece of fucking Japanese shit, that's what!' I whirled it round my head, for a moment debating whether to hurl it into the rapid. The battery had drained in two weeks, and everything had gone dead. Peter had no camera. Martin and Tanis had offered me the loan of theirs, but I had turned it down. (That was stupid – I should have known that electronic cameras don't get over a soaking that easily.)

'I will have to start my sketching,' said Peter, and from that point he passed the quiet moments with his sketch book.

We ate well during this journey – the men placed a gill net every night and frequently caught 70 kilos of fish or more. Once they made us *acai* – a drink made from the fruit of the Acai palm. I'd had it before and really liked the stuff. Mixed with farinha and sugar it is delicious. The Brazilians stress its high vitamin and iron content, and obviously consider it a powerful aphrodisiac. Each time I have taken it there has been much winking and pumping actions with the fist and laughter. There, in the jungle, it was wasted on us.

After nine days we finally made it to Carecaru, and went straight round to the house where I had left our canoe and equipment to see if they were okay.

'Who did you leave the canoe with?' Peter had asked the day before.

'Oh, a couple who live up there.'

'You know them well?'

'No, not at all, really. They just happened to be at the airstrip when Mark and I were leaving.'

He had frowned. 'Can you trust them? I mean, will the canoe still be there?'

This had been a worry to me. I had said I would be back in a fortnight and nearly a month had passed. Had they assumed I would not be coming back and sold the canoe? Or maybe a garimpeiro had stolen it? Maybe they had used it themselves and smashed it on the rocks?

We walked briskly and apprehensively down the trail to their home. We had returned with so many new provisions, and had had such a long, tedious trip to get back, that it would be disastrous if the canoe were gone. The local dug-outs would be impractical as they were far too heavy for the 15-kilometre portage we were planning. Once again the trip would fizzle out.

The couple's twelve-year-old daughter greeted us shyly, and seemed to be under instructions to keep us out of the house. She waylaid every attempt we made to get in the front door, and from inside we could hear her parents whispering and rushing about. It was all horribly suspicious. We walked to the river bank, and felt even more alarmed when we saw our canoe was not moored among the others.

We squatted in the yard for over ten minutes before the couple finally emerged flushed and breathless. We need not have worried. The delay had merely been due to that universal phobia about receiving guests into a disordered parlour. They had obviously been using some of the equipment (and why not?), but they wanted to have it all ready for us to see in one neat pile. The woman had even washed our blankets and sewn up an old pair of shorts. Moreover the canoe was missing because their son had gone fishing in it up the Rio Carecaru. It was wonderful that everything worked out so well. I was glad I had brought a few small presents to show our gratitude for their honesty and kindness.

We now had everything we needed: abundant provisions, and a canoe returned to its former glory by a fibreglassing of the external joints. We were keen to be on our way, and under our own power. The Jari awaited us with all her usual surprises. In the stretch before Burnt Foot Camp she had presented a more serene and languorous appearance. Would she offer a bit of slack at last? We were eager to find out.

At first paddling seemed extra hard work after the long lay-off and sickness, and even worse of course for Peter who had never paddled before. The canoe was full to the gunwales, and we still had more to pick up at Burnt Foot Camp. However, we would surely soon eat our way through the edible stores, and better too much than too little.

About 1.5 kilometres upstream we stopped to visit an Indian family Mark and I had met on the previous trip. The man was a twinkling, chubby extrovert, always bubbling into song or laughter. His wife was a serene, silent madonna, and their children black-eyed charmers. We pulled alongside their jetty, and I was surprised at how strangely quiet the place was. I could see smoke, so someone was at home. We climbed up the steps cut into the steep bank, and walked over to a figure lying still in a hammock outside the hut.

It was our friend but he stared impassively at me.

'Ah, voltou (You came back),' he murmured, without interest or inflection. I was shocked at his appearance. He had lost more than 10 kilos and his eyes had a dull stricken look in the gauntness of his face.

'Yes, I'm back. Are you sick Manolo? Where's Teresa, and the kids?'

A large solitary tear rolled down his cheek.

'Teresa's dead.' He gestured weakly to a white, wooden cross that I had not noticed on the edge of the clearing.

'Oh, Lord, I'm so sorry Manolo! When? How?'

'Twelve days ago. She just died. Fell down and died. I don't know why.'

More tears were now coursing down his crumpled face.

'They took the children away.'

'Who did?'

'They did, and he rolled his head to one side, making it clear it was too much to try and explain.

I walked around his clearing. The pets were still there – the parrots, the snuffling baby wild pig and the tame monkey at the end of a string – but they looked neglected and pitiful, and not the cheerful menagerie of a month before.

'When did you last eat?' I asked.

'I'm not hungry.'

'Well, you should be. Peter and I'll go fishing and we'll prepare you a good meal. You need it.'

'I don't want it.'

'You have to eat, Manolo.'

His voice gained the barest hint of animation.

'Look, Joao, you're being kind, but I don't want your kindness. I'd rather you left. I want to be left alone.'

He turned his back to us, and after hanging around feeling helpless and awkward, we fed and watered the animals, and went on our way.

We paddled in silence for several minutes.

'He's just going to lie there and let himself die,' said Peter.

Yes, it looked as if he would.

* * *

We took it easy for the first few days to avoid the risk of strained muscles. It was still raining repeatedly in those short sharp showers that seemed to be part of the Jari dry season. They made no change in the level of the river which was a good deal lower, and that seemed to be to our advantage. Several times on the way to the Ipitinga we were able to wade up stretches where Mark and I had been forced to portage six weeks previously. We had in fact been very lucky to get a canoe from Monte Dourado — most of the boatmen had stopped doing the run until the rainy season returned. The river was too low and difficult by motor. We were told that the river then (mid-September) was at a level not normally reached until the end of November. This was because the earlier rains had been scarcer than usual and the river had not reached its normal peak. We wondered if there might not be enough water at the headwaters to float our canoe.

We reached Burnt Foot Camp four days later and found all my stuff still there. To celebrate our return we consumed a gourmet dried dinner, and spent a day organising the gear so as to cram it into the canoe. We had to burn a few items that would not fit or that we weren't going to use — among them some of Mark's old clothing. I was just about to burn his old combat jacket, when Peter told me to stop and showed me a note.

'In return for sending my combat jacket to me in Australia, I donate my Swiss Army knife, compass and any other of my personal effects left at Carecaru or Burnt Foot Camp to Peter.'

I was furious to find Mark still taunting me.

'That's a really heavy jacket. We'll have to carry it for the next five months up and over the Tumucumaque mountains. Throw it on the fire.'

Peter's face hardened.

'I promised Mark I'd send it to him.'

'Well, we're hardly a hundred metres from the post office, are we? It's an unreasonable demand.'

I admit, too, that I had had my eye on Mark's knife and compass.

'I'm not going to burn it,' continued Peter, wrapping the jacket in a polythene bag.

'Well, I assure you the first time I feel we need to lighten the load, that bloody jacket will be the first item to go.'

For the moment I had to be content with burning Mark's strange reading matter. On to the fire went Debrett's 'Etiquette and Modern Manners', and the English grammar was consigned for use as toilet paper. The opportunity to leave the jungle impeccably-mannered, socially adept and smoothly erudite had been lost.

It was a relief to leave Burnt Foot Camp with its mosquitoes and bad memories and journey on into the unknown. If the Jari was kind to us we might reach the mouth of the Cuc in five weeks, and be ready to portage over the hills to French Guiana in less than three months. We had a long, long way to go but we were in excellent spirits as we left that camp. The rapid just above the camp that had looked so formidable a few weeks before now delayed us only a few minutes. After that the river was smooth and easy for the rest of the day. Maybe the Jari felt we had passed the tough initiation test and were men enough to be allowed the chance to explore her further. Suddenly there seemed to be much more wildlife. We saw a tapir, a deer, an otter and some monkeys. When we stopped for lunch on a sandbank I cast the spinner and caught a trairao and five piranhas in less than five minutes. We put the piranhas back into the river, which was more than the little ghouls deserved, but everything seemed to give grounds for optimism.

One should never trust the Jari to be consistently benevolent. That afternoon Peter began to feel ill, so we camped early. He vomited several times in the night, had shivers, and a temperature of 103 degrees. It looked like malaria to me, though it seemed unreasonably early for him to get it since we had been on the river for less than three weeks. I started him on a course of treatment just in case, and we stayed at that camp for four days until he felt better. It was an unpleasant camp too, full of mosquitoes and surrounded by unattractive jungle. To me, such areas of jungle are those submerged in the rainy season — jungle that is thorny, tangled and covered with debris deposited by the floods and rotting flotsam lodged in the low branches. When you look for firewood it all seems to crumble in your hands and the termites run up your wrists. I went hunting every day, but not far. Too much effort and noise was involved in getting through such thick vegetation. I shot one small jungle fowl that foolishly alighted in a tree above our camp — but there was only enough meat for one — so I gutted it for Peter as he had been eating very little.

I crossed the river to see if it would be easier hunting over there, and I came upon a magnificently spooky place. It was a pool — an old channel of the river that had been cut off by the river changing course, or by the drop in water level perhaps. The water was dark and littered with fallen debris, and trees met over the top. Cobwebs as resilient as cotton clutched my face, and a little group of bats that had been invisible against the bark of a tree detached themselves silently and flew like wind-blown leaves to another perch, immediately vanishing again.

The water had a stagnant look, but it was far from lifeless. Skirmishes and battles were taking place down there. The surface was furrowed by racing dorsal fins as big fish chased little fish, and even bigger fish chased big fish. Shoals of tucunare, fierce golden predators, cruised the shallows causing fry to scatter in panic.

I went back to the canoe to get the fishing rod and some bait, and seated myself on a rock. It was not a place to fall in. Blasé though I am about piranha and the dangers they present, I would not trust them in a place where food was so obviously in short supply. I was also concerned about anaconda. It seemed just the type of habitat that they would love, and I glanced nervously over my shoulder at frequent intervals. I could imagine that heavy muscular loop of snake dropping around my neck.

I baited up a large hook with a piece of fish, and cast into the centre of the pool. I could see fish racing from all sides, but a ½-kilo something got there first. Disappointed, I began to reel it in, but almost immediately a 3-kilo tucunare swallowed the previous one whole, and I had a bit more of a struggle on my hands.

During the excitement the line got wound round a sunken branch a few metres from the bank, and as I was tweaking the line to free it I saw a massive dark shape appear from the depths, grab the tucunare across the back and make off. I tried to hold on but the 20-kilo line snapped like cotton, and I was left shaken and fishless.

* * *

When we finally got going again we had to wade through a few small rapids but between times the river was slow and deep. The map marked seven major rapids between there and the mouth of the Cuc, and we thought these would help us pinpoint our position accurately. With a 1:1,000,000-scale map, which did not show every twist and turn, nor the many islands, we needed to take care we did not miss the Cuc altogether. The map had been the best we could find but it was originally designed for use by pilots. Apart from the blue lines of rivers (which we hoped were accurate), the map was mainly blank, with 'Relief Data Incomplete' or 'Altitude not believed to exceed 3,000 metres' stamped across the Tumucumaque hills. Well, that was jolly encouraging news.

As we were eating our supper we heard a commotion in the jungle and I grabbed the shotgun, hoping it might be a wild pig or deer. The vegetation parted and two tapirs strolled casually into our camp, grazing and oblivious to our presence. I grinned and lowered the shotgun. Tapirs were far too large to be on our hunting list, and we were happy to sit and watch them. (It was lucky for them they did not wander into our camps a few months later when circumstances were to force us to reconsider our attitude to hunting.) They stood at 5 metres' distance, blinking stupidly and deaf to the insulting comments we were making about their intelligence. Evidently we were downwind. It is a privilege and a pleasure to get these sightings of wildlife. They provide the very special highlights to this type of trip.

Within two days we had managed to pass two of the falls, and they were not especially hard compared to what Mark and I had had to negotiate.

After Peter's first brush with malaria I considered it was fortunate that the river itself was giving him a fairly easy introduction. We got into a routine of travel. Up at first light (five o'clock), we had a large breakfast and got on the river before seven. We paddled for four hours or so, had lunch, went on for another two hours, and then stopped to make camp. As we were making good progress we could afford to stop early, and it was much more pleasant to do so. That way we had a few hours of daylight in which to relax, read, write diaries, swim, fish, hunt and get supper prepared before the sun went down around seven. After that the mosquitoes would come out and we would be driven to our hammocks and nets. Six o'clock was cocktail hour. We wished we had brought more booze with us because we finished our 10 litres in no time at all. Near Carecaru we had found an abandoned house with a tree full of little limes, so for a while we made *caipirinhas* — rum, sugar and lime — and it made a civilised end to the day. When the limes ran out the rum alone was hard to take. A very coarse, fiery spirit made from sugar cane, it is not a drink for sipping and savouring. However, get it past the taste buds and the effect is most agreeable.

We found the best campsites were those with an expanse of flat rock in the foreground. Here we could make our campfire as far away from the jungle as possible, so that the mosquitoes would take longer to find us. Of course if it looked like rain we had to make our fire among the trees near the hammocks, where we would rig up a shelter. It would have been nice to spread blankets on the rocks and sleep under the stars, or lie there chatting or star-gazing until late, but the mosquitoes put paid to that. Also, judging by the number of sloughed-off skins, snakes were abundant among the rocks. There were other dangers too. One morning, when it was Peter's turn to make breakfast and mine to have a fifteen-minute lie-in, I was watching him rummage in the food-bag when suddenly he leapt 2 feet off the ground and gave a yell.

'Ah, shit, shit, shit, shit!' he cried, hopping around clutching his finger.

'What happened?' I giggled. The sight of him prancing naked around the fire had its touch of comedy.

'Bastard animal. It is not funny!'

'What animal?'

'I don't know the name in English.' He gave a word in German that rang no bells.

'You know — it is a sign of the astrology.'

'Astrology? I don't know much about that. Aries? Taurus? Did a bull bite you, Pete?' I giggled.

'You are very funny,' he said as he sucked his finger. 'It is an animal, that has a tail that sticks up above his back, and which stings you.'

'Scorpion?'

'Ya, that's right. Jesus, it hurts.'

A few minutes later I was searching in the food-bag to get some coffee when another scorpion ran over the back of my hand and dropped to the ground.

* * *

Eleven days after leaving Carecaru we were negotiating a little channel that was becoming narrower and narrower, when we looked up and saw a man sitting on a rock 50 metres ahead. The unexpectedness gave us quite a nasty shock, and we quickly covered our nakedness before we paddled up to him. At first we thought he must be an Indian but from nearer we saw he was a light-skinned Brazilian. He was fishing and seemed very, very wary of us. We never found out who he was, or what he was doing there because he evaded all our questions, then asked us plenty which we evaded in turn. It was not a basis for a lively conversation, and there was something unsettling about his impassiveness. He squatted with his fishing line in his fingers, not shifting his position once in the ten minutes we were there. He was not going to miss any fish through idle chit-chat. We had the impression he had been a very long time alone. His voice had a rusty, unused quality, and if he ever had any social graces or humour the jungle had robbed him of them. He gave us the creeps, so curiosity unsatisfied, we paddled on our way.

The channel we were following soon became clogged with more rocks and more shallows, so that it was easier to get out and walk. Finally we were forced to do our first portage since Carecaru. It had been a good run, eleven days without a portage, and Mark would have been incredulous that the Jari permitted such relaxation. There is nothing like a portage to make you realise just how many provisions you are carrying, and we had to do three that day before we finally emerged into a wider channel. There we were faced with a large rapid which we roped our way up, a section of quiet water, and then a worse rapid cascading over several drops round a jumble of islands. That took us all the next day to negotiate, with only the briefest moments of paddling, and a lot of wading through fast dangerous water.

I shouted at Peter several times. He seemed too casual when walking the canoe up rapids. All casualness had left me after that near disaster with Mark, and I preferred to walk up extremely cautiously. We would take up positions on either side of the bow, and whenever the water was very fast, or the rocks slippery, I preferred one of us to move forward at a time so as to get a firm footing before nodding to the other who then moved up too. Without this precaution there was the risk that we would both slip together. Something went wrong with our manoeuvres that day because we both lost our footing simultaneously. We floundered in the waist-deep torrent and the bow of the canoe turned slightly across the current. That's all it takes. Just a few degrees to one side and she becomes too heavy to hold. She tips and fills with water. Mercifully we were wading up a very narrow channel, and the swinging bow hit the bank which delayed her progress long enough for us to hang on. A few of our belongings started to float away but Peter managed to grab them. It was a very close shave. In Amazonia disaster is only a moment's carelessness away. Generally you are given no chance to learn from your mistakes. We had been lucky.

A short time later I noticed a piece of wood hanging from the bottom of the canoe. This turned out to be the keel, or rather half the keel – the rest had broken off and disappeared. When working on the canoe at Carecaru I had seen that there were a couple of screws missing but had assumed all would be okay. Well, I was wrong, so of course we had to stop, take her out of the water to dry, and fix half the keel back with fibreglass. It had been a day of hard-learned lessons. Do not be careless. And do not be lazy.

The next day started with a large rapid that forced us to portage, and continued difficult until we camped in the early evening. We had endured three days of continuous rapids – disconcertingly like the Jari that Mark and I had known and loved. We camped that night in a small gorge with huge boulders on both banks, and round the corner we could hear an ominous roaring. It was depressing to lie in our hammocks and listen to the sound of the next day's toil and misery. Impossible to reassure ourselves that we must be over the worst by now; not with the thunder of falling waters drowning the jungle chorus.

We set off heavy-hearted next morning, and there just around the bend were all the obstacles we had been imagining. The river had narrowed and now ran through vertical-sided rocky channels, falling over no less than eight drops. There was no way we could paddle, or walk the canoe up there. It meant eight separate portages over the sharp rocks, dotted with dangerous blow-holes and sculptured caves. Judging by the expanse of water-hewn rock at present 5 metres above water level, this was an awesome place in the rainy season. Huge tree trunks had been stranded by the retreating water, and were waiting for the next flood to continue their journey. Every one of these portages required six or seven trips for each of us with the equipment, before we carried the canoe and relaunched her above the fall. Then we reloaded, paddled 20 metres, and did it all again. So we passed the day, and by evening had covered a kilometre or less and still not reached calm waters.

While waiting for supper to cook, I wandered upstream to check things out. I could see the need for at least three more portages in the first 200 metres, but it was a positive pleasure to stroll over the rocks in the relative cool of the late afternoon when the light softened, and when, for once, I was not humping a heavy load. From under the rocks and down inside the holes I could hear the gurgle of water, and once or twice the cheeping of young birds in their nest. The parents would try to decoy me away by feigning injury or, in one case, dive-bombing. This was a fairly small bird but the sharp whistle of wind through its feathers made me duck each time. Next I surprised a jaguar on the rocks. He paused for a second – his spotted coat glowing gold in the orange light of the setting sun, then turned and bounded for the jungle, kicking up spurts of sand across a small beach. From his tracks I paced out the size of his leaps: over 5 metres. I saw many other tracks too that evening: tapir, alligator, ocelot and deer.

Recently we had caught a new species of fish – one very similar to the tambaqui found in the Amazon, with delicious, white, firm, juicy meat reminiscent of veal. I am told that the Santo Antonio falls act as a barrier to certain fish. For example the tambaqui and the fresh-water porpoise are found below them on the Jari, but not above. Also there are no stingrays above the falls. This was an enormous relief for men who had to wade so much.

We had 1.5 kilos of fish each for supper with rice, and although it had been a hard day, we felt terrific. Nothing like paddling and portaging to get you fit, and now that our malaria was under control we felt supremely healthy. The portages were a bore and hard work, but the scenery at rapids was always stunning: sparkling cascades, rocky islets with miniature jungles in their centres, flowers, bleached driftwood, black rocks, blue sky, herons fishing, and parrots and butterflies to provide some gaudy touches. Being fit we could carry all the gear several times and not get particularly tired, and as we hopped over the rocks with 40-kilo sacks on our shoulders sometimes we would realise that we were whistling or singing.

However the week that followed gave us less and less to sing about. On the next day we set off straight into a portage, just a small, quick one. Then there was a big one over 100 metres, then we waded up a fast section to another portage, then crossed to the other bank and did one more. Total distance covered? About 400 metres. In front of us was another series of falls, and after getting past two of them the next morning, we reached a place where the right bank was impossible to walk over with gear on our backs. We were faced with huge boulders and large gaps between them. On the left, the jungle came right down to the water's edge so we could not portage on that side either. We decided on a reccy and found the river looped round to the left with five or six drops in quick succession.

We sat on the rocks and stared at each other gloomily.

'What are you thinking?' Peter asked.

'You remember that people told us about a rapid called Macocoara — somewhere up here — where it's necessary to portage over a hillside? This could be it. It would be quicker to cut across the loop by carrying everything over this hill, wouldn't it?'

'Oh, Christ,' muttered Peter, looking at the steep climb. 'I think we have no choice.'

There was no alternative, so we cut a trail, humped the sacks over, and the next morning we completed the portage by taking the canoe across. It was a long, awkward load with which to scramble up a jungle hillside. It got wedged between trees, tangled in vines, and was heavy enough to have us gasping.

'This is how it will be when we portage into French Guiana,' Peter panted, 'except it will be fifteen kilometres instead of five hundred metres. We are crazy, it is madness.'

We lay on the jungle floor and giggled.

'We'll also have to climb over a three-hundred-metre mountain too, not a thirty-metre hillock like this one! It's utter lunacy,' I said, and we giggled some more.

We were cheerful because we felt instinctively that we had got over the worst and reached quiet water at last. However after five minutes' paddling we rounded a bend only to curse: more of the same! During the rest of the day we did four more portages, and the following day we had a 200-metre portage, a long wade, then brief peace and quiet before another portage, a little paddle, a wade and then another portage.

My feet were beginning to give me the same trouble I'd had earlier. It was a type of foot-rot caused by always being in the water, and always wearing wet tennis shoes with sand or small stones in them. Little patches of raw flesh developed between and under the toes, and along part of the instep. It would heal quickly with a few days of dry feet. Small chance of that.

It became hard to get started in the morning, knowing the sort of monotonous activity that lay ahead. Every day it was portaging, wading under overhanging branches, moving rocks and driftwood from channels to deepen them, dragging the canoe through the shallows, loading and unloading the sacks, cutting bushes and sunken branches, banging our scabby, infected legs and shins, getting our ankles trapped down crevices, and being whipped by thorny branches while our feet rotted away. We had spent nine days like this before we finally emerged into quiet water. Nine days to cover 20 kilometres at the most.

What a great holiday we were having.

8 Up the Cuc

Ah, the simple pleasure of sitting quietly in the canoe all day long, with the sun on one's back, feet dry, just dipping that paddle! The Jari had put us through yet a further trial, and having proved we were worthy to see a little more of her, was giving us a breather. We covered over 15 kilometres in one day, passing the Mapari tributary (which enabled us to pinpoint our position on the map), and getting through two more rapids. They were kids' stuff: one tiny portage for each and on our way.

'But, Peter,' I would complain with mock puzzlement, 'the map shows a big rapid here.' I surveyed the 2-metre fall that we were negotiating. 'I see no rapid here. Maybe a few bubbles, but not what I'd call a rapid'

'Lord, no,' Peter would agree. 'We used to do ten of these before breakfast.'

If our map was to be trusted there were only three more major rapids before the Cuc. This was greatly encouraging, but we did not dare to build up our hopes too high. Suppose there were so many rapids the cartographer had grown lazy and omitted a lot of them? And was the Jari really likely to be so sweet? We got on with our daily toil and enjoyed any respite that we were offered.

Once a week we permitted ourselves the luxury of a rest day, or as much of a rest day as the mosquitoes would allow. It hadn't rained for ten days, and the jungle was very dry, but that seemed to make no difference to their numbers. Each time we arrived at a new camp it took them a few hours to find us, but once they did they stayed day and night until we left. After dusk, the only refuge was the hammock, but that meant a long, long night.

The equator runs across the river Jari a few kilometres south of the confluence with the Ipitinga, so we were dominated by the equatorial pattern of almost equal days and nights. It would be dark by seven o'clock, and dawn would break at about five-thirty. Usually we had taken enough exercise during the day to be pretty tired, and that helped us to sleep quickly. At other times we lay awake for five or six hours, sweating and tossing in the airlessness of the net, with the whine of the swarms outside and the itching caused by the dozen or so which had broken through the defences. In normal life I have always been one for going to bed late, and for me the worst aspect of jungle trips are the enforced early nights and the long hours of darkness. Sleeplessness at home is a question of worry about how one is going to feel next morning at work, but can be made more tolerable by turning on the light and reading, listening to the radio, or getting up and raiding the fridge. In the jungle one can't waste torch batteries for reading, so there is nothing to do but sweat it out, think of home and make little plans or projects.

We had one more easy day, and then new difficulties arose. The Jari became shallow with almost dry channels full of rocks and only an inch or two of water. Frequently there was no gap between the rocks wide enough to get the canoe through, so irksome 3-metre portages were necessary. We spent most of the day either walking the canoe or dragging it. Bits of fibreglass were ripped off the bottom and floated away. Peter broke his paddle trying to fend off a rock, and the whole thing was agony on our backs and formerly-on-the-mend feet. We made five long portages, and in the afternoon came to a cascade that fell over 10 metres. This forced us to do a portage of over half a kilometre, and above it the view was depressing: rocks as far as the eye could see — just like a wave-cut platform at low tide, complete with rock pools. The river was spread through so many channels that not one of them was deep.

'Oh, Jari, you mean bitch,' I muttered, 'do you always have to be so bloody spiteful?'

We spent the next day and a half walking up this maze, getting progressively more demoralised and bad-tempered. Stopping for lunch on the second day we had a strange experience. I had shot a curassow, so Peter was sitting on some rocks plucking it and frying up its liver and heart with a little rice, while I repaired his broken paddle with fibreglass. Looking up, I saw a figure several hundred metres away up ahead. We waved, and he seemed to reply in kind, but made no move towards us. We were there for well over an hour, and all that time the figure stood out in the hot sun and in the same place watching us. We wished we had binoculars to examine him. From that distance he seemed naked and pale-skinned, but we could not be sure. Finally we set off wading through a difficult section towards him and he disappeared from sight. We reached where he had been, called and whistled, but there was no sign. Perplexed, we left the canoe and spent twenty minutes wandering around the islands, before we grew worried about leaving our canoe and stuff unattended, and sat on the rocks near it to have a smoke.

'Bloody strange character, isn't he?' I remarked to Peter.

'I'm thinking he is somewhere on one of those islands hiding in the trees watching us,' he said.

'Must be,' and we glanced around in apprehension.

'I'm thinking that he is pointing the arrow at you, just now. He won't shoot at me. Too skinny. But you are a nice, big, fat, easy shot,' offered Peter kindly, and we laughed nervously. We felt sure our elusive stranger was an Indian, and the situation was creepy.

'Come our redskin!' we shouted facetiously in English. 'Come and see the super presents we've got for you!'

Nothing stirred.

'Let's get the hell out of here.'

'Good idea!' said Peter, and we waded on our way with many a glance over our shoulders, determined to get away as far as possible before nightfall. Later we saw on the map that there was a tributary entering the Jari thereabouts, and thought that the Indian could have been from a settlement up there.

We continued to see a lot of wildlife – families of capybara that gave a warning bark and galloped into the river, tapir, coatis, numerous monkeys and three giant otters. These latter are charming animals, and a rare sight on so many Amazonian rivers where they have been widely hunted for their skins. One of them saw us coming and slipped off the rocks into the water. The other two stayed lying on their backs paws in the air, unaware of our presence and ignoring the warning chattering that their companion was making. We got to within 3 metres before they saw us, and then they dived and swam around the canoe, popping their heads up like periscopes.

The river was a little deeper at last – it had carved a channel through some rocky areas, and for the most part we were able to paddle although the current was swift. We learned that the difficult rapid of the previous week had not been Macocoara at all, because we found it the next day. The river fell over 25 metres, but to get round it we found a trail cut by past portages. Our first glimpse of the falls had taken us by surprise. First of all we heard it, and from the volume of the roar presumed it to be near. Then we rounded a bend, and the water was smooth in front of us, but way up on the hillsides that bordered the river we saw a glint of white, still too far away to be easily discernible. Five hundred metres further on we were able to see that the glint of white was the top of the falls and that the bulk of the water was falling into the gorge from the right.

The portage was surprisingly short and painless considering the height of the falls. Yet at Carecaru this was the most fearsome rapid that everyone had heard about. By the side of the trail there was a little plinth with the names of a past Brazilian expedition, dated October 1937. The thirties seemed to have been a very busy time on the Jari. We had already seen the cross of the dead German expeditionary at Santo Antonio.

The falls themselves were magnificent – cascading in a dozen places over rocks festooned with moss and flowers. The water sparkled in the sunlight, and hummingbirds and green parrots flashed through the spray and rainbows. In the rainy season it must be spectacular indeed, although how one would get past then I don't know, as the trail would be under water and the rapids above the falls too dangerous.

The next day I felt ill again and my feet had given up on me. We had to do a portage over sharp rocks and I was hobbling along doing only one trip to Peter's three. The foot-rot had spread all along my insteps, so there was no relief. It would have been all right if we had been given a day or two of calm paddling, but that day began with over a kilometre of wading, and after 300 metres I called a halt.

'We're going to have to camp for a day or two, Pete. If I don't rest them now, they'll only take longer to heal later. I'm sorry.'

'No problem,' he replied. 'If you do not rest, I would soon have to carry you as well as all the sacks,' and he grinned.

Good old Peter; he was as keen to press on as I was, but never complained. He slung my hammock for me and I crawled in. It was bliss to rest the tootsies — but I was feeling decidedly rough in general, and I recognised the symptoms all too well.

Through the mosquito net I watched Peter wading up the rapid, casting the spinner. Apart from a few minor details like his lack of clothing, the hot sun and the lush vegetation he could have been a trout fisherman on a Scottish stream. Suddenly I saw him reach into the water and come up with a .32-calibre shotgun — a bit rusty, but perhaps still serviceable. The result of some overturned canoe in the last dry season, we supposed.

Later I had a classic malaria attack, shivers, temperature to 104 degrees and then sweats. I took three Fansider. Doctors warn of the toxicity of Fansidar — saying that you should never take more than three in any one week. Certainly every time I took three they did strange things to me. I felt numb and floaty, and my hearing became distorted. Sounds came in circular waves. A wind rustling the jungle canopy would sound like the whirring of helicopter blades. In short I was stoned, and it was a welcome distraction from the miseries of malaria attacks.

In common with most people of my age my pre-malaria experience of sickness had been no more than 'flu and the usual childhood maladies. I was unprepared for that feeling of utter misery, which presented intimations of mortality — a new, frightening and disturbing idea to a fit young person. By the time I had this attack at Macocoara I was an old hand, having experienced eight malarial bouts already, yet the fear remained and I suffered the same. In some ways perhaps I had more to worry about because I was more informed about the possible complications of the disease, and aware of how different my self-medication in the jungle was from the treatment given in hospital. Falciparum malaria can cause kidney failure, permanent damage to the liver, brain haemorrhaging and death within three weeks. All that stood between me and such disasters was quinine and Fansidar — two good drugs admittedly — but God help me if they got lost in a rapid or ran out.

With such cheerful topics to think about we stayed put the next day, and even with a short spell of rest my feet had improved a lot. I had a temperature of 101 degrees, but compared with the previous evening I felt positively sprightly and even went on a short shuffling walk to look for gold. With the knowledge that the Jari was a gold area we always kept an eye out. We didn't want to pan for it, move tons of sand or earth, or do any hard work, we just wanted to find a few nuggets of half a kilo each. Near the camp was a little creek which to our untrained eyes shrieked 'Bonanza,' and we spent the afternoon grabbing handfuls of sand and shingle to sift through. Having spent so much time walking up the river we felt it would be only fair if we stubbed our toes on the occasional golden pebble and returned home wealthy. We used to fantasize about which items in the canoe would be thrown away to make room for our cache of gold and of finding a gold field up there on the Jari, where in future years we could return periodically and secretly when our extravagant, debauched lifestyles needed new financing. Needless to say we never found one speck of the stuff — but no doubt over the weeks we frequently trod on it, slept on it, or built fires on it.

There was a colony of hoatzin in some bushes that overhung the river near our camp. These pheasant-sized brown birds hissed and squabbled incessantly, and it was only their inedibility that spared them a few pellets up the back-side. Their flesh gives off a strong, disagreeable smell, and that offensiveness is their protection. Scientists regard the hoatzin as a living link between primitive and modern forms of bird, as it is the only survivor that resembles the oldest of all known birds — the archaeopteryx — reconstructed from fossil remains found in Bavaria. The baby hoatzin, I had read, has a two-clawed 'finger' at the angle of each wing. The new-born bird can creep around in the branches, and in times of danger, drop out of the nest into the water where it swims with astonishing speed. Using its wings like hands, it then climbs to the nest once the threat has passed. I sat and watched them for a time, but unfortunately their eggs had not yet hatched, and I could not test these observations with some baby-baiting.

Although I had another fever that night, I felt strong enough to move on the next day. As Macocoara was the last major rapid marked on our map we had good reason to feel optimistic. The Cuc was only 75 kilometres away now, and perhaps the Jari would be moved to bestow upon us a kind farewell so that we would remember her with a touch of affection? Surely she would not want us to desert her for the Cuc in our present mood? It was time she revealed to us her sweet nature if she had such a thing, and atoned for all the toil and hardship she had caused us.

As if in answer to our prayers the river did change for the better. Suddenly she was island-free and fairly deep. Almost unrecognisable. This was the first time since Monte Dourado that she had kept to one channel for more than a kilometre, and the absence of islands made it much easier for us to follow her twists and turns on the map. We now knew where we were to the nearest kilometre and could check our progress. The chances of missing the mouth of the Cuc because it was hidden the other side of an isalnd had receded.

However it now became Peter's turn to be sick. There had been a strong breeze all morning that I had found pleasant, but Peter complained of feeling cold, and put on a sweatshirt and wrapped a blanket over his shoulders. The temperature was in the eighties. I don't know what I look like when I've got malaria — not too good, I expect — but Peter always looks ghastly. Having a naturally dark complexion, he got very tanned in the course of the trip, but when he was ill his face went a sickly grey. He vomited frequently and his temperature went over 105 degrees. That used to worry me. God, he might die and leave me up there on my own! We nursed each other with concern during these malaria attacks, and fortunately they never once coincided on the trip, otherwise we should have stopped eating for a day or two. We both found that if food was presented to us we could eat it, however feverish we were. But preparing it would have been beyond our strength.

We spent three days waiting for him to recover and I kept boredom at bay by doing a few chores. First I checked all our food supplies to see if anything was damp and which items were getting low. We still had plenty of staple foodstuffs, but most of our luxuries — onions, drinking chocolate, tomato paste, etc — were finished. I washed some clothes, fished with a fair amount of success, went hunting with none, and forced myself to read long passages from 'History of the World'. I suddenly had the urge to have short hair, so hacked away at it with the tiny scissors of my Swiss Army knife. I cut the front and sides to one centimetre long all round, and Peter did the back. Finally I trimmed my beard, and finished up looking like an escaped convict. What the hell? It felt cooler, and who was going to see me for a while anyway?

I also repaired one of our camp stools that had begun to fall apart. 'You're getting a bit old and soft,' Mark laughed when he saw my purchase of a little folding stool in London the week before we set out for Brazil. Despite excess baggage charges I had decided that a stool would be worth taking to improve the quality of life on the Jari: a little concession to luxury. I know well enough that without it, at the end of a hard day, you end up leaning against trees aswarm with ants, or sitting in the debris on the jungle floor.

Mark considered it unnecessary, or so he said at first. However the day before we left Manaus he appeared in the hotel with a big grin and a package. Inside was a folding stool — larger, lighter, cheaper and much more comfortable than my own. These stools made the period we spent together even more of a galling experience. Mine had a tendency to collapse, almost pinching my testicles off, or to sink slowly into the soft soil until I was sitting on the ground anyhow. Furthermore, it was so low that ten minutes on it would cause my feet to go to sleep.

Mark's stool, on the other hand, behaved itself perfectly, and judging by his comfortable expression had no defects on that score either.

After Mark and I split up, and I returned with Peter, I was tempted to tell him that for some reason Mark had bought that absurd little stool and I had bought the other. Honesty and friendship won the day, and to save a squabble every evening we designated it the cook's chair. If anything stopped us shirking our cooking duties it was the idea of sitting on that ridiculous little thing.

As I repaired it with a piece of wire, I thought that next time I go to Amazonia I shall go one better. I want a folding chair with arm rests and a back. On second thoughts, I'd better take two otherwise my companion might murder me for it.

* * *

Hunting trips were rarely successful, but they did take us away from the river and reward us with some pleasant and interesting sights. Apart from the usual glimpse of the rear-end of fleeing deer, we saw other creatures. There were marmosets, tortoises, the occasional sloth hanging upside-down from a branch and peering round sleepily, but not nearly so many animals as one might expect. Usually that was because we were making so much bloody noise; but once we accepted the fact that we were unlikely to shoot anything, and began to treat the excursion as an interesting nature walk, we found it absorbing.

We came across giant trees with trunks so massive and straight that they made us giddy looking up to their crown 65 metres above. They were supported by huge buttress roots often higher than our heads and only 2 or 3 centimetres thick, and it was pleasant to sit down and recline against their fibrous, russet bark and listen to the sounds of the jungle.

Woodpeckers scampered up the trees, cocked their heads to listen for the burrowing grubs and launched into an attack sometimes with incredible loud staccato, perhaps six strikes to a second.

A great variety of jungle sounds were familiar to me by now, but I was often not sure if they were the sounds of bird or insect. These were the wold-whistler and the knife sharpener, the football fan's rotating ratchet, and something that went ohhhhhhh-si, si, si, si, si, si, si. I recognised the squawking green parrots, and the raucous macaws which always flew in pairs conducting their screeching conversation, and the whirr of tiny hummingbirds which hung suspended nearby with their wings a blur, before darting a metre or two up, down or to the side. There were the beautiful irridescent morpho butterflies too, the size of a human hand, catching the occasional ray of sunlight in a dazzling flash of turquoise. They were seemingly clumsy in flight, but could fly through a tangle of lianas with great ease.

The jungle could be thick and inpenetrable, or as easy to walk in as an English beechwood — when it was like entering a cathedral. The tree trunks rose like pillars in the coolness of the shady half-light. Insects ruled the jungle floor. Lines of leaf-cutter ants carried pieces of greenery four times their size and cleared bare paths through the debris. Termites had constructed covered tunnels up the outside of any dead tree they were working on. The leaves of the lower bushes were often totally stripped by caterpillars. If you raked the dead leaves dozens of beetles would be revealed, and always the air was filled with the hum of bees and the drone of insects. Fortunately the blood-sucking ones were fairly rare during the day.

We usually returned to camp sweaty, covered in debris and cobwebs, scratched and still carrying the shotgun but having murdered nothing. Each time we would have found something interesting or new to observe: a tiny bird's nest for example, glued to the leaf of a sapling, and so small and light that it, and the three eggs it held, did not even bend the slender stem, or a tree that was obviously a favourite scratching post for jaguars. As much as 3 metres off the ground we could see that the bark had been gouged, raked and shredded by those powerful claws. A hunting trip also served as a pretext to get away on our own for an hour or two; important on a trip where we were together for twenty-four hours a day.

Peter was remarkably even-tempered and we rarely bickered or quarrelled. When we did it was invariably me who started it. He was very quiet, and since his English was not perfect, I felt sometimes he was just nodding his head without understanding all I was saying. But the silences were companionable, and I'm no chatterbox anyway. I would rather travel with someone who talks too little than one who talks too much.

Everyone likes to think that in times of stress and hardship they behave coolly, rationally, with good humour and in a manner supportive to their fellows. This trip really tested these assumptions, and sadly I often did not score too well. I became sulky and moody and threw little tantrums when I kicked the canoe, hurled sacks of food or hopped up and down swearing. Whenever I did behave like this a calm, rational voice would refuse to be silent in my head. 'God, you're being childish and petulant,' it would reprimand with infuriating smugness, and I would carry on with my tantrum feeling pretty ridiculous. Peter did not produce many such outbursts. He would calmly take over whatever I had left undone when I stalked off to sit in the river and brood. That angered me even more.

Generally, however, we kept remarkably cheerful throughout the trip. We would laugh, and clown a little, and although the constant singing of the first weeks was not kept up, we did occasionally hum and sing through the never-ending routine of daily chores.

Every morning camp had to be broken, everything packed away, breakfast cooked, items of food fetched from the stores in the canoe and transferred to the food-bag, clothes washed (although less and less frequently), pots scrubbed, fish gutted and scaled, birds plucked, lunch and supper cooked, hammocks and plastic sheet put up, things repaired and machetes sharpened. All this and the trials of paddling and portaging as well. Yet not once did we argue about whose turn it was to do any of these chores. Each of us knew it had to be done, and got down to it. Bloody commendable, I think.

One night a jaguar strolled into our camp and gave me a scare. We were sleeping on an island, and had noticed numerous jaguar tracks criss-crossing a beach on the far side. Even so, we had not bothered keeping the fire going, letting it die once supper was cooked. Jaguars were abundant on the Jari but we felt they would stay away from man. According to the best book written on the subject, 'The World of the Jaguar' by Richard Perry, the animal is not aggressive and is only likely to attack if wounded or protecting its cubs. However, owing to the terrain it inhabits and the extent of its habitual territory, the jaguar is the least studied of the big cats.

That particular night I awoke suddenly, with the certainty that something menacing was near me in the darkness. I lay motionless, staring in the blackness, but it was a moonless night and so dark I began to wonder if I'd been struck by sudden blindness. There was a clunk of a cooking-pot. Was it Peter, having a snack? 'Pete,' I whispered, but instantly regretted opening my mouth. He would be using his torch if he was up and about. Silence returned, except for the thumping of my heart. Everything was quiet for so long I wondered why I felt so strangely apprehensive. We often had visits from creatures in the night. Why was I on edge? I sniffed. Cat! I could smell the rank odour of tom-cat. Then I heard the stealthy movement of a large animal taking a few paces towards my hammock before stopping again. Oh Christ. A jaguar. I could imagine him 2 metres away, powerfully muscled, head raised as he checked my scent. I lay as if paralysed; any movement and he might pounce and I would be trapped in the folds of my net. And if jaguars shared the habits of domestic cats I did not relish the idea of having my hammock swung by a playful kitty with paws as big as my hand.

I began to realise that I was lying all cramped. I would have to move soon. My throat was itching; I would have to cough. The jaguar was also motionless, but once or twice I heard it sniff the air. I had to do something or this could go on all night. I said a little prayer, drew in a lungful of air, and leapt up in the hammock, emitting a banshee wail. I don't know who got the bigger fright, the jaguar or Peter. The animal leapt through a pile of our dirty plates, crashed away through the jungle, splashed across the shallow river and kept on going. Peter was plucked from his peaceful slumbers by my scream and by a large, powerful form colliding with one of the ropes holding up his hammock.

Nearly the whole length of the Jari had a large frog population, and at night they began their croaking chorus − often twenty or more together. Usually I was able to ignore them, but one night, unable to get to sleep, I started to count the croaks of one frog. It had already been croaking for some time, croaking about once a second or a bit faster. I swear this little bugger croaked 10,000 times without a rest before I gave up counting. That means I lay there for two and a half hours counting the bastard − so we were equally deranged. I rose in the dark, grabbed the shotgun and spent half an hour trying to locate it so as to blow its head off.

Peter recovered, and we moved on up the river. The Jari remained island-free, fairly deep and calm. She was about 50 metres wide at this point and serene and friendly. All day long we met no obstacles − just sat there and paddled, travelling over 15 kilometres. There were an enormous number of fish around, mainly piranha, which were probably congregating to spawn. We passed areas where over difty dorsal fins protruded above the surface, and more fish splashed in the shallows. We could never catch any when they were massed together like that. They must have had other things on their minds than food.

It was when we were casting the spinner among these fish in the hope of foul-hooking one across the back, that our fishing reel gave up on us. The handle stripped its thread and then broke off. It was a serious blow. There seemed to be no repair we could improvise. Fishing was our main source of food and from now on we were going to be much less successful. We would have to supplement our food supplies more efficiently. So we turned to the shotgun.

Our appetites were enormous, and food became an obsession. We tried to make our diet as varied and interesting as possible, but were obviously limited. We used to make rice cakes stiffened with flour and fried, porridge or oat cakes, farinha cakes − either sweet or savoury − and pancakes. A treat we looked forward to twice a week was spaghetti with an oil and garlic sauce. During the first weeks we had enjoyed onion, tomato puree and even parmesan cheese, too, but they ran out. We also fried up any rice left over from previous meals, and ate plenty of beans, fried lumps of dough or made stick bread.

Stick bread is delicious — or seems so to the hungry expeditionary. You mix flour, water and a pinch of baking powder to a smooth dough and knead it thoroughly. Then you wind a long length round a green stick in a spiral and bake it over the hot coals of a fire. It takes about an hour to cook, so you have plenty of time to yearn for civilisation where you can pop into a bakery and buy something much nicer. I had been slightly put off stick bread just before our trip started by reading of two travellers who died in East Africa after wrapping the dough round a poisonous stick, a danger I had never considered before. However I decided the danger did not outweigh the pleasure.

Bean sprouts were something we also tried to cultivate several times. These are normally easy to produce by putting a handful of raw beans into a large plastic bag and covering with warm water overnight. In the morning you prick holes in the bag and drain the beans, then you refill and drain two or three times a day until the sprouts are ready four days later. However we found we had bought a really dud batch of beans for this trip. They were obviously so old and dry that just cooking them took over twelve hours, even after soaking. They never produced so much as one sprout before the whole lot grew mouldy and had to be thrown away. A shame. We fancied a salad of raw sprouts.

Until now fish had accompanied most of the above delicacies — either filleted, fried or boiled in a soup. Amazonian fish are generally very tasty but eating so many had become boring and repetitive, so when the reel packed up we were happy to lift the moratorium we had imposed on certain animals and go after some juicy red meat.

We shot a capybara one morning. There were eleven in the group: six adults and the rest youngsters. We pursued them across the river and shot an adult female. Fortunately the river was shallow because after thrashing for a few seconds she died and sank, contrary to expectations, and it was only by wading around that we were able to find her. She was very fat and heavy and we spent the rest of the day skinning and butchering her. It was a lengthy job just removing the skin, and then the meat had to be cut into steaks for frying with the liver and heart. Other parts we cubed for stew, and then cut the remainder into thin strips which we salted and started to dry in the sun. We had meat for several days.

We were camped in a beautiful place, a grassy hollow obviously covered by water for most of the year but now lush and dry. It seemed like a park with soft grass underfoot and a few trees to provide shade. This was a welcome break from exuberant vegetation. There were animal tracks everywhere — tapir, capybara, jaguar, ocelot, otter, deer and alligator. To our

relief, too, mosquitoes were fewer, and we sat under a full moon with almost daylight visibility. Peter measured that we had covered 250 kilometres since the Ipitinga, which was not bad going. He estimated we should reach the mouth of the Cuc the following afternoon.

We set off at first light, keen to begin what would be the second leg of our trip, the Cuc.

We saw our first anaconda. It was sleeping half out of the water and we paddled very close before it woke and slipped below the surface. About 3 metres long we estimated: a baby. The largest anaconda ever measured was 37 feet 6½ inches (11.5 metres). according to many sources, yet much larger ones have wriggled their way into travellers' accounts and folk-lore. In fact there have been so many absurd exaggerations and touched-up photos of gigantic specimens that everyone has grown wary. For example a Brazilian told me in 1980 of an incident when he was a guide on the Juruena river.

'I know every metre of that river, Senhor,' he told me, 'and every rapid and fall. But one day we rounded a bend and saw a fall that had never been there, that shouldn't have been there. Getting closer we saw that it was a giant *sucuriju* stretched half-submerged from bank to bank, with the water pouring over its back. It looked like a cascade from a distance.' The river, he said, was about 60 metres wide at that point.

Such nonsense fuels the disbelievers. They also cite the reward of $5,000 that Theodore Roosevelt offered in 1913 to anyone who could produce the skin and vertebrae of any anaconda of over 11 metres. That was an enormous sum in those days, and many people were destitute after the collapse of the rubber boom, but the reward was never claimed. However, I remain open-minded, and think it is probable that giant anacondas do exist in Amazonia. Colonel Fawcett, while obsessive about his quest for El Dorado, was usually very restrained and matter-of-fact in describing jungle perils, and he measured a 62-foot (19.5-metre) specimen on the lower Amazon in 1907. Other reliable travellers have measured equally large anacondas.

Anyway, unless extremely hungry or angry, the anaconda won't attack people. It preys on caimans, water-birds and capybaras and can swallow animals of up to 70 kilograms. Contrary to popular belief, it does not crush its victim, but compresses it just enough for it to asphyxiate, and then swallows it whole. The anaconda has about seventy teeth in each jaw, the longest being about 14 millimetres and the thickness of a needle. Set at an angle towards the throat, these are used to grip the prey and to assist the labour of swallowing such a huge meal. An anaconda in a zoo thrives on six large meals a year, but no doubt in the wild it would hunt every few weeks.

The Jari here continued free of rapids but it was often so shallow we could walk from bank to bank with the water not above our knees. This was irritating because we could not dig our paddles in as deep as usual without hitting the bottom so had to jab rather futilely at the surface. There were dazzling white sandbanks where we stopped for rests or to swim, and where on other rivers I might have hoped to find turtle eggs. There seemed to be no turtles on the Jari. Perhaps Santo Antonio was a barrier to them too, as it was to sting rays and other fish.

* * *

There can be few creatures in this world of tooth and claw that give off such an air of benign inoffensiveness as the turtle. Perhaps it's that slow, waddling gait on land, or that rather absurd carapace. Most likely it's that wrinkled neck, bald head and myopic eye that reminds us of kindly old men. There are two species of turtle in Amazonia. The tartaruga is the largest freshwater turtle in the world, living over thirty years and growing to 80 kilos. Its carapace is greenish-brown and round. The Tracaja is smaller with a more elliptical, greyer, carapace. Unfortunately they are both succulent and flavoursome, and the locals catch them either by harpooning or by using floating lines with baited hooks under fruit trees.

Only once have I killed a turtle on my river trips. I shot a tracaja from 100 metres with a .22 rifle as it sat basking on a rock in midstream, and then I paddled over to retrieve it. It was still very much alive and when I got it to the campfire I was in a dilemma as to how to finish it off. I saw a Brazilian once chop through the carapace with a machete and yank the beast out, and I rebelled at the cruelty. Yet now I was forced to consider the practical difficulties of butchering a well-defended turtle.

I placed it the right way up and stood beside it quietly waiting for the head to emerge. Sensibly the head stayed under cover for over fifteen minutes before it considered the danger had passed, and it headed for the river to soothe its pain. Swiftly I swung the machete and chopped the head off smoothly, congratulating myself on achieving a difficult task with the minimum of cruelty.

I then chopped the two places where the lower half of the carapace joins the upper and pulled it apart. To my consternation I discovered the heart was still pumping, the lungs still billowing, the legs were waving, and even the severed head was opening and shutting its mouth. My appetite was fading fast as I separated the guts and bunged the rest in a pan of boiling water, slamming the lid down shut. Even then the waving legs twice kicked the lid off before the dismembered creature consented to die. Never again.

* * *

In 1970 when I travelled by steamer down the Rio Madeira the cargo of live turtles grew at every stop. Passengers embarked with them carried on their heads, in sacks, or under their arms. Men paddled out to the steamer and sold them to the captain. Soon even the floor space under the hammocks had its cargo of mute suffering. Laid on their backs, they were rendered helpless, undignified and pitiful. They waved their legs, extended their grandfatherly necks and spent the journey trying to right themselves. Very occasionally one would succeed if its legs could get a purchase, and many had their legs tied tightly across the underneath of the carapace to prevent this.

Many turtles had been caught a week or more before, and kept in pens waiting for the steamer to arrive. No one had watered or fed them. Turtles can live for much longer without sustenance so it was deemed unnecessary. Several had the puncture hole of the harpoon in the carapace which oozed a watery blood. Very soon nearly all had rubbed raw patches in their legs and necks from chaffing against their inverted shells. Others had bleeding wounds from the cords that tied their legs.

There was only one other gringo on board, an America, who viewed the pitiful cargo with even more outrage than I. We remonstrated with the passengers and the captain that the creatures should at least be watered and fed, kept untethered in the hold, should not be taken in September when some of the captives were undoubtedly egg-carrying females. All to no avail.

If we'd been richer we might have bought the lot and released them – but from talking to the passengers we realised we'd have to be rich indeed. Every kilometre nearer to Manaus their value increased. A large tartaruga would sell for over $35, a small one for at least $7. Turtles are a delicacy and everyone was going to profit from their sale – especially the captain who had purchased several dozen for less than $2 apiece.

The idea of a commando raid to release the hostages came to the American and me one night as we lay side by side in our hammocks passing a bottle of *cachaca* between us. We were still two days out from Manaus and by now every part of the deck had its turtles.

Cachaca is a fiery, fairly loathesome, cane spirit that has to be gulped to minimise contact with the taste buds. Once inside however it makes the stomach glow; the coward brave; the meek proud; the proud unbearable; the uncertain resolute and the cautious reckless.

It made us embark on a foolhardy mission while the passengers lay snoring in their hammocks with only the pilot awake at the wheel on the upper deck. We flitted about on our bare feet, shivering in the 2 am chill, running our hands over the turtles' shells checking for harpoon punctures. Any without, we untied, carried to the rail and dropped overboard.

It took only half an hour and in that time we liberated sixty or seventy. That was only about a third of the total, but there seemed no point in releasing the wounded ones, and I think we hoped that no one would notice any were missing.

Some hope. By the time we awoke, hung-over and exhausted by our nocturnal mission, it was very clear that bad feeling was afoot.

Every visitor to Brazil comments on the gentleness and lack of violence in the average Brazilian. They are a warm-hearted, easy-going, amusing race, welcoming to foreigners.

Well, I can assure you that they had undergone a transformation on that particular boat. For the next two days the atmosphere was distinctly uncomfortable. Everyone stared at us with murder in their eyes, and the American and I took it in turns to go to sleep. No one voiced an accusation. Not once. But people would get up and eat elsewhere when we sat next to them at

meals; stop talking when we approached, spit pointedly when we leant on
the rail near them.

As for us, we felt a mixture of guilt and glee. We had deprived some poor
people of a deserved addition to their meagre income — but we had thrown
overboard three-quarters of the captain's personal cargo and he could afford
the loss. We felt that self-righteous, persecuted glow of reformers and once we
got off the boat we had no doubt we'd done the right thing.

* * *

We hugged the right bank of the river in our anxiety not to miss the confluence with the Cuc. We craned our necks round every bend expecting to see
it there, and by five o'clock we were tired and keen to stop and camp. No
offence Jari, old girl, but we felt like sleeping beside another river and drinking
from fresh streams. We paddled on. An hour later we were rewarded. The
turbulence caused by the two currents meeting had formed a large sandbank
in the middle of the Jari, and the Cuc's waters were slightly clearer. We let
out a whoop of excitement and rested our weary arms. It had taken us five
weeks from Carecaru. We were on schedule and pleased with ourselves.

As we drove the canoe into a small beach at the confluence Peter pointed
excitedly at something in the sand. A footprint. But it was not the imprint of
some splay-toed savage that had never known the imprisonment of shoes —
this was a size nine boot with a heavy tread. Somehow that worried us more.
A military boot perhaps?

We made our camp in the jungle behind the beach, and the coffee was
brewing nicely on the fire, when we suddenly heard the intrusive sound of an
outboard motor approaching.

'Oh, shit, it could be men from a military post,' I said to Peter. 'Let me
do the talking.' We had been warned of a place called Molocopote where the
army would stop us from going any further, though no one had been able to
tell us exactly where it was. Could this be it? Would we be stopped at the
scene of our small triumph? We skulked in the jungle hoping somehow the
canoe would go right past and not spot us. Small chance. Our fire was belching
smoke across the river. The outboard slowed its roar and turned into the Cuc.
Excited voices greeted the sight of our canoe. Time to go and welcome our
visitors.

Peter and I emerged from the jungle and were relieved to see that the three
men were not dressed in army fatigues. They had come prepared for trouble
though. Each carried a firearm: there was one rifle that Mark would have
liked, powerful enough to knock a double-decker bus on its side, one shotgun
and a revolver. All were trained on us, but dropped shamefacedly when we
greeted them with smiles and the offer of coffee. We sat round the camp-fire
while I tried to find out who they were and to evade every question they
asked us. We smiled a lot, shrugged our shoulders and played cat and mouse.
We were two very mysterious gringos.

Finally it emerged that they were geologists up there for a month doing a survey of the mineral deposits. Several years previously there had been an Indian post at the mouth of the Cuc and the airstrip still existed, but the Indians retreated and the post had been abandoned. A military zone did start there, but when we asked if there were any troops about, they laughed and assured us we would meet no one. Our fears evaporated. They were camped at the airstrip a few hundred metres away and invited us to spend the night there. However it had been a hard day, our camp was already set up, and we had no further energy to face a barrage of friendly questions. We promised to call in for breakfast, and they said they would mail letters for us next time the helicopter came with supplies.

So we celebrated our arrival at the Cuc with another precious dried dinner and some capybara stew, though I felt the onset of fever again and could not really enjoy it. In the morning we called at the camp where there were about fifteen men, had a coffee and handed over some letters. Then we set off up the Cuc. We learned that this party was staying until late November – useful if we met with disaster upstream. The beginning of the Cuc was all right, but after 2 or 3 kilometres we were already in difficulties.There was so little water that soon we were getting out every 20 or 30 metres to wade the canoe. The geologists had been measuring the water level on the Jari, and told us it had dropped 10 centimetres in the past week, so we assumed the Cuc would be falling fast too. By midday we had to stop because I had a bad attack of malaria and that was disconcerting. I swallowed another three Fansidar, felt better next morning, and we pushed on.

The Cuc was lovely: only 10 or 15 metres wide, and twisty with abundant golden sandbanks. We saw a deer and two tapirs, and although we spent more time walking than paddling we were enjoying ourselves. Until the early afternoon, that is, when I had another bad attack of the rigours and my temperature soared even higher than the day before. The night passed slowly. When I got up now and then for a pee everything spun around, and I found my legs would barely support me. I felt sweaty, achy and very, very old. Yet the next morning I again felt stronger so we continued, but progress was slow. We stopped for lunch.

'How're you feeling?' Peter asked me.

'Not too bad. I feel I'll have an attack this evening – but I'm okay for now. Just wish this bloody headache would go away.'

'Take some more of those strong aspirin.'

'I've already had six today – I'd better go easy on them.'

Ten minutes later, before even the water had time to boil, I was lying in the sun wrapped in all our blankets and spare clothing, and it was the worst attack of the trip so far. The chill came in waves that I tried to control until I was too exhausted. My teeth chattered, my body vibrated, and my mind wandered off into hallucinogenic realms of nightmare and paranoia. Peter carried me to the hammock, and there I shivered, muttered, shouted and sweated until late evening. It was obvious that the Fansidar had not worked at all, so I started on a course of quinine, boosted with tetracycline – a combination that the hospital had used on me to good effect in 1980. A party of four men from the camp passed us as I lay there, and I sent Peter to ask them about helicopters. It seemed that one had arrived that day and another one would be coming in ten days' time.

We had to decide what to do. The Cuc was so dry it promised to be impassable in another week or two — especially further upstream. It was over 100 kilometres to the point where we were to begin our portage into French Guiana, and the headwaters must be almost dry. We might reach a point where we could not go any further, and by then the river would be dry, cutting off our retreat. It was then the end of October, so the rainy season would not start for another month or more. Would we have to make camp until the rains raised the level of the river? If so, how long would we have to wait? Presumably it would take a lot of rain before there was enough run-off to make the river easy. We might have to camp until January. Did we want to be inactive that long? On the river that long? Moreover we would be doing the portage and final part of the trip in the rains. What about malaria? We only had two courses of quinine left, and if the disease returned as often as this we would soon run out of the drug and die.

Whenever malaria gave me a respite, Peter and I discussed these alarming possibilities. In our conversation, ironically, I could see similarities with that stressful time at Burnt Foot Camp when Mark wanted to quit and I didn't. Now the roles were reversed, because the geologists' helicopter was unmanning me. It afforded an unexpected chance to get off the river and out of the jungle, and I very much wanted to be whisked to the comforts and medical facilities of Belem. I put forward all the difficulties of the Cuc as good reasons for going back to the airstrip. Peter, however, would hear none of it.

'We can't give up now,' he said angrily. 'Imagine the helicopter does not exist. If it was not there we would have to carry on, yes?'

'But we can't carry on up that little creek, can we? Look at it — not even enough water to float the canoe here. Imagine how dry it'll be up in the hills. I'm not going to portage it for fifty kilometres.'

'You need a rest — and then you will feel better,' said Peter and set about preparing supper. I felt like crying. How could I ignore the helicopter? Why had I picked this mule-headed Swiss macho man for a companion? How could he be so stubborn? Oh, to be lifted up and away in a clatter of rotor blades, to float over the rivers and jungle, and be deposited a couple of hours later in the reassuring bustle of Belem. In a few days we could be sitting in a bar with a bunch of lovely girls, clean, fresh shirts on our backs, and with ice-cold beers in our hands. We could gorge ourselves in restaurants, go to the cinema, read the newspapers, listen to music. All this could be ours so soon. Surely he must succumb to temptation?

Meanwhile the strips of capybara we had tried to dry had gone off after three cloudy days. It tasted foul and had to be thrown away, but the weather did look as though it was changing. Great banks of cloud rolled up from the east, though apart from one brief shower it remained dry. We began to place sticks in the river to monitor its changes of level, and we developed faith in the weather-forecasting of frogs. They had scooped out circular depressions in the sand for depositing their spawn – positioned just on the edge of the present water level, but where the sand was wet enough to fill their pools. The spawn and tadpoles were thereby safe from fish until they had matured. (Why birds like the herons do not scoop up the lot I don't know.) Clearly any rise of more than 2 or 3 centimetres in the level of the river would sweep away all this work and their offspring, so was their knowledge of the start of the rains infallible? Certainly they were still building these pools – so it seemed probable it would stay dry for a while yet.

It was two more days before I could face travelling again. I had no energy at all and shuffled around like a geriatric on the rare occasions when I did get up. The incident of the Milo was during this period. By this stage in our journey the tastier foodstuffs were getting scarce. We had run out of saccharine that we used to sweeten our drinks (avoiding the weight and bulk of sugar), so we were therefore getting through our remaining kilos of sugar at a great rate, and we needed it for our porridge and pancakes. At the same time we both suffered a terrible craving for sweet things, and frequently wolfed spoonfuls of neat sugar when the other was not looking. The last tin of Milo (a chocolate drink, fortified with vitamins) was a huge temptation. Although beautiful as a hot drink to end the day, it seemed even better eaten surreptitiously as a powder.

A little rain had recently fallen and the jungle was dripping onto our pots and pans, but as I lay in my semi-delirium I imagined I could hear Peter taking advantage of my weakness to have a few spoonfuls of Milo. 'You're eating the bloody Milo, aren't you, you bastard!' I shouted, and Peter who was in his hammock at the time and nowhere near the food supplies, started in surprise. The truth was that he had eaten a couple of spoonfuls of sugar just before turning in, so this he confessed to guiltily.

'Oh, great! Just when we're short of sugar you start stealing it all. . . .' (I'm really charming when I'm sick.)

Feeling rather better now I drifted off into semi-consciousness. But after a few minutes I again imagined the stealthy clink of spoon on Milo tin.

'You're still eating it, aren't you, you bugger?' I yelled, quivering with rage, and Peter awoke with a start.

'John, you are going mad,' he shouted back. 'Too much malaria, your brain has cooked. Now are you going to let me sleep?'

When I felt better we decided on an alternative plan. The boatmen had told Mark and me weeks before that the Mapaoni tributary would be better than the Cuc for reaching a portage point over the Tumucumaque Hills. It also had the great advantage of the supposed trail cut at the top, connecting it to the Litanie River in Surinam. We had rejected the Mapaoni initially because of fears of trouble with Surinamese officialdom and opted for the Cuc which 'connected' via a portage with the rivers of French Guiana. Now, however, the idea that the Surinamese—Brazilian border would be a tense military area seemed extremely unlikely. We would risk it anyway. The Cuc seemed impassable, and although getting to the mouth of the Mapaoni meant continuing up the Jari for a further 200 kilometres, at least the rains would have two or three weeks to do something about raising the level of these tributaries.

So back we paddled to the confluence. We had hoped to spend the night at the geologists' camp, but everyone was off on surveys except the cook and a male nurse, and they would not let us stay without authorisation from the boss. The cook sat at the table nervously fiddling with a ball-point pen as he dredged up excuse after excuse for this lack of hospitality.

'We can't let you stay without authorisation,' (click—click went the retractable pen tip) 'and the radio isn't working otherwise I'd radio the boss for permission' (click—click).

On and on he went, and we just stood there making him more and more nervous. We were tired and were just having a break and rolling a cigarette before returning to the canoe and finding a camp site. I made some comments about how we knew it was traditional in Amazonia for people to provide shelter to passing strangers, and mentioned how six nights previously the boss himself had invited us to the camp. The clicks of the ball-point became more and more frantic, and after enjoying his discomfort for a while we departed. Perhaps we looked a mean couple of characters by then; the wild beards, faces gaunt from malaria, and tattered clothing: I looked Peter over objectively. He did look pretty unsavoury. We had hoped to swap cooking oil for some sugar but it didn't even seem worth asking. The cook was the type who wouldn't pick his nose without written permission.

We camped on a sandbank near the other side and discussed whether to do a night raid on the cook's supplies. We had seen boxes of forgotten delights piled high over there — tomato paste, stock cubes, canned meat, tons of sugar, tins of drinking chocolate and much more. Our diet was now so bland that the highlight of our day was our candy-coated multivitamin pill. We had even gone through the medical kit and wolfed all the peppermint-flavoured indigestion tablets.

'We will go at about two in the morning,' said Peter.

'Okay, but we'd better be careful. They have revolvers and a lot of guns over there. That cook is so twitchy that he'd shoot for sure.'

We retired to our hammocks, dozed off, and never woke again until dawn. We'd missed the chance. I'm sorry to say it would not have been the first time I had helped myself to someone's food. . . .

* * *

In the summer of 1980 I canoed down a section of the Teles Pires with an Italian friend, Andrea Betella. We were using a home-made plank canoe — so heavy and robust that we could barely lift it. While we managed small portages we knew we would be in trouble if we hit some long rapids.

After a fairly quiet beginning the river got progressively worse. The Teles Pires had not read those geography textbooks where rivers get quieter and more sedate the nearer they get to the sea. She was calm at the source and meaner with every mile. It took us two weeks to get through a 15-kilometre stretch of rapids, and the weight of the canoe prevented us taking the sane option of portaging. We had to paddle through them or use the ropes while one of us floundered chest-deep in foam trying to control the bucking craft. One false move and everything would have been lost.

Finally the river dropped over a 7-metre fall and cascaded through a 2-kilometre gorge with steep sides littered with giant boulders impossible to walk across. The end had come. It would have been too difficult to retrace our steps back upstream so we had to abandon the canoe and everything we could not carry and walk 100 kilometres to the nearest road.

A hundred kilometres is a long walk under any conditions; in thick jungle with 30 kilos on our backs it was nearly the end of us. Fifteen days of terrible thirst, of stumbling fight with jungle creepers, of sweat and rain and sodden nights when we slept where we fell. We were short of food and our strength went so fast that we never expected to get out alive.

On the seventh day we suddenly came across a faint trail in the bush – not a game trail like so many others that criss-cross the jungle – but a man-made one as shown by the machete-cut saplings and one discarded tobacco packet. It was going in approximately our direction so we willingly followed it, spared the work of cutting our way, and as dusk was approaching we came to a hollow and a deserted camp.

A trestle table held cooking utensils and one or two personal possessions. Underneath we found a pick, shovel, gold pan, and some provisions wrapped in plastic sacking. A hundred metres away were the two water-filled pits where the owner had been excavating for gold. He had obviously gone away for a day or two, taking hammock, plastic sheet and shotgun, but he intended returning soon because he had left a large monkey stew in one of the saucepans. We knew it was monkey because he had cooked it head and all, and it came as a shock to lift the lid and see the little skull grinning up at us.

I am not very proud of what followed so I shall quickly make some excuses. We were in a desperate state, having only eaten meat once in the previous seven days. Rice and flour were inadequate fuel for such strenuous activity: we were exhausted, weak and ravenous.

It started modestly. We cooked some rice and decided to have two pieces of monkey with it. This we did, and then another piece and then another. Soon only the head was left, and deciding it would look even more insulting if we only left that, cracked it open, ate the tongue and sucked out the brains.

'The guy will kill us if he comes back,' we said as we rooted through his sack of provisions to see what else could be found. A tin of corned beef was opened, mashed up with rice and wolfed down.

Time for dessert, and we started on a large jar of 'Toddy' – a chocolate drink 'fortified with vitamins' as the label said. Sounded just the ticket, and there to go with it was a large tin of powdered milk and sugar. We made a great pot of the stuff and drank it down thirstily.

'We'd better stop now,' we told each other as we discovered that if you put Toddy, powdered milk and sugar in a cup and mix it up dry it tastes as good as any Swiss chocolate bar.

Soon the spoon was clinking against the bottom of what had been an almost full jar of Toddy, and we had tried, we had tried so hard, to stop.

'We really mustn't take any more,' we'd say, and retire to our hammocks after stowing away all the temptations, 'after all, these garimpeiros can be very violent men. For all we know he might be on his way back at this very moment.'

Yet we knew there was no stopping us now, and soon one of us would lead a new assault on the goodies.

Eventually the stuff ran out and we began to feel apprehensive. It was unlikely the man would arrive that night as it was already dark — but perhaps he had nearly made it back and was camped a kilometre or two away and would arrive at first light? We made plans for an early start.

In the scrubbed, empty stew pot we placed ten dollars in cruzeiros and a good sheath knife. We thought of composing a note to go with it, but the man was probably illiterate and words were superfluous anyway. In financial terms it was a generous payment — but in jungle terms it was meaningless. It was not a question of nipping round to the corner shop and replacing the stuff — that would probably require a six-day round trip.

The next morning, with the sun barely lightening the eastern sky, we were on our way, and seven days later reached the road.

I still think of the poor garimpeiro racing against the fading light to get back to his camp, having walked 20 kilometres that day. Weary and keen to get home he consoles himself with the glad thought that at least he had the foresight to leave some food prepared so he can eat quickly and get in his hammock.

'Perhaps a little cup of Toddy after the stew would go down well,' he muses and smiles contentedly, adjusting the load and quickening his pace through the jungle gloom.

9 The Jari again

Our decision to return to the Jari was a gamble. It was 200 kilometres up to the mouth of the Mapaoni, and if she gave us a hard time it would add several weeks to our trip. She had proved fairly easy for the last 75 kilometres before joining the Cuc, but there was no guarantee she would stay that way. From our past experiences it was probable she would not.

Paddling away from the lure of the geologists' camp that morning was heartbreaking. I'd hoped that Peter would weaken and submit to the temptation of a helicopter, but he never gave so much as a backward glance. I sat crestfallen in the stern, still weak from malaria and with an appalling headache that the glare of the river did nothing to improve. I felt the discomfort, the insects, the hard work, the sickness, the bland food. The whole trip had degenerated into a joyless endurance test, and I wanted to go home. We'd been presented with a marvellous opportunity to escape without having to retrace our steps, and here we were paddling away from it!

I kept these thoughts pretty much to myself. I had already suggested quitting twice to Peter, and he had wanted nothing to do with it. I didn't persist in trying to persuade him. That was unusual: generally I make repeated attempts to get my own way. In retrospect I think I was relieved that he didn't let me persuade him to abandon the trip at a moment when malaria had left me so utterly dispirited and depressed. On a more practical level I suppose I knew a helicopter was not due for at least another week. So there was time enough to discover whether I would recover my enthusiasm. Meanwhile it was surely better to be on the move than hanging around the airstrip.

Next day continued easy as far as the travelling was concerned, and we gobbled up the kilometres. In the week after leaving the Cuc we saw more wildlife than at any time on the trip. The river and her creatures seemed to be trying to cheer me up and rid me of my lethargy. We drifted to within 15 metres of a puma as it reclined on the river-bank enjoying the breeze, and it watched us quizzically from golden eyes. Then it caught our scent and bounded up and away with marvellous fluid grace. It was the first time I had seen a puma in Amazonia, and the best view I'd had of one of the large cats.

A few kilometres further on we saw a group of six giant otters. We could see why they are threatened with extinction. They popped up cheerfully a few metres from the canoe and would have been extremely easy to shoot. They have a beautiful thick pelt which fetches a better price than a jaguar's, so they stand little chance of survival along a populated river. I have been told that their skins retail at $1,800 apiece. They are social creatures, and live in groups of up to twelve, so that each group requires a large home range —

perhaps as much as 30 kilometres of river. They trample the vegetation down in characteristic clearings, and this betrays their haunts to any hunter. Their only enemy appears to be man, and up there on the uninhabited rivers of Amazonia we found them still abundant, as were the small species of otter. Unfortunately, once the giant otter has been hunted out of an area it has no great ability to make a comeback. They reproduce very slowly — about two years between births — with an average litter of only two cubs.

We ate well over the next few days, because we were not only viewing this abundant wildlife with aesthetic pleasure. We shot a monkey, two curassows and a small alligator. The alligator has suffered severe persecution in Amazonia over the last century because of the value of its skin, but we shot it for its soft, fishy-tasting meat. In 1950 five million alligator skins were exported from the state of Amazonas alone, which comprises about a quarter of Brazilian Amazonia. Taking into account that for every skin exported two more are very likely lost owing to bad curing, or because the wounded alligator sinks and cannot be retrieved, that means about 12 million alligators were killed. This figure has now dropped considerably — partly owing to tougher controls and the US ban on imports, and partly because on the more populated rivers the alligator is actually hunted out. On the Jari we saw numerous small alligators that slid into the water as we approached — but the largest we saw on the whole trip was no more than 2.5 metres long.

We were prepared to eat anything once in an attempt to vary our diet. We boiled up some water snails to eat one day, which were revolting. Another time on a gravel bank where we had stopped for a rest we found some freshwater clams, so we collected them to make a 'spaghetti alle vongole'. More successful — but we only found the clams once more after that. There were a lot of crabs on the Jari. They were quite small, and we boiled one up now and again, but we never saw enough together to make it worthwhile catching them for a feast.

We found the new-look Jari was psychologically hard work. There were long, calm, wide stretches where we had to slog along wilting in the heat. We covered large distances but it was dull and monotonous. I was still depressed and dispirited — aware that if we turned round we could still make it back to the Cuc in time to catch the flight out. I had been taking the quinine/tetracycline mix for over a week now, and I was beginning to feel stronger. It was a complicated regime of pill-taking: four tablets at noon, two at 6 pm, two at 8 pm, two at midnight, two at 4 am and two at 6 am. Considering we had no watch, there was no way I could be very accurate, especially in the hours of darkness. I'd just take two whenever I woke up in the night. It was only after I returned to England that I learnt of the side-effects of tetracycline. I could not understand why it was that any part of my skin exposed to the sun stung and itched excruciatingly, especially after I had been exposed to its rays for so many weeks. At night the itching and stinging continued, and I had to take anti-histamines, get up in torment and sit in the river. I thought the sun must have changed character — perhaps as a prelude to the start of the rains. Not at all: that is a side-effect of the drug.

I must have been miserable company all that week. I sulked in silence for much of the day to punish Peter for being so strong-willed. Finally I suggested a rest-day, and that did me good. We decided to check over the presents we had for the Indians we expected to meet soon. We had brought 150 fishing hooks, 700 metres of fishing line, spare salt, beans, and some cheap mirrors and combs. We had been very mean in the buying of these presents. What Indians really like are knives, axes, machetes, pots and pans – considerably more bulky and costly. The mirrors were horrible little things stuck on to plywood, and we hoped our lives would not depend on such trash. By the end of the day of rest I felt transformed: keen and eager to push on. The depression had lifted away.

Early next morning there was a setback. I woke up to hear the tweets of a couple of curassow near the camp, and in my haste to get in my contact lenses and nip out for the slaughter, I dropped a lens on the jungle floor.

'Peter,' I called. 'There're some curassow. See if you can shoot one.'

I had done all the hunting so far, and he had been reluctant to participate. He was still reluctant that morning.

'I never shoot an animal in my life. I don't like to kill things.'

'Look,' I said angrily, 'I can't because I've dropped my bloody lens and I can't see bugger all. I don't enjoy killing creatures either but we both enjoy eating them. It's time you took a share of the burden.'

This conversation was conducted in a fierce whisper; the birds were near. Peter was still reluctant.

'Peter, I'm not your bloody hired-gun, you know. I won't do your killing for you, your dirty work. I've done it up to now, but enough's enough. Go and shoot one of those birds before they fly away.'

Off he went, and I concentrated on the area of jungle floor where my lens must have landed. Talk about a needle in a haystack – leaves and twigs in a layer several centimetres deep – but I knelt down and began to sift through them. I only had one spare lens. Peter returned, the birds had flown off just as he was taking aim, so he joined me in this different type of hunt. For one and a half hours we gently separated each leaf over a 2-metre square area, and miraculously in the end we found it.

Two days later we passed the mouth of the river Ximin-Ximin. At one time Mark and I had considered taking this river to the Tumucumaque instead of the Cuc or the Mapaoni. We were thankful we had dropped that idea. What a feeble trickle it was.

'I have pissed more liquid than this after a night on the beer,' said Peter as we nosed the bow of the canoe up the choked waterway. Just past its mouth was a little rapid – the first on the Jari since Macocoara, which must have been over 200 kilometres behind us by now. We were developing a belated attachment to the Jari – she had been very kind to us lately, just when we needed peace and quiet. She was also getting lovelier by the day, narrow and twisting, with steep hillsides, sandbanks and rocks. She discourages

the casual visitor by all the obstacles between Monte Dourado and Macocoara. The faint-hearted, the weak, the wimps — and the sensible — give up
and turn back. Yet the loonies who persevere earn their reward. The wildlife continued abundant. We saw several groups of giant otters and tapir,
caught a glimpse of a jaguar and watched an eagle swoop and snatch a fish.
Finally, draped and coiled on a fallen tree, was a 7-metre anaconda. I'd never
seen one wholly out of the water before and we sat for a long time only
5 metres away while Peter did a quick sketch. It was a beautiful creature,
its green, black and brown markings gleaming in the sunlight. It still had not
moved when we left.

It came about very slowly, so slowly that we were unaware of it at first:
the mosquitoes steadily declined in number from about Macocoara onwards.
They were still around, but in tolerable numbers, and we found we could sit
after dark without being eaten alive. Why there should be less was a mystery.
It could not have been altitude only, because later on the lower Mapaoni
they became more numerous again. Others factors must play a part. Why had
Martin and Tanis Jordan found the Rio Mapuera mosquito-free? It is some
quality of the water that destroys their larvae, perhaps.

As we approached the mouth of the Mapaoni we came across a few signs
of humanity, an old shelter of the type Indians make while on hunting trips,
an abandoned house and an old canoe. We checked out the house. The
thatched roof had collapsed and we had to hack our way across what had
been the cultivated clearing. To our joy we discovered a papaya tree with
some ripe fruit. Being unable to shin up its smooth trunk, we chopped it
down. An act of vandalism, but nothing was going to keep us from that
succulent fruit. The house must have belonged to Indians we thought, and
that impression was reinforced by the overgrown garden being full of the
little red berries they use for dyeing and decoration. We paddled on expecting
to meet Indians at any moment, so when we saw a clearing on the left bank
we donned shorts and climbed up to investigate. We reached the crest of the
bank, took one look and dived for cover. There, dominating the bend in the
river, was an encampment, though it was not an Indian village; several Brazilians and a radio mast were visible.

We squatted there and discussed what to do. This looked like Molocopote,
the control we had been told about, and it looked too bloody official for our
liking. We debated whether to confront them openly, or sneak by later under
cover of darkness. We decided on the former, and paddled round the bend.
There was a young guy having a wash on a rock. Covered in soap suds and
singing lustily he did not see us until we were 2 metres away. His face was a
treat. The song dropped abruptly as his mouth gaped open, the soap flew out
of his fingers, and Peter and I were convulsed with laughter.

We moored the canoe and went up to the camp with all sorts of stories
prepared to try and bluff our way past officialdom. It proved unnecessary —
they were not officials at all, just another group of geologists. They responded
admirably to the surprise of our arrival by piling good food on us and inviting

us to spend the night.

This place was Molocopote and there had been a FUNAI post until two years previously, with over fifty Indians living there. However another tribe had come down from the Cuc on a raid, so the survivors had moved over to the Paru river. There was a large area cleared, the remains of some huts, a long airstrip, and a herd of water buffalo that had run wild. There were also several graves of Indians who had been killed.

One of the team had dug up two graves out of curiosity. He stressed that it was not grave-robbing, but more in the nature of an archaeological dig! One skull was not reburied, however. He chose to hang it from a post of the hut. He found that the Indians were buried with a strange assortment of prized possessions: a hammock, a tube of Colgate toothpaste, shotgun cartridges, pots, pans, and an empty Coca-Cola bottle. He was also interested that they had been killed with shotguns rather than bow and arrow.

One of the group, Paulo, played the guitar and sang for us, and he had a marvellous voice that soared in the cool, star-filled night, and echoed back from the jungle of the far bank. He knew a lot of songs in English that he had committed to memory with no idea of their meaning – and he sang them beautifully. We realised that we had missed music a great deal. At the beginning of the trip, when I was with Mark, we'd had a little cassette player and a few tapes which had been an appreciated luxury. However it had been Mark's; Peter and I had nothing.

Four of the men had been up the Mapaoni for about 30 kilometres two weeks before. They said it was really hard going with little water and many rapids. This sounded more or less what we had expected. They had a good map of the river with a scale of 1:250,000 and we made a tracing of it.

We slung our hammocks near the fifteen others, and like all Brazilian camps it was not a peaceful night. One man listened to a football commentary for two hours. Brazilian commentators are even more irritating then the English ones. Jabber, jabber, jabber they go at breakneck speed, but when a team scores the commentator yells GOALLLLLLLLL! in a shouting crescendo and holds it for about twenty seconds or more. Well before dawn other guys were fiddling about with the wave-bands of their radios. Others coughed, spat, scratched and farted. It had been a nice interlude and a change of routine, but we were keen to depart.

Peter looked pale, and continued to clutch a blanket round him long after the sun had chased away the dawn chill. However he said he wanted to move on, so after some coffee we shook hands with the men and paddled away. We had only gone a kilometre before he was violently sick and began to shake uncontrollably. He lay on a small beach wrapped in our bedding until I persuaded him that we should return to the camp. I paddled him back, and found that most of the men were about to depart for a place upstream beyond the mouth of the Mapaoni where they had found gold in workable quantities. Peter crawled into his hammock, and I spent the day talking to the four or five guys who had stayed, and from them I heard some world news. It seemed that the US had invaded Grenada, which I imagined might well make the Surinamese even more paranoid about the threat of mercenaries crossing their border. However, up there in that remote spot it seemed extremely unlikely that there would be troops on either side of the border, so we were not too alarmed.

The boss and Paulo had a bitter row that evening that was embarrassing for the non-participants. I liked Elcio, the boss. He was a well-educated geologist who had done his doctorate at a university in France. He listened to Radio French Guiana a lot, which irritated the other members of the group who were of humble origins. He felt there should be a hierarchy in the camp, and that he should be at the apex. So he sat around giving orders — while the others felt, rightly perhaps, that this was the sort of work where everyone should muck in and help with the chores. In the course of their argument Paulo brought up all these grievances, whereupon Elicio decided to quit the project and return to Belem. He told me he would only return to the jungle if Paulo were sacked. However Paulo seemed too capable a man for that. Elcio was probably the more dispensable.

Everyone departed upstream next day except Elcio, who was waiting for a plane due in four days' time, and Peter and myself. Peter's malaria attacks responded well to chloroquine, so it looked as though he had the Vivax strain. Mine would only respond to quinine, indicating Falciparum. It was very fortunate we had different strains because we were by now short of both chloroquine and quinine. I decided to stop taking my two-weekly chloroquine tablets — a futile attempt at malaria prevention — leaving Peter more for the control of his attacks. We were very concerned about running out of these two crucial drugs and frequently counted them. I had forty-three quinine tablets: not even enough for a complete course of treatment — but enough, I hoped, to keep the disease at bay and me alive. By the next day Peter felt well enough for us to set off again, and I had to admire his resistance to the temptation to call off the whole trip. When I'd had my last malaria attack there had been the helicopter to seduce me, and here at Molocopote he knew a plane would arrive within a week. Yet never once did he falter in his determination to carry on. I was fortunate to have found a companion of Peter's calibre.

For the end of our journey on her waters the Jari continued quiet and peaceful and we were almost sorry to leave her. As we were stopping for lunch I saw a paca (a large cat-sized rodent) crouched under a tree by the water's edge and shot it. We could not understand what a nocturnal animal was doing out in the daytime until we saw that it had already been shot and wounded. I don't know how the poor thing had lived so long: it had a horrible putrid hole blown in its neck that looked two days old. It must have crouched here in agony since being shot by some group from the camp. This is the aspect of hunting I find most hateful since inevitably sometimes an animal or bird will be wounded and not finished off. We were glad to put this one out of its misery, and were also undeniably glad of the meat it was going to provide for our dinner.

An hour or two later we reached the mouth of the Mapaoni and paused on a sandbank for a breather and to say goodbye to the Jari. We had a last swim in her green waters and gulped water from each of the two rivers to see if we detected a difference in taste. Peter was convinced the Mapaoni tasted of gold – optimistic to the end. A few months before leaving England I attended a medical seminar at the Royal Geographical Society which had impressed me with dire warnings against drinking untreated water. I had been scared enough to buy a filter bag and sterilising tablets for this trip, although I had never bothered on other rivers. However if the river has no towns, factories or dwellings along its banks, I can't see what dangers it can hold. Surely it is just rainwater with natural vegetable and mineral matter? Anyway our fil-tering and sterilising had only been kept up for a few weeks.

Peter got bad worms on the Mapaoni and each morning would find him prodding his deposit with a stick to see what would emerge. I was often dragged away from my breakfast to give an opinion on his findings, and there was no doubt about the quality of some of the specimens that waved their heads at me.

'Don't take that medicine yet, Peter,' I'd tell him as he stood looking down shocked at the horrors he had fathered. 'A bit fatter, and we'll be able to use them for fishing bait.'

When cleaning monkeys we noticed how worm-ridden they were. Our favourite delicacy from any kill was its liver – but we often had to throw away the monkey livers because they were alive with thick white wrigglers. Their stomachs and intestines would often contain a nauseating ball of worms, some as juicy as fat earth worms.

That first day on the Mapaoni we covered about 4 kilometres before stop-ping to camp. We were encouraged: not nearly so many shallows as the Cuc and a surprising amount of water for the time of year. Elcio had told us that the river had rapids, but we could not imagine them being very big affairs on a river this size. Next day we covered over 20 kilometres and apart from a few minor rapids which we had to wade through, all was easy going. Arro-gantly we mimicked Elcio and his party as we went along. 'There's no water, many rocks, many rapids. It's very hard,' and laughed. They should have seen the Cuc or the lower Jari. Obviously the poor boys had no idea what a shallow, difficult river was all about.

The Mapaoni was the most beautiful river I had ever travelled on. At the top, the Jari had become narrower and more interesting, but this was a paddler's dream. It was 10 metres wide and twisting, with constantly-changing vistas, sandbanks, little rocky inlets and lovely jungle-clad hillsides. I feel strongly about jungle on hillsides, perhaps because I have travelled on so many rivers in flat terrain, where you have only one line of jungle on either bank. When it is hilly you can see the canopies of a host of trees, and really appreciate the infinitely-varied shades of green. And not only green, because in mid-November there were a lot of trees in flower, showing great bursting crowns of yellow or mauve.

On the map we had measured the distances we should have to cover in order to achieve our objective. To the border was about 120 kilometres, and the last big tributary (the Caripi) entered the river after about 80 kilometres, leaving us some 35 which promised to be very hard, with little water. We were rejuvenated by the change of river. The last part of the Jari had been easy so that we made good progress, but it had been a monotonous slog. Now we forgot about aching muscles, the heat, the constant headaches that malaria gave us throughout the trip, and delighted in the Mapaoni. In contrast to the Cuc, we scarcely even touched the bottom or had to walk.

The second day was a little more difficult, but we still covered 15 kilometres or so. One rapid forced us to do our first portage since Macacoara a month before, but we didn't care − in between the rapids there was barely any current and the jungle wildlife continued to entertain us. Where we stopped for lunch we had a large troupe of spider monkeys on one bank, as big as two-year-old children, another troupe of capuchin behind us, and an otter dragged a fish on to the rocks 10 metres away and ate it, seemingly quite indifferent to our presence. A flock of six blue and scarlet macaws squabbled and shrieked as they passed overhead and landed to feed in a nearby tree, filling it with their gaudiness. I collected some of the feathers from one of these birds later in the trip after a Brazilian had shot one and found that some feathers have at least five colours. Others are red on one side and blue on the other. The tail feathers are 55 centimetres long.

That afternoon I experienced a chilling moment with the shotgun. I wounded a curassow at the water's edge and, quickly reloading, cocked the gun to finish it off, but the bird flapped into the jungle before I could take aim. So throwing the gun down on the gear between us, I grabbed the paddle, thrust the canoe to shore, scrambled up a steep bank and through some thick undergrowth till I spotted the bird. When I raised the gun and made to cock the hammer with my thumb, I found to my horror it had been cocked all the time. It was an unnerving reminder that I am very much an amateur with firearms, without the discipline and safety-consciousness that are driven into people who hunt regularly and are taught properly from the beginning. It was a sobering lesson, mercifully learned without a tragedy.

That evening, after a huge meal of curassow, I tried to catch a few catfish for breakfast next day. I sat on the rocks near our camp in the moonlight, smoking, and had no shortage of bites. In fact I caught twelve piranha in fifteen minutes and put them all back. We had eaten enough piranha − we wanted something better. It was enjoyable fishing with the moonlight on the water, the cruising fireflies, the accompaniment of Peter's singing from the jungle behind me, and the nocturnal chorus swelling into full voice. There were more mosquitoes on this stretch of the Mapaoni, but they were not bothering me too much that evening. Occasional bats dipped and swept within an inch or two of me, invisible in the dark but ruffling my hair with the beat of their wings. They were after mosquitoes and they were welcome.

Have another mosquito, my friend, I thought. I mused about the possibility of having four bats on strings, one tied to each shoulder and one to each kneecap as the ultimate mosquito-repellent. I caught another piranha, and killed it to provide a nice large piece of bait, then changed hook and put half the piranha on. No way would they be able to swallow that whole anyhow. I cast out, gripped the line between my knees, rolled a cigarette, sipped on a mug of coffee and daydreamed.

The sudden rasp of the line being pulled out in a rush made me spill coffee down my shirt front. This was no piranha. Indeed, after a lot of mad rushes and splashes a 2.5 kilo trairao was out and gasping on the rocks. When I think of all the hours I have spent fishing English rivers to catch nothing or some mere 100-gram roach, Amazonian fishing really was a delight. It has ruined fishing in England for me for ever. I dispatched the trairao with a blow behind the eyes and scaled it with the back of a knife. Not a job I enjoy much, since I seem to transfer all the scales to my hair, beard and shirt. I slit out the guts where I found a 7-centimetre fish still perfect and intact in the stomach − and tossed the mess into the stream. Then running the knife flat along the backbone I removed two juicy fillets to fry for breakfast, preserving them in a pot of brine.

Next morning I threw up my trairao fillet. A bloated, dead tapir floated by just as we were eating breakfast. What a stench! The corpse caught on a submerged tree right next to us and when I attempted to nudge it along with a stick, I prodded too hard so that it deflated like a balloon, sending out a huge whiff of stinking gas. Holding our noses we grabbed our gear and departed.

The geologists' party had been up here the week before and from what they told us shot everything that moved. It seemed they did not always follow up wounded animals either. Brazilians shoot a wide range of animals for food, and tapir is the most prized for the quality of its meat − over 200 kilos on a large specimen. However, being such a large animal it can absorb a lot of shot before it dies, especially if the hunter is shooting from a distance. Brazilians also shoot monkeys, capybara, peccary, wild pig, deer, paca, agouti − in fact everything. I have personally eaten armadillo, turtle, macaw, toucan, snake, alligator, iguana, porcupine, sloth, puma and ant-eater at various times after they have been shot by Brazilians. I found them all tasty, but then there is no food I don't like. The Brazilians must have had a field day on the Mapaoni − the animals had little or no fear of man and frequently just stood there sniffing at the strange unfamiliar scent. The iguanas, on the other hand, went to the other extreme. We often disturbed them sunbathing on the top branches of trees. Their reaction was to let go and drop like stones into the water 20 metres below, bouncing off the lower branches and somersaulting before smashing into the water with huge splashes. How they avoided injury I don't know. Had they stayed put we would never have seen them up there anyhow. And presumably once we had passed they had to drag themselves laboriously back up the trees.

During these days on the Mapaoni there was still a lot of cloud but no rain fell. The river water was usually deep, and we certainly did not want rain unless it was really necessary. We saw that one of our maps marked Indian villages near the headwaters, and we prepared ourselves for the first meetings and wondered whether a trail would still exist. We had mixed feelings about meeting Indians. We hoped they would be there because without them the trail would be overgrown from not being used, and it would obviously be an interesting experience to meet Indians. But we were apprehensive about our first encounter because one can never be confident that Amazonian Indians will be friendly. There are so many factors that can influence their behaviour: how they have been treated by outsiders in the past, whether they feel threatened, whether the tribe in question is generally war-like or pacific. We were intruders, and we had no right to be there. Once contact was made we felt confident enough about our sensitivity and diplomacy: we were not going to upset them by our behaviour. But we might not even get the chance to prove what smashing chaps we were and just walk into an ambush from unseen attackers. We were not too keen to go that way, but we vowed not to use guns to defend ourselves should we be attacked. We were trespassers on their land, and we were not going to compound the crime by killing Indians.

Meanwhile we were meeting bigger rapids. It is very difficult to portage the canoe across rocky terrain where you have to hop from one boulder to another. Unless you try to keep in unison the canoe is yanked out of the hands of the guy at the back, or the one in front is pushed off his precarious perch. We fell frequently, but fortunately the canoe landed on something soft — us — and was undamaged. We took advantage of the opportunity to look at the state of the bottom of the canoe. Not bad, considering the scraping, scrunching and abuse it had received since we fibreglassed it two months before. However most of the fibreglass tape had been stripped off the external points and we would not be able to leave it much longer. We only had 1.5 litres of resin left and we wanted to keep most of that for emergencies.

We had grown soft on the long rapid-free section of the Jari, but five days of rapids whipped us quickly back into shape. Quite large rapids, too. Some of them fell 15 or 20 metres. Our progress dropped to less than 5 kilometres a day, and we waited impatiently to find the Caripi, the last major tributary. With so many islands and channels, we were worried we might miss the turn-off. Although our map was 1:250,000, it was still too small a scale to be of much use. The river was twisting and turning all over the place and most of the loops were not marked.

10 Choked waters

Eight days after leaving the Jari we reached the confluence with the Caripi. Neither stream looked exactly imposing, but the Caripi was perhaps slightly the larger and easier. Anyhow we were happy to have reached here relatively easily. Over 80 kilometres in eight days was far faster than we had expected, but now it was apparent that the good times were over. The river was only 3 metres wide, and the main problem was fallen trees. Amazonian trees are notoriously unstable, often having roots only a few centimetres below the surface, and where they were exposed to swirling river flood waters they heeled over right across the stream. About every 15 metres there was another fallen tree, and looking along the stream was a demoralising vista of obstructions. If we were lucky the banks were high and the trees had fallen across from one high bank to the other, leaving the necessary gap underneath for our canoe. Again, if we were lucky, the tree had broken either on impact — or later after rotting, so there would be a place in the centre we could float over, or at one of the ends near the bank. Or sometimes we found a gap near the bank that we could slide under.

Usually, however, we were not so lucky. Some trees lay half-submerged across our path and we had to carry everything over them. If they only stuck up a few centimetres above the water, we could drag the canoe across still laden. If they protruded a little higher we unloaded some of the gear before this exercise. If they were 30 centimetres or more out of the water we had to unload everything, and then balance it on the trunk while we carried the canoe across. Paddling was almost impossible, although the river was still quite deep in parts. Instead we were walking, and while walking chopping at dead branches with machetes, jumping up and down on the rotten logs to break them, and moving smaller logs out of the way.

In many places the jungle had taken advantage of these log bridges to nip over to the bank on the other side. Somewhere in the centre of the stream must be the rotten remains of a log, but the jungle had formed a luxuriant barricade of liana, thorns and bushes several metres thick. These we had to cut a channel through. Standing up to our waists or chests in water full of evil flotsam that had piled up behind the barrier over the years, we slashed and cursed. The chopping and shaking of course disturbed ants, spiders, stick insects and biting flies, and cobwebby dust and bits of rotten wood rained down on us. Then we had to tug the canoe through our little tunnel, only to face more of the same.

The canoe had done very well on this trip, but in these conditions it rapidly showed signs of strain. The designer in England had warned us that one thing the canoe might not withstand was being hauled fully laden over logs. The back might break. He advised us to put struts down from the thwarts to brace the bottom. We should have done this in Santarem when building the canoe, but we had hoped for the best and now we were taking a risk with every log. Even with the canoe empty we could see the strain we were putting on her. The bottom would bulge up as it passed over the log, the thwarts popped out of their gunwale blocks as the shape distorted, and we could only imagine what stress was imposed when we left it laden. We wired up the thwarts, but continued doggedly for another day before deciding we must take a rest day and fix the canoe up properly. The half-keel had come off too, so we had a lot of work to do.

In the afternoon we heard the warning chatter of a troupe of capuchin monkeys and Peter pursued them into the jungle and shot an adult male. I heard him cursing and swearing and he yelled that the monkey had fallen dead but was lodged in a branch 10 metres up. I joined him and we tugged at nearby lianas and shook the tree to try to knock it off, but it was firmly wedged, dripping bright splotches of blood on to us and leering at our efforts with its death grimace.

Peter courageously shinned up a nearby liana like a Swiss Tarzan, while I stood anxiously at the bottom. The liana was as thick as my wrist and well-attached at the top. At least we hoped it was. We were eager for the monkey meat, but a fall and broken limb would be an unacceptably high price to pay. Mark had learnt to set a limb, but Peter and I had no idea. That was the sort of disaster we were very vulnerable to so far from medical help. I would not be able to transport an injured Peter and the canoe downstream unaided. A fractured skull or pelvis, moreover, would almost certainly prove fatal. All these thoughts were in line with the expeditionary's dread of appendicitis (although we had been told that a combination of Co-Trimaxazole and Flagyl would control the infection for a few weeks). Anyway, tree- or liana-climbing was altogether best avoided, and it was a relief when Peter returned safely to earth clutching our supper. Ours wasn't the sort of expedition where help was a radio call and a short helicopter ride away.

We stopped for the night soon after, and Peter set up the camp while I skinned the monkey. Another tedious job. It is always easier if the animal is still warm, but even so a lengthy, unpleasant task. Once again we found the liver too worm-ridden and it had to be discarded, but we kept the heart and kidneys. I put aside some of the guts to use for fishing bait and cut the monkey into portions. Monkeys are so horribly human. Hands complete with little fingernails, little penis and balls (the males always seem to have ejaculated when shot — is it the same with humans?), and the eyes — although filmy in death — seem to have a sad 'What have I done to you to deserve this?' sort of expression. Our victim was an old-timer judging by the wear of his teeth. When hunting monkeys you tend to get the dominant male as he stays behind covering the retreat of his brood. Sorry, old boy, but I guess you had a long and full life and perhaps soon some young upstart blade would have kicked you out to a lonely retirement. I peeled the fur off his face, as Peter and I had developed a taste for the brains and tongue and took turns to have the head. The flavour was great, but as in tackling a crab, half the fun was getting inside. Peel the flesh off the cheeks, dislocate the lower jaw and prise out the tongue, and then suck out the brains. Delicious. Foolishly we decided to fry a bit of this monkey, but being elderly it was tough as an old boot and about as tasty. We nearly broke our teeth on one piece and threw the rest in a pot to be boiled up.

My foot-rot was becoming increasingly painful as it dried out each night, and I had to place a soft shirt round my feet to protect them from the coarse fabric of the hammock. By wandering around the jungle naked I had also collected dozens of ticks. Ideally you should let ticks suck and bloat up before trying to remove them. This way they come off more easily, but there were too many to allow such hospitality. I scratched them off with my nails, no doubt leaving a lot of heads embedded to cause further little infections.

However the mosquitoes had suddenly vanished, this time for good. Like an animal emerging from its burrow after an early fright we waited one more night to make sure, before removing the nets. When we did life was so different. No more stuffy, sweaty nights worrying that heads or faces might inadvertently rest against the net. No more distractions to our view of the stars and animals that approached. Just cool breezes and better nights' sleep. Also there were certain odours that did not have to be tolerated any more. Probably from being immersed in the river for so much of the day, we used to find we had to urinate four or five times a night. Getting up so often and walking a few steps in the dark, with the risk of treading on something, became a bore, and when we were sick it was just too much effort. Consequently we got quite adept at unzipping and directing the jet over the edge of the hammock. Quite adept. Occasionally part of the net would get a splashing and as a result they were beginning to pong a bit.

The next day we worked long and hard on the canoe. Some rest day. I suppose such work is all jolly character-building and helps you overcome your lazy, slothful personality, but we would have preferred to swing in the hammocks all day. I removed a lot of screws from the useless watertight hatches to secure the half-keel back on, and roughly shaped a piece of wood to replace the rest. It did not look as though it would last many days – but would protect the bottom of the canoe from a lot of scraping. We roughly strutted out the centre thwart. Then we checked through our food supplies to see what was left. A lot was damp and we spread it out round the fire because the sun did not penetrate down to the narrow stream through the jungle.

A family of capybara came swimming towards us. Two adults and three youngsters came within 2 metres before they saw us. At first I grabbed the shotgun, intending to get a juicy youngster, but I did not fire. It was such a nice family scene, and I'd had enough of killing. Instead I did some fishing with a piece of monkey gut. I caught a trairao of 2 kilos, which seemed a big fish for such a little river.

Next day we commenced battle with what remained of the Mapaoni. It might be only 30 kilometres more to the headwaters. In the morning we found we could get under or round quite a few of the fallen trees and moved fairly fast, and a lot of other trees could be scraped over without unloading, as they only protruded a few centimetres above the surface. We would stand on either side and heave in unison — 'One—two—three—heave!', and in three or four pulls she would be over and we were on our way again. Worse were the tangles of vegetation. We would take it in turns to cut through these, the other just sitting and resting until a tunnel had been cut and before he pushed the canoe through to his companion on the other side. I was having a smoke and watching Peter swinging the machete energetically, when he let out a yell and came thrashing back through the waist-deep water.

'Electricity! Electricity!' He shouted. He looked scared stiff, and I guessed immediately that he'd had a shock from an electric eel. He got back to the canoe and leant against it, shivering violently.

'Shit,' he muttered. 'What the hell was that? It felt like an electricity shock!'

'It's a type of eel, Peter.'

'Eel? What is an eel?'

'A fish that looks like a snake — long and thin.'

'A fish with electricity? Are you serious?'

'Yeah. Another Amazonian curiosity.'

He smiled weakly. 'This fucking jungle has some surprises eh? Well, it's your turn to use the machete.'

'Oh, no it's not! You haven't finished your job. One tangle each.'

'I'm not going back there with that electricity fish, and the land round here is too swampy to portage. You have to go and finish the cutting.'

I knew that was fair, with Peter still looking so shaken, so I took the machete and cut a long pole from a tree on the bank. I then headed slowly and reluctantly for the tangle, slapping the water with the flat of the machete blade and jabbing the river-bed with the pole. It was scary. Electric eels can deliver a shock of up to 650 volts, more than enough to stun a man and cause him to drown. This one must have moved on. But it was a cheerful thought that for the rest of the trip these eels would be about.

Electric eels are actually not true eels — rather a freshwater fish related to the catfish. They grow up to 2 metres in length and feed on frogs, crustaceans and fish. They have to surface every fifteen minutes to take breath. The head is the positive pole, and the tail the negative pole, and both must touch the victim to transmit the shock.

We had expected the Mapaoni to have a lot of rapids. In fact they were not a major problem, which was just as well because from the two or three little ones we passed that day we could see that the combination of rapids and fallen trees was unpleasant. It was bad enough hauling the canoe in calm waters but doing so in rocky, swirling current would have been nightmarish.

Our map marked the first Indian village about 5 kilometres ahead and we found ourselves scanning the jungle for watching faces and checking sand-banks for footprints, but there was no sign as yet. It made us apprehensive — we felt that they would not attack a couple of nice guys like us (with all those super presents) who wished them no harm. But how were they to know how lovable we were? As we headed on we kept a look-out for signs of any other lunatics trying to get a boat up here, but there were none. No doubt the Indians would not use canoes on rivers of this sort, but we did complain that really they should keep their waterways in rather better condition.

We saw less wildlife now than we had before the Caripi, not because of scarcity, I feel, but simply because the ringing blows of machete on hard wood, the coarse oaths in German and English, and the splashings gave every creature plenty of warning about our approach. We did see monkeys and marmosets, however, and disturbed several alligators only a metre or two in front of us. Fortunately they scrambled away forward even faster than we ran away backward.

At times the river entered swampy regions with grassy banks and here progress was much easier as there were fewer tall trees along the river to topple over and block it. On the banks of one of these sections we saw signs of what seemed to be Indian activity — a section of broad-leaved plants had been trimmed at their base over a wide area. We got out and checked for machete cuts — but it looked on closer inspection as though the stems had been broken off rather than cut, probably meaning that the Indians in this area were as yet uncontacted and so without steel tools. We scanned the horizon for smoke, and our nervous tension increased. When two capybara suddenly 'barked' and leapt off a high bank into the water 3 metres in front of us, we jumped so violently we almost capsized.

At this time we became reluctant to use the gun at all. The sound would carry too far and alert all the Indians for kilometres around. Mindful of 'Etiquette and Modern Manners', we even dug out our shorts to keep them at hand for our first meeting. This tension continued for another couple of days, but we never had the expected contact and gradually we stopped looking for human signs.

'I don't think there are any Indians in this area,' I commented to Peter.

'Oh. Why are you thinking that?' he replied.

'Well. They are intelligent people. No one with any sense would live in this shit hole, would they?'

We averaged 3 or 4 kilometres a day up this stretch. They were tremendously hard days, made just tolerable by the anticipation of the evening's pleasures. First the wash that had been a ritual throughout the trip now became even more of a treat. Soaping the cuts and scratches, soothing the stings and itches, removing the debris and sweat, and sluicing ants out of hair and beard never failed to restore us to a good mood. We could dress leisurely in our evening wear — long trousers and shirts — because there were no mosquitoes to hasten the process, settle down to a large mug of coffee and

our meal. Alas, the tea, Milo and powdered milk had all long since been used up, but we still had lots of coffee. We sat and discussed the day, moaned and complained, talked of the world outside that seemed so far away, wrote up our diaries and I smoked a few cigarettes.

In Manaus I had bought a roll of 'Fumo'. This is compressed tobacco leaves in a long cylinder that is ideal for jungle travel, being so tightly compacted that I could shave slivers off the end with a knife as I needed it. It could get wet — and frequently did — without spoiling, and a kilo of it lasted me for over four months. It was exceptionally strong and pretty revolting, and any attempt to inhale incautiously induced violent coughing. Unfortunately, when I returned the second time to the jungle with Peter, I discovered that I had mislaid the huge supply of cigarette papers that I had bought to accompany it. We therefore had to rely on airmail paper at first, and later on pages out of notebooks. Peter sensibly decided that the time was right for giving up the stupid habit, and stopped after a week, but I persisted. Somehow smoking seemed one of the least important of our health problems during this trip, and anyway our lives were vice-free enough.

In one swampy area here the river divided into several channels and we were uncertain which to follow. We separated and explored one each, wading with the water up to our necks, and sometimes above our heads when the river bottom shelved unexpectedly. I wished I had left the shotgun behind because it would have been easier to swim. As it was my feet disturbed large bubbles of foul gas from the deep slime on the bottom, and the stagnant water was too murky for me to be able to see the sunken logs. I would raise my leg to take a step forward and bash my scabby shins and knees yet again.

I had gone half a kilometre like this when suddenly and unexpectedly I went into a funk about electric eels. This was just the sort of territory they love, and I was slap-bang up to my neck in it. I stood, paralysed with fear, convinced that if I took another step forward I would get the shock of my life. I stood still for over five minutes fighting the panic before I could will myself to proceed. I wanted to get out of the water, but the adjacent land was too swampy. The river was the only way. To cheer myself up I composed a ditty and sang as I went along.

'Down in the slime where my white feet tread
Oh Lordy, Lordy
Lives a ten-foot eel, dozing on its bed.
Oh Lordy, Lordy.
Will he give me a shock, will he bite off my cock?
Oh Lordy, Lordy
Will he let me pass, or will he nip up my arse?'

There is nothing like a coarse and banal song, sung lustily, to raise the spirits (rugby players will vouch for that).

I had struggled along a kilometre when I heard splashing round the bend. Tapir or Indians? Fear returned anew. The splashing was coming my way. Turning on my back I swam clumsily for the cover of some overhanging bushes, clutching the shotgun above the water, and there concealed myself among the vegetation. The splashing came nearer — whatever it was would pass very close to my shelter; it was hugging my bank. I drew even further into the cover and peeped through the fronds. Suddenly the suspense was broken by a stream of oaths in accented English. Peter had got into the habit of swearing in English. It was one area of the language that I'd been coaching him in pretty regularly recently.

'Oh, shit, you fucking bastard,' he groaned, raising a bloodied kneecap out of the water where some sunken log had removed the scab. I let him pass before I gave out a yell and sprang on his back.

Once his heart-rate had dropped to a level that permitted him to speak, he told me that his channel and mine connected upstream, so that it made no difference which way we took. The last two hours had been a waste of time. We trudged back to collect the canoe.

A bit later, however, the river was so totally clogged with tedious tangles of thorns and lianas, that after cutting through three we decided to portage the canoe for 300 metres rather than hack our way through five more. We camped at the spot where we relaunched the canoe.

The old tick-heads I had left in my legs had turned into pus-filled pimples, and we both began to have painful sessions with the iodine night and morning. By the time we had finished annointing all our cuts, scratches, spots and abrasions we were more yellow than flesh-toned, and we reckoned the Indians might consider us tastefully decorated. Our hands were also battered from accidents with the campfire, the knife when skinning animals, or bumps and scrapes with the trees that blocked our path. Periodically, too, we had to sterilise a needle and pick out the egg-sacs of the *chigoes* from our feet. These are deposited by sand-fleas, and they announce their presence by a tenderness and itching. You see a white area the size of a shirt button, with a bluish spot in its centre, and when you prise the lid of skin away a large white blob pops out, leaving a gaping hole. There was a perverse pleasure in this activity, and it was essential to pick the eggs out before they hatched because otherwise the maggots would burrow over a large area.

By now we were amazed at the amount of water still in the river. It seemed to us that since this was the very end of the dry season and we were only 20 kilometres or so from the top of the river, it must be fed by some pretty enormous springs. Or else it never stopped raining up there at the source. Occasionally there were shallow sections with a sandy bottom where the canoe could not float and we would have to drag it laboriously along the grip of the sand, but generally the water was at least knee-deep. Of course paddling was now a rare pleasure — it just was not worth embarking for the brief unimpeded 10 metres between obstacles.

At lunchtime next day Peter shot a monkey from among a troupe that were feeding on a tree overhanging the stream. All the monkeys scattered except that one, which stayed rocking gently and making little cries. Peter tried to put in another cartridge to finish it off, but the old one would not eject and he had to get a knife to prize it out. In the meantime the monkey slipped, hung for a second by one hand, and dropped into the river. I waited for the current to bring it to me and saw it was still alive, jerking spasmodically, staining the water from the wounds in its chest. I grabbed it and held it under, while it kicked and struggled in my hand. 'What's happening to me?' I pondered, as I felt the little chest gulping for air, but only filling with water. Was I feeling remorse, guilt or revulsion? No, I'd come to regard killing as a necessary evil, part of our daily routine. Even as the creature fought for life in my hand I was assessing its body for plumpness, and thinking of the meal ahead. What was this trip doing to me? Was this what 'back to nature' was all about? We stopped for a brew of coffee while I skinned it, and several large trairao came up, attracted by the blood and offal that I was tossing into the river. I amused myself for a while by feeding them from my hand – gingerly, because I know what large teeth they have. Tiring of that I put a hook into the next piece and after a brief struggle we had a fish starter for that evening's feast. I put the lot in brine to keep it fresh until later. Then we got on with our work, and the afternoon passed in the usual wearisome way: hacking, slashing and chopping at our enemy: vegetation most vile.

In the evening when I was reaching round a tree to fix the rope of a hammock, I was stung on the little finger by a scorpion. That was the third time on the trip. The pain was excruciating. I hopped up and down cursing the Mapaoni, the Jari, the rain-forest, Amazonia and all South America. After the pain diminished to a dull ache we began to laugh, and Peter hopped around the camp imitating my tantrum. As far as we were concerned at that moment the quicker they cut down all the rain-forests and made one great cattle ranch the better. We vowed that when we got home we would throw out all our houseplants. We'd had enough vegetation for a lifetime. Peter said he was going to give up his job as a landscape gardener. He was not going to fraternise with and care for the enemy any more. I suggested he should devote his talents to defoliant research.

I lost my cool again the next morning, this time with fire ants. They are aptly named – tiny red ants that burn like flames licking your body. I had unloaded the gear and placed it on a log in approved fashion, while we hauled the canoe over. When I picked up the bags again dozens of ants ran on to me and began to bite ferociously. These ants favour the warmer, moister, tender parts of the body, and my groin and armpits were on fire. I'm sorry to say I did not take this very stoically. I kicked the canoe, swore, hurled a sack of food across the sandbank and jumped in and out of the water seeking relief. The canoe was full of the little bastards, and so Peter was getting a taste of the same torture. I sometimes wonder why South American dictators spend so much money on sophisticated torture machines. No doubt there are foreign businessmen with briefcases and brochures calling at their doors like brush salesmen, offering the latest 'Shockometer Turbo Deluxe' model. What a waste of money. Two hours plonked in a fire ants' nest, or a week in the jungle without a mosquito net and any freedom-fighter would be squealing.

We took anti-histamine tablets and after a while the torment began to ease, but not before I'd rubbed a raw patch in my groin. Peter already had a nasty one in his. I'm not sure what it was, a fungal growth perhaps from sweat and humidity, but a large area around his scrotum and upper thigh was permanently raw. He coated it with vaseline during the day, and dusted it with Mycil powder at night. But it never went away — in fact it slowly spread.

Peter already had a thing about ants that had been developing for quite a time, and I got a laugh out of his 'antics'. The large black ones would crawl over us, and then invariably decide among themselves to sting and bite simultaneously. Peter's sense of fair play was outraged. 'For no reason! They're biting me for no reason at all!' was a frequent outburst. Earlier on in the trip he had begun to imagine that the canoe was aswarm with ants, which sometimes it was — when they invaded the canoe at night via the rope. As we paddled along Peter began to lay down his paddle at frequent intervals to examine his body and pick off the ants. He would stand up, shake out the towel that he had under him on the seat, and mutter, 'Little bastards, why don't you leave me alone?' I watched half-entertained and half-irritated, as we began to drift backwards in the strong current.

Ants are no joke I will admit. Even the normal black ones could make some camps unbearable. They nipped up our trouser legs, dropped from branches onto our heads and bit at the hair roots, and trickled down our necks and into any food-bag left open. There were also lots of *sauba* — the leaf-cutter ants — but at least on this trip they left our nylon goods alone. I remember one rainy night on the Rio Verde, when Glen, my Australian companion-in-misery, began yelling that the ants were carrying away his mosquito net. I shone the torch over mine and was relieved to see that it was ant-free. It was one of those wet, windy nights for staying under the blanket. Selfishly I lay there listening to Glen cursing and stumbling around in the dark, and saw him moving our food-bags into the canoe. I dozed off. The laugh was on me, however. The next morning I picked up my pack and everything dropped out. The ants had carried away most of the bottom! Considering that these ants normally cut leaves to take to underground chambers to cultivate a fungal growth that provides food, I can't understand why they are attracted to nylon. Maybe they just want to line their burrows and make them waterproof? Or were the little fungi off their greens so that the ants were desperately trying to find an alternative food supply? Most probably their burrows were a little drab, and they were cheering things up with blue nylon-screened windows.

We estimated we were about 10 kilometres from where we thought the trail should be. Ten kilometres is nothing in most environments — half an hour by bicycle, or two hours' walking. We reckoned we might get there in four days if everything went well.

11 Dire Straits

The canoe deteriorated with alarming speed. At our previous inspection she had seemed to be in pretty good shape. A week later she was a terrible mess. There were two places on the bottom where the plywood was completely worn through, and all the fibreglassing on the external joints had been ripped off. As we lifted her we could feel that the structure was losing rigidity – she sagged and flopped, and the whole craft was only held together by the fibreglass matting we had sensibly put over the inside. It was time for an overhaul in dry dock, so we took her out of the water that night. Next morning we found the wood was still saturated and as most of the river was in permanent shade we had to carry her a couple of hundred metres to a sandbank to catch a bit of sun. I put aside one small half-kilo of resin to keep for emergencies and we used the rest to do an adequate job. It was only just in the nick of time. The plywood was paper-thin over much of the bottom. As we returned to our hammocks for a well-deserved rest, Peter and I discussed the situation.

'That will be the last time we can fibreglass her on this trip,' I sighed, flopping into the comfort of my smelly hammock. 'That little tin has to be kept for emergencies only.'

'I suppose when we have carried the canoe over the hills, the river over there will be similar to this one,' said Peter, gesturing at the choked waterway, 'a hundred kilometres of fallen trees and rapids. We know what that will do to the canoe.'

'It's the sliding over logs that does it. We're as careful as we can be. Hell, we can't carry her all the bloody way!'

'I'm thinking we do that already,' Peter muttered with a smile. 'Do you think she'll survive?'

'She'll have to,' I answered, swinging out of the hammock. I'd just remembered it was my turn to cook supper. I gathered some little sticks and stuck them into the sand leaning against each other to form a pyramid. 'She'll be in a lousy state when we get to the end, that's for sure – but so will we!' We laughed. I cut a piece of rubber from the old car inner tube that was our trusty fire-lighter, lit it and pushed it gently into the centre of the pyramid. The dry sticks crackled and a little flame appeared. I leaned a few slightly larger pieces of wood against the pyramid and prepared some others by attacking a dry log with a machete.

'We've got to be really careful we don't break her back though. That tin of resin wouldn't be enough to put her back together again.'

The fire was going nicely. I began to prepare the rice and tossed over to Peter a large bird that we had shot earlier. 'Pluck that for me, will you?'

'Ah, work, work, work,' he said good-naturedly, and got up to sit on a stool. Feathers flew.

'Waiter, I'm thinking I would like my pheasant with potatoes and peas,' he said with a smile.

I raised my hands in mock regret. 'Oh, so sorry, Senhor. No potatoes or peas today.'

'Salad?'

'No.'

'French beans?'

'Very sorry, Senhor. May I recommend the rice?'

'Rice? What is rice?' asked Peter.

It was an old routine.

'Rice is a succulent vegetable from the mystic East,' I answered. I heated some oil in a pan and chopped up six cloves of garlic into it. After they had browned slightly I added the rice, stirred it up for a minute and then poured in the water and covered the pot.

Garlic had been one of our best purchases. We had bought 1.5 kilos and used it abundantly — to spice up pancakes, in rice, to make a sauce for spaghetti, and once, and only once, in porridge. At Molocopote I remembered bending over Elcio's shoulder to look at his map while he gagged and flapped his hand in front of his nose.

'Shit, John,' he gasped. 'Are you afraid of vampires, or what?'

Oh, yes, we must have stunk: a mingling of sweat, grimy clothing, woodsmoke and garlic breath. We could have emptied a rush-hour train in seconds! As for vampires, well I think we were out of Count Dracula territory, but vampire bats were probably around. One of the risks of removing the mosquito nets was that they'd be able to bite us as we slept, but the pleasures had outweighed that risk. It was not so much a risk of blood loss as of rabies. Vampire bats can be rabies carriers. Not that the blood loss is insignificant. As they bite their prey they introduce an anti-coagulant that causes blood to continue to flow for a while after the bats have finished their snack.

Supper and coffee finished, I climbed into the hammock, but could not get to sleep for hours. I was worrying about the deterioration of the canoe. It would be so easy to break her back in these conditions, and that one little tin of fibreglass would not be nearly enough. Without a canoe of course Peter and I would almost certainly perish. It was over 200 kilometres to the nearest habitation (Maripasoula in French Guiana), and to get there we would have to leave the waterways and cross the hills on foot. From my previous experience with Andrea Bettella on the Rio Teles Pires trip, when we had to abandon our heavy canoe and walk 100 kilometres through the jungle to the nearest road, I knew how slim our chances of survival would be. We would be very limited in the quantity of food and equipment we could carry with us, and in our already weakened state we would rapidly be overcome by the exertion of crossing such terrible terrain. We would meet our end in some squalid little jungle camp and expire from hunger, exhaustion and disease.

It was not a pleasant prospect, and to shift my thoughts from such morbid contemplation I rolled a cigarette in the dark and sat up in my hammock to smoke. We'd just have to treat the canoe as gently as possible, that was all. As for meeting death on this trip, well, that had always been a possibility. One old man in Egypt had regarded it as much more than a possibility for me, and still I had come to Brazil. We might perish from the most trivial accident, from a moment of carelessness, or from a stroke of bad luck. It would be a pathetic and rather pointless fate; but these had always been the odds for expeditionaries in the past, and are the essence of adventure. We had not been just quixotically romantic in neglecting the modern developments and security of a radio and back-up for emergencies. We could not afford them.

I lay back in the hammock, but still could not get to sleep. As I listened to the jungle noises my imagination began to play tricks. A strong wind was jostling the tree canopy, although no breeze touched us down below, and I seemed to hear the singing of a massed choir away in the distance. At other times I heard a radio playing, a police siren and racing tyres squealing. Were the Caipora and Mapinguary out there too? The Caipora is a conservationist; a small, boy-like figure with his feet turned backwards. His friends are the animals of the rain-forest that he protects and heals when they are wounded. Any human hunter who kills wildlife too frequently or who leaves wounded animals to suffer incurs the Caipora's wrath: they'll become lost and will themselves perish.

Unfortunately not all hunters in Amazonia respect the Caipora. Many fear him a lot less than the other bogey-man − the Mapinguary. This is not your gentle, caring protector of animals. The Mapinguary just likes biting a hole in the top of your head and sucking your brains out. Instead of having his feet turned backwards, he has no feet at all on his hairy, ape-like body. He has one eye in the middle of his forehead, and his scream is so loud that it can knock you over at close range. He is especially active on Sundays.

I've met quite a few homesteaders in Amazonia who believe in these two characters: perhaps there really are some Yeti-like figures in that huge area − who knows? Certainly I have heard some distant roars and screams that might have been the Mapinguary on the prowl for my brains. And what about those eerie moments when the jungle suddenly goes deathly quiet? When those background chirpings, warblings, croakings, rustlings and whoopings suddenly cease? They are usually so omnipresent that the sudden silence is alarming. You can imagine all these little birds and beasts pricking up their ears to some sound you can't hear. Could it be the bogey-man?

'Nonsense,' you mutter, but the little hairs on the nape of your neck are not convinced.

* * *

I got up and stuck the coffee-pot on the embers of the fire. It probably was not even midnight yet − we turned in so early, so there were five more hours to dawn. The frogs croaked repetitively and in the distance I heard the rasping grunt of a hunting jaguar, but as I sipped on my coffee I became aware of a breathy whistling that I had never heard before. Immediately I thought it must be Indians, which seemed to be confirmed when from the other bank I heard an answering whistle. Nearer and nearer the sounds came, and although I tried to reassure myself that no Indian would attack in pitch darkness (in the westerns it's always at dawn, isn't it?), I began to get frightened. Soon I could hear actual footsteps approaching, and a stealthy swishing in the undergrowth as I sat there sweating and regretting my vow not to shoot Indians if I were attacked.

There came a colossal fart from a few metres away, followed by the rumble of dung hitting the deck. Only one Amazonian creature produces that amount of wind and excrement: our old friend the tapir. My pounding heart eased as I remembered being told how they whistle to each other. I relaxed and listened, amused at their seeming inability to get together. This one walked through our camp whistling forlornly, and was answered from the other only a hundred metres away on the other bank. Yet I knew they were rather deaf animals and their attempt at a rendezvous seemed doomed to failure. The situation became pitiful as they both crossed the river, whistling all the time, but ended up again on opposite banks. Poor lonesome tapirs. When I last heard them they were still calling plaintively to each other, further apart than ever.

I returned to my hammock, but was still awake when the howler monkeys started their chorus just before dawn. Weighing up to 15 kilos and standing a metre tall, they are the largest of the South American monkeys (although the gangly spider monkeys look bigger). Their chorus is an extraordinary sound — especially when heard close-to. Audible for 4 or 5 kilometres, it sounds like a roaring wind when the monkeys are distant. From nearby you can hear far more subtleties. The male starts the proceedings by gradually cranking himself into action. He utters long, rasping, vibrating exhalations, followed by almost equally powerful inhalations. After ten or so of these he attains a crescendo that becomes a sustained roar. When this falters slightly, presumably as he is drawing breath, you become aware of a falsetto trilling in the chorus. This must be the females. The chorus ends after three or four minutes with a last few coughs from the male. Peter and I found their almost nightly performances both wonderful and comforting. Many travellers disagree. 'It touched some secret chord of long lost fear, when speech was yet unformed. While it lasted, the sense of peace which had been inspired by the calmness and silence of the jungle gave place to a hidden portent of evil,' wrote C W Beebe dramatically. Mind you, if you did not know it was monkeys making that racket, then you would be alarmed.

We set off pretty late the next morning. I felt drowsy, and we spent some time improving the strutting of the canoe. However, we made reasonable progress, managing to squeeze under or round more trees than usual, and during the morning we only unloaded the canoe eight times and portaged twice. Easy stuff. After lunch I heard the alarm call of curassow, and clambered up the bank. Sure enough, there were four of them, and they flapped up into the low branches as I approached. I fired, and one toppled dead to the ground. The others seemed unaware of what was going on, so I reloaded and bagged another. I was getting greedy, and perhaps better at hunting too — though still sick at the bloodshed. The trouble was that as our foodstocks dwindled to unrelieved blandness we relished meat more and more. Anyway, our overall supplies were now so low we could not afford to let slip any opportunity to live off the land.

You might imagine that after three or four months of celibacy and all-male company our thoughts would be turning to women. Not at all. We lusted and craved for only one pleasure: food. Our conversation and yearnings were wholly concentrated on titillation of taste buds and orgies of gluttony. We lingered and slobbered in masochistic detail over the great feasts of the past and those we planned for the future. This had been a feature of every jungle trip I had done in the past. Andrea Bettella, on the Rio Teles Pires, had taken me each night on a gourmet tour of Italy's provinces, discussing intimately the regional dishes and the wines, and telling me how they are prepared. 'You take the oil, onions and garlic, and fry them gently ('sssst' — he'd hiss softly) until golden brown . . . ,' and I would listen, drooling as I spooned down my boiled white rice.

That afternoon we glanced up and saw a large, hazy outline towering over 300 metres above us. For a while we were not sure if it was cloud or mountain. But it did not move. It must be mountain. After seeing nothing more than a few little hills for so long this mountain mass seemed pretty awesome and we realised with excitement that it was part of the Massif de Mitaraca. Our portage! There are two major peaks in this massif — Paloulouni-meenepeu (phew), 707 metres, and another of 690 metres. We would be portaging over the lesser Mapaoni—Epoyane (300 m) and Temomairen (453 m). That still gave us over 100 metres or more of a climb, but we thought they would seem easy after the last couple of weeks. It would be lovely to be on dry land for a while and damp only from sweat. Elated at being so near our goal, we camped early and gorged ourselves on curassow. They have a lot of meat on them and, if one could roast them in the oven with spices, I'm sure they would be delicious. Boiled in river water they are merely tough and tasteless, but we did not care. We ate half a bird each with a good helping of rice. Next morning we had fried rice with curassow pieces, and still had plenty left over for lunch and supper. The Mapaoni had become a tiresome little river, but she was bountiful.

We were expecting one last tributary — the one that marked the trail over the mountains. The trail might be overgrown by now, but we thought there could be some sign of its old starting point, like abandoned tin cans, bits of plastic or perhaps a collapsed shelter. By lunchtime, after a morning of unloading and carrying, we still had not reached the tributary and were growing despondent. Then a couple of hours later the river veered west, which would mean (if we had identified the start of the trail correctly) only about four kilometres to go. A little later we saw another place on the bank that seemed to have been cleared by man, and that encouraged us. We needed Indians now. Our earlier fears of meeting them had been replaced by positive eagerness for contact. If there were no tribes on the upper Mapaoni using the trail regularly it would be completely overgrown, but Indians would be able to save us time by showing us the way. Also, we had a couple of heavy bags of junk to hand over, which we were getting tired of humping around. To warn them of our approach, and to attract attention, we fired six shots into the air, and made camp cheerfully hoping that shortly we would receive visitors.

We were in good spirits. The end seemed to be in sight — well, at least the end of the second stage. Now all depended on the trail. Did it exist? The whole idea of the Surinamese and Brazilian governments deciding to connect two rivers in this remote region seemed so unlikely, yet the boatman said it had been done when the frontier was surveyed and demarcated. As for our initial fears that we would stumble on garrisons of crack troops resisting the Cuban-inspired invasion of Brazil from Surinam — well, that seemed laughable. Perhaps we might meet a few soldiers on the Surinamese side because access to the border was a little easier over there. But no, it was not an idea we could take seriously.

In this mood we set off enthusiastically the next morning, but after a couple of kilometres our hopes were dashed. There was a tributary entering from the left, which according to our map should not have been there at all. It was also much too large to ignore. This was the sort of development we had feared. It made us doubt our position and shook our faith in the map. Once a map has proved unreliable, you never trust it again.

This was not the sort of terrain over which to drag a canoe if you were not dead sure you were going the right way. We tied her up and set off on foot up the larger of the two streams. We covered over 4 kilometres wading the shallows, swimming across the deep pools, and sometimes walking through the jungle, all the time checking likely places for some sign of the trail. Once we thought we had found it because on high ground near some rocks we found an old saucepan. Completely rusted through, it had obviously lain there for many years, but it was the sort of rubbish we expected to find. We climbed up the hill behind, looking desperately for any further signs, but had to give up when the compass told us we were heading south rather than north. Bitterly disappointed, we carried on upstream, the only consolation being that someone had been up here before. Half a kilometre further on, the river again divided in two, making our confusion complete. We had three maps and none of them coincided with what we were finding. We had expected the 1:250,000 scale one to be more help, but it too was letting us down.

We returned to the canoe and made camp. It had been a tough and miserable day — only marginally improved by Peter shooting a curassow so we could have a meat supper. While we ate we decided to push on up the way we had walked that day and take any fork of the river that looked to have the most water, as long as it went approximately north. After all, if the trail did not exist we would have to cut a new one, so the further we travelled in the right direction the better. Still, it was worrying that no big peaks were visible. If we were only a few kilometres from the planned portage point surely we would see them by now? To the northwest there should have been a peak rising 300 metres above us, like the one we had seen three days before. It should be only 10 kilometres away at the most, and clearly visible over the tall forest. Yet through the breaks in the cloud we saw only flat scenery to the northwest.

The following morning we took the canoe up to where we had walked and camped a little way along the right-hand fork. With each division of the river it became still smaller and shallower. There were a few deep pools, but in many places there was not enough water to float the canoe. The obstructions remained as numerous as ever, and that day we were treated to a new and particularly unpleasant experience. As Peter was slashing through a tangle of vegetation, I saw a large dark mass, that I'd assumed to be a bird's nest, suddenly separate and drift outwards in a cloud.

'Look out, Pete!' I yelled, but he had already heard the buzzing and seen the size of the hornets heading his way. He began to run like hell for the deeper water. A bit too slow. Just before I dived under the surface he let out a scream and clutched his head. We stayed in the water for over five minutes, only popping our heads up briefly for air. The hornets continued to fly about agitatedly. They were massive and terrifying. Peter told me later that sting had been far more painful than that of the scorpion a few weeks before.

'Ten of those stings, man, and you'd be dead,' he said with conviction, fingering the swelling on his head. 'Shit, that hurts!'

The hornets had now formed a new swarm, and I had to volunteer to go and retrieve Peter's machete. I crept towards my quarry, eyeing that seething mass and debating whether we could not do without the machete after all. The hornets were still angry and unsettled, and many cruised around looking for trouble. With their legs trailing below them, they reminded me of Harrier jump jets, and I inched through the shallows keeping as submerged as possible. I grabbed the machete almost directly below the swarm and retreated with considerable relief.

At this juncture we decided we'd better portage the canoe through the jungle rather than risk any more stings, but to get our revenge we sneaked up to within 5 metres, fired the shotgun at the swarm, then turned and sprinted for our lives. But we collided with each other and fell in a heap in the shallows as the first of the hornets reached us. One landed on my arm. I remember seeing it alight a split second before I submerged, but it must have been washed off just in time. The water was about 50 centimetres deep, and we crawled our way along the bottom, heading for a pool upstream. Lungs bursting we clawed our way over the shingle, concerned above all that our bare arses should not stick out above the surface. We reached deeper water and surfaced at last. All clear. We looked at each other, gasping and pop-eyed from the fright, and burst out laughing. That would teach us to mess with hornets.

As we had come across two half-mouldy onions mislaid at the bottom of the food-bag, we decided to treat ourselves to one of our dried dinners, and use the onions in style. The next dried dinner had in fact been earmarked for celebration when we found the trail, but we were in need of encouragement now. Tired though we were, we went to great lengths to prepare a memorable meal. We made a dough from flour and rolled it out on a paddle blade using an empty bottle, then wrapped it round some fried rice with onion and garlic, and fried the patties until crisp before serving them with a curry sauce.

Next morning we began to haul the canoe up the tributary, but after battling with our worst kilometre to date, we stopped to reconsider. This stream was surely impossible: almost no water, more rocky than usual, and fallen trees everywhere. We could not move more than 5 metres at a time without having to lift the canoe over an obstruction, usually after unloading all the gear. Our cheerfulness was wearing thin. You can keep moderately cheerful for the first ten times you unload and load the canoe (four sacks, two back-packs, two bags, one large sack of bedding, one sack of cooking utensils and bloody Peter's two smelly monkey skins, not to mention Mark's army jacket). You can force a smile for the first ten times you carry the canoe over obstructions. You can manage to twitch the mouth corners when dragging smaller logs out of the way, or pulling 200 kilos of canoe and gear against the grip of sandy shallows. But, try as you may, no smiles can be mustered when you cut through 10 metres of tangled creepers and thorns that seem to leap back into place however frenziedly you slash at them. Try cutting a tunnel through a tangle like that and then meeting rocks and logs in the middle so that you have to unload all the stuff, haul the canoe over, and reload while you're bent double and throttled by creepers. The ants drop all over you, the sticks gouge those old, festering wounds and you collect a new crop of scrapes, bruises, bites, scratches and cuts. Just see if you smile.

Nothing was more guaranteed to produce flaring tempers than such tangles of vegetation. The person at the bow of the canoe had to do the cutting, while the other shoved the canoe up the tunnel behind. The bow was six metres away in front, so it was not easy to see how near it was to your companion floundering amid the vegetation. The danger was that you shoved enthusiastically and rammed him in the back or pushed him on to that column of ants he'd been trying so carefully to avoid.

'Wait! Wait! Wait you stupid bastard!' came the muffled scream of rage. 'Pull it back, you've got my leg trapped. Ouch! Shit! Ouch! Why the hell don't you wait? Jesus Christ, I've got enough trouble in here without you pushing me on to these thorns!'

We decided to leave the canoe once more and reconnoitre on foot. We walked about 5 kilometres I suppose, and managed to establish nothing definite, apart from the fact that getting a canoe any further up there would be sheer torture. There were sections difficult enough for us to walk through unladen. I thought we would be lucky to advance a kilometre a day in those conditions. Fortunately, anyway, the stream seemed to be bearing mainly east, and that seemed to indicate it was the wrong tributary. Hunger forced us to return to camp, but we decided to have a better look at the terrain next day. We set off at dawn armed with a plastic bag of rice cakes and the shotgun. We walked all day, explored every likely place for a trail, checked the compass frequently, and climbed any hillsides to gain a better view. No luck. Not a sign of major mountains either to the northeast or anywhere else. What was certain was that the stream carried on running east, which ruled it out. Thank God. It was a bitch of a stream. We turned back for camp.

Peter's malaria returned that evening and he had a night of shakes and vomiting. What a fantastic holiday we were having! Who the hell wants to stay in some beach-side hotel with a temperate, dry heat, a game of tennis before breakfast — orange juice, crunchy croissants and coffee with creamy milk? What pleasure in a morning of beach, reading and swimming, followed by a light salad and siesta in an air-conditioned bedroom? Then more beach, a shower, and an evening of good food, wine, dancing and moonlight strolls? How bloody boring. How mundane. How fantastic!

As I sat staring into the embers of the fire, smoking and reflecting on life and leisure, I heard a jet pass overhead. At one stage of the trip — when we had been near the mouth of the Cuc — we must have been on the main Buenos Aires—Rio—Miami—New York route, because we would hear three or four jets a day (without actually seeing them). Now it was over six weeks since we'd heard one. The sound of this plane was made more poignant by the knowledge that it must be the Air France flight Manaus—Cayenne—Paris. My flight home. It was a Thursday, about 7 pm, and I could imagine the passengers up there nursing their pre-dinner drinks, and the pretty hostesses, the film. God, how I wished I could be up there on my way home. I wanted my family, my friends, some home comforts, varied food, girls and some intellectual stimulation.

I sighed, prodded the fire with a stick, and thought of Raymond Maufrais who had disappeared not so very far from here in 1951. I had come across his journal, 'Journey without Return', in a second-hand bookshop years before, and found it a very moving story. When he was seventeen, Maufrais had been awarded the Croix de Guerre for his bravery with the World War II Maquis, and he later became a parachutist in Indo-China. Then he embarked on a career as a journalist and joined an expedition to the Mato Grosso in 1946. In 1950, at the age of twenty-four, he undertook an ambitious expedition in the jungles of French Guiana to attempt a lone crossing of the Tumucumaque hills. An Indian found his diary, rifle, camera and other possessions on the banks of the Tamouri river in early 1951, and Maufrais himself was never seen again.

His father published the unedited diary to raise money for his own attempt to find his son, who he was convinced was still alive. This humble workman-turned-explorer undertook two expeditions in the search, and became the first westerner to cross the Tumucumaque from French Guiana to Brazil.

To impartial readers of the book, it seems that his son must have perished. By the end of the diary account Maufrais was suffering from dysentery and starvation, and decided to swim the 75 kilometres downstream to the nearest village.

'I feel it's going to be an amazing experience. This, after all, is the real primitive life that I love. A civilised man turned into an amphibian on a river in Guiana with nothing to rely on but his skill, his strength, his will-power . . . with no firearm, half-naked, no roof to return to . . . it's fascinating.' Obviously frightening too.

These lines are rich in morale-boosting, bluster and courage. They come on the last pages of the journal that recount his sufferings over six months. Reading the account, you cannot help but feel that he was ill-equipped and his plan too ambitious. People advised him to head straight for the Tumucu-maque via the Oyapok or the Litanie (the river Peter and I were planning to cross to), rather than taking the difficult, exhausting route he chose. He was plagued by lack of funds and forced into delays that made him miss much of the dry season. He could not afford a light canoe which would have saved him so much hard work, and right at the start he had to sell several items of useful equipment.

More important, he planned a trip across the jungle mostly on foot, and that is far harder than any journey by river. It severely limits you to what supplies you can comfortably carry on your back. Maufrais was soon to become wholly dependent on living off the land, and found the jungle an erratic provider, over-generous one day, miserly the next.

'In the forest, providence is my maitre d'hôtel. You can walk for hours and days together, exploring every inch of the forest without finding a thing, and then when you pause for breath at the foot of a big tree you see a hocco (curassow), a tortoise or a partridge.'

He journeyed up the Maroni river from the coast, and up the Ouaqui in the company of the bush negroes of the interior. He was then on his own, and crossed from the Ouaqui to the Tamouri rivers by land. His only com-panion a little terrier called Bobby.

The intense solitude of the forest quickly began to affect his spirits, and he poured out his homesickness, fears and uncertainties in the diary. Perhaps if he had survived he might have edited out these passages before publication and concentrated more on the moments of feeling buoyant and confident. If so, we would have lost a fascinating and unique account.

'I hunted once again – drew blank. Yet I want to live, I want to be strong. I want to come through all this. I want to eat. I want to see my parents again and make them rich and happy. I have such great stores of love for them; it doesn't matter if we're rich or poor, so long as we're together. Oh, God, let me live. Suffer me to return to France!'

His search for food became more and more desperate: almost all his time was taken up with it, and he ate snails, tortoises, palm hearts and grubs, but on many days he found nothing, or not nearly enough to prevent his decline into weakness. On the 3rd January 1951 he killed his dog.

'I killed Bobby this evening. I was just strong enough to cut him up in front of the fire. I ate him. I was ill afterwards; my constricted stomach caused me agonies of indigestion. I suddenly felt so alone that I realised what I had just done and began to cry. I was angry and disgusted with myself . . .' Two days later he wrote, 'I thought of Bobby and realised how necessary to me was his silent companionship. There's nobody in camp now to welcome me in the evening. No more barking, no more eager licking. Poor Bobby!'

Poor Raymond. The borderline between recklessness and audacity is narrow, and the determining factor is success or failure. If he had succeeded he would have been considered extraordinary, brave and daring. But he failed, and it is easy to be unkind and unsympathetic to failure. 'That unhappy, deluded young Frenchman, who in order apparently to prove to himself that he was not a coward, persisted in adventuring on various expeditions, virtually without equipment, into the most inaccessible South American jungles . . .' said one writer. Reckless he was, but he had courage, tenacity and the ability to bounce back from the black moments.

He reached the banks of the Tamouri, but by then he was in severe trouble. He camped there and began to build a raft — a job that took him a couple of weeks, as he had to spend most of the day scavenging for food, and was often too weak to work afterwards. Most of what he ate aggravated his dysentery or would not stay down. Even when he did finish the raft and set off, he travelled only one kilometre before it was wrecked.

'I ought to have realised that a raft would never get far on such a creek. You need a light, narrow boat that can slip along anywhere.'

He started work on a dug-out, but soon realised that it was beyond his strength. He could not walk any further on land, his shoes had disintegrated, one ankle was swollen and painful, and his back-pack had fallen to pieces. He decided to swim, leaving the gun and hammock behind.

'I can only count on providence to give me the chance of knifing a sleeping crocodile, or a serpent on its liana, or a ray in a shallow pool, or a fish sleeping between two rocks. . . . All these are entirely speculative of course . . . I promised to come back; and come back I will, God willing.'

It was a desperate move, but his situation was equally so. Swimming or wading down a creek would be less arduous than walking through the jungle, or getting a canoe through, and he would cover more distance each day. However the decision to leave his rifle was a bad mistake. Perhaps he should have made a small raft to carry the gun, and to push in front of him?

After the Indian discovered his diary and belongings in February 1951, the Prefect of Guiana organised an expedition to look for Maufrais. In October it was found that he had reached a point 50 kilometres from his last camp, and had built a native shelter. This was only 22 kilometres from the nearest village, but he was never seen again.

It was a small consolation that he left the journal, and in his moments of loneliness and discomfort he wrote many touching entries.

'I'm rather ashamed of my weakness. I feel that I'm behaving like a washed-out, fretful creature. But I'm a man after all, and I've a loving heart inside me. I'm not like an animal that thinks only of getting something to eat in the fields. And I've nothing to love in this forest.

'There's always a struggle inside me between my continual need for affection and my love of solitude and adventure. I've nobody to stretch out a hand to me, nobody to smile and wave me on, and so I talk to myself and curse myself. I've got to get out of this apathy, this dreamland; I've got to break through. When I don't think, I'm happy; and I take delight in the way of life − free, pure and primitive − that we all long to experience, even if only for a while.'

* * *

I sat by the fire smoking and trying to imagine what it would be like to be alone in that place. Days of struggle with no one to moan or joke to, no one to share the work. A crushing solitude that would stifle the song on my lips, that would make the shadows menacing and the imagination lurid. Any accident would mean death, and the idea of Indians around would be much more disturbing for someone alone.

I did one short canoe journey in Amazonia by myself and I found it a very lonely experience. Yet the Rio Guapore had quite a few houses, so every now and then I could spend an evening in company. Up here it was different. You were beyond help, prey to any chance fate that might break your leg or topple a tree to crush your canoe (always one of my recurring nightmares, that one), or you might so easily fall on a knife, or cut an artery when the machete slipped in your wet palm. Admittedly the same mishaps could occur to a pair of you with equally disastrous results − but how comforting to have someone to share the worst − even to die with.

I looked over at Peter who was retching over the side of his hammock. We were both exhausted, plagued by headaches and sickness, never-ending toil, painfully slow progress, and now confusion as to exactly where we were. We had been on the river for fourteen weeks, and while we wanted to achieve our objective it seemed to be degenerating into a joyless endurance test. The fate of most expeditions, I suppose, as they go on for too long or too far.

12 Dilemmas

Peter had a bad night and in the morning did not feel up to doing another long reconnoitre. I decided to explore the left-hand tributary by myself, so I crammed some tobacco, cooked rice and cartridges in a plastic bag, strapped the compass on my wrist, picked up the shotgun and machete, and departed. This stream was substantially easier than the other one: deeper, a few less fallen trees, and no rapids. It also seemed to be heading in the right direction, northwest, so after about a kilometre I decided to cut through as many of the tangles as I could to save time later when we returned with the canoe. Indeed often it was the only way I could walk through.

After an hour I came to a bend with the deepest water we had seen for a long time. Holding the gun above my head I was swimming awkwardly across and got the fright of my life when what I had taken for a piece of driftwood suddenly thrashed the surface and duck-dived 2 metres away. A caiman. I kicked my way to shallow water aware what a tempting target my waving legs must make, and pulled myself on to some rocks heavy with relief. As I stood up, a squawking flock of large birds legged it into the jungle. I threw the gun to my shoulder and snapped off a blind shot as they began to get airborne. Miraculously I hit one. It was an attractive bird that I had not seen before — mainly black with a long elegant neck and head, pale blue legs and a half dozen rainbow feathers on its breast. A common trumpeter, I learned later. There seemed no point in continuing with the shotgun, as we had our supper and it was heavy and awkward to keep dry while one hand was constantly in the water with the machete. So I left the gun and the bird in the fork of a small tree and continued relatively unencumbered.

It occurred to me that I was running a grave risk of bumping into Indians while by myself that day. That first contact would be preferable if I were accompanied by Peter. I began to wish I had waited until the next day when he would have been feeling stronger, and I peered into the undergrowth apprehensively for the rest of the way. I walked for five or six hours and must have covered over 7 kilometres. The direction of the stream seemed right, but there was still the perplexing absence of mountains. They should have been towering overhead by now. I scanned the horizon for mountains but saw nothing larger than a few low hills.

At one point I was half crawling under a tangle of creepers when a swarm of bees set upon me and stung me ten or fifteen times before I could scramble out. Cursing and smarting I edged back to see where the nest was. I soon spotted it hanging from the tangled vegetation and effectively blocking any attempt to pass. I was looking gloomily at the prospect when the little bastards set on me again and gave me half a dozen new stings. I had to cut a lengthy detour through the jungle to get round and continue on my way. To my consternation the stream gradually narrowed down, getting more and more choked with vegetation, although it still had a few chest-deep sections. At about 3 pm I had to turn back to be sure of making camp before dark. Even so, I only just made it, arriving at dusk, weary, rubber-legged and carrying the bird for our supper.

When I retrieved the bird from the place I had left it four hours previously I found it aswarm with the little black bees that seem to be the first agents of decomposition in Amazonia. They soon find any fish or meat and collect in hordes. Fortunately they are stingless, because there must have been several hundred on the bird and they had already nibbled away quite a bit. They had attacked the weak points — eyelids, anus and around the shotgun pellet wounds. Imagine what their honey must taste like!

It made me ponder just how long one's own body would last on the jungle floor. A meal for the bees, wasps, maggots, ants, beetles and perhaps termites too, and the carrion-eating rodents and birds. I would not be surprised if within two weeks everything would be devoured: skeleton, the lot. Maybe even sooner. There were some mean, ugly little rodents around at night. We often heard them crunching up the discarded bones from our supper, and as they are fairly small creatures their jaws must be disproportionately powerful. By shining the torch we obtained only a glimpse of glowing eyes and a small, furry outline. We had to wait until a visit to the zoo in Manaus before we saw what they looked like. Now I am in general quite sentimental about animals. I find most of them attractive. Not all are cuddly, but usually they have something appealing — a lustrous coat, an appealing inquisitiveness, an alert intelligence. Well, these creatures were the exception. They were shifty-eyed, mangy-furred, bare-tailed, vermin-ridden and foul-smelling. They had pointed snouts full of yellowed teeth. They were quarrelsome and aggressive to each other, and no doubt they also sprayed their piss about and dropped their shit indiscriminately. They were that sort. They made the brown rat look sweet and cuddly in comparison.

Back at camp, I found Peter had recovered enough to move himself from his hammock to a stool by the fire. He slumped there looking ghastly. The malarial fevers of shakes and sweats are bad enough, but I think the immediate aftermath is the worst part of the whole cycle. Your temperature has returned to normal, but you feel an overwhelming weakness. Every joint and muscle aches and the hallucinations and delirium have left you with a feeling of unreality and depression.

I prepared the bird, and Peter forced a bit down before he returned to his hammock. We decided that if he felt up to it the following day we would take the canoe up this second tributary. It seemed the best option, and at least it was heading in approximately the right direction. However, if we still hadn't seen any mountains within two or three days we would have to rethink and assume that somehow we had gone wrong.

Next morning after only a couple of hundred metres we had holed the side of the canoe. We were pushing it through a narrow gap at the time, and Peter saw that it would not fit.

'Do not push any more, John. It will not go through here.'

I continued obstinately shoving. The alternative was a portage, and it was too early in the day.

'Stop pushing for Christ's sake!' shouted Peter.

Too late. A sharp piece of wood pierced the thin plywood just above the waterline.

'There, see what you did!' said Peter angrily. 'That was bloody stupid.'

'Oh, shut up, Peter!' I was in no mood to take criticism lightly. 'If we're talking about stupid mistakes what about you the other day chopping the canoe with your machete? Jesus, that was a smart move!'

The incident had happened while Peter was chopping at some vegetation and the canoe had drifted a little too close, so that his swinging machete cut a chunk out of the bow — but well above the water-line. We had laughed at the time.

I notice that when under strain I get increasingly sensitive to criticism. The most extreme example occurred on the Rio Teles Pires with Andrea. We were paddling down a rapid, and I made a cock-up which caused us to crash into a rock.

Andrea turned around in his seat at the bow, 'Come on, John, get it right!' he said angrily. 'We had plenty of time to avoid that one!'

'It's all right for you to sit there in the bow — you don't have to do any steering at all!' I snapped. There was still a lot of rapid left and the canoe was picking up speed. 'If you think you can bloody well do better, come back here and try it.'

I stood up in the canoe, and waved him to take my seat.

'For Christ's sake, John, this isn't the moment to change seats!' cried Andrea as the first waves sent spray over his lap.

'No, come on. If you're so bloody clever, you come and try it, smart arse!'

'Not now, John. Steer the canoe or we'll turn over!'

I sat down reluctantly and picked up my paddle.

'Jesus! After eight weeks I make one little mistake, and you start shouting at me. You're welcome to sit back here any time you like!'

'Okay, John, I'm sorry. I'm sorry. You're a marvellous steerer. I couldn't hope to match you. You're the tops. Now look out! That rock!'

It's sad to see yourself reacting so poorly in times of stress. Where was the noble spirit? The stoical, long-suffering good humour you always liked to think was just below the surface? These trips put me to the test, and I was found wanting. I wasn't a figure of heroic stature after all. It was a tough truth to swallow.

* * *

We covered about half the distance I had walked the day before. On one high section of bank we found a very rusty piece of metal. It crumbled in our hands, but we thought it had once been a kerosene can. There were no other signs of a camp or trail, but at least it meant that some other poor bastards had been up here years before. Perhaps we were on the right tributary after all.

That night it rained very hard, which did little to lift our spirits. It hadn't rained seriously for so long that we had grown lazy about erecting the plastic awning. It came suddenly and torrentially, dowsing the fire before supper was cooked, soaking our hammocks and the clothes we slept in. We turned in hungry and cold, and the next morning we awoke to a disaster. The canoe was three-quarters full of water; in fact it would have sunk completely if the stream had been deep enough. The combination of the leaks and the rain water had weighed it down until that hole was below the water-line, and then the canoe had rapidly filled.

All our gear was submerged or floating, and the food sacks had been under water for several hours. Even the treble-wrapping in plastic bags had not been enough to protect our stocks. This was a bitter blow. The rice was swollen and damp, the spaghetti had congealed into solid lumps, and the beans were soaked. It did not matter about the salt and the sugar, they would not spoil, but the rest we must at all costs dry out, and that would not be easy on an overcast day on the upper Mapaoni. We made a large fire and spread out all the rice and beans. The spaghetti had definitely had it. We ate it up over the next three days – boiling it for five minutes and then cutting it into thin strips which we fried until crisp. These were moderately palatable eaten with salt or sugar.

We reckoned we had only food for another two weeks, and it seemed likely that a lot of the rice and beans would spoil and be wasted. Game seemed quite plentiful and we felt we need not starve, despite the lesson of Raymond Maufrais, but we hoped to avoid a total dependence on living off the land.

It was the worry that we might be up the wrong creek that was beginning to undermine our resolve. It we could just find the trail, or discover where to cut a new one, we'd get stuck in and do it. This uncertainty was causing delay and virtually ensured that we would run out of both food and malaria pills. We decided to give it just four more days of reconnoitre and if we found nothing in that time should consider returning back downstream. We pulled the canoe out of the water to start drying her off prior to some more repairs, and set off walking. We examined every possible place for signs of a trail. We climbed a large hill, and excited by the glimpse to the north of a higher hill, wondered if we could be standing on Mapaoni—Epoyane. And could the bigger one be Temomairan? But there were no hills visible to the north-east, not even from up there 100 metres above the river, and with a reasonably unobstructed view.

We had been wandering around up the hill, following a ridge and looking for a place to get a good view, and I had only been taking casual glances at the compass bearing. When the time came to return to the river the bearing I had remembered seemed totally wrong and to be heading right away from where we thought the river should be. How easy it is to get lost in the jungle – a moment's distraction or the pursuit of an animal, and you suddenly have no notion where camp lies. The compass is an absolutely essential guide, but at that moment it needed all our self-discipline to believe in it. However, contrary to expectation, it did lead us safely back to the river and we were so relieved to get there that I totally forgot about the bees' nest and we were severely reprimanded.

On another trip I once spent a very uncomfortable and frightening night in the jungle after getting lost. I'd had the compass with me but had not bothered to check it. I felt confident that I knew my way back and I had not intended to go far. It was a troupe of monkeys that led me astray. In my attempt to bag one for supper I pursued them avidly as they swung through the treetops always tantalisingly out of range. I gave up as the sun was going down. It was time I headed back. I strolled confidently back to where I knew the camp was, but after half a mile I hit a huge area of swamp, something I had not seen on the way out and which was impassable. I felt the first stab of panic. The sun was on the horizon already and the light was fading. I hurried along the fringe of the swamp, tripping and stumbling, scrabbling at the vegetation. I headed off in a new direction. But by the time night fell I was hopelessly lost. It was a terrifying experience. I could have been 200 metres from camp, but it might as well have been 2 kilometres. I fired the rifle into the air to try to attract my companion – but the crack of the .22 was absorbed by the jungle. Fortunately, being a smoker, I had matches on me so was able to build a fire for comfort; but the mosquitoes ate me alive that night. By morning I had so many bites on my eyelids that they were closed to two little slits. During the night I had controlled my panic, and at dawn I headed north marking my way as I went. I covered over 2 kilometres on that bearing and nothing looked familiar. I returned to the starting point and headed south for a similar distance. Again nothing. Back to the beginning and off east. To my joy that led me to the river. It's all so simple when you keep calm.

I staggered into camp expecting to find my companion pacing up and down in panic and concern. The son of a bitch was fast asleep in his hammock!

'Hey,' I shouted, giving his cradle a rock. 'Sorry I'm back so late. One hell of a party. Went on all night!'

'I stayed up for three hours, calling and whistling, banging saucepans etc – but when you didn't show up I though, what's the point? And I went to bed.'

Peter and I walked for another two hours without finding anything conclusive, and then returned to camp. We were absolutely wiped out, stumbling like zombies, and we had spells of feeling dizzy and faint, and had to rest for

a while. We were in need of a good long rest. A total sort of rest, that we
were unlikely to find in the jungle. We reached camp and flopped out in the
hammocks for an hour or two, contemplating the effort of making a fire and
cooking supper. We had no meat, so when we heard the commotion of a
troupe of monkeys (chattering, swishing of branches, and the plop of discarded fruit), Peter grabbed the gun and set off in pursuit. After fifteen
minutes I heard two shots and assumed he'd got one. A bit later he returned,
but instead of a monkey, he carried a dead fawn — a spotted, limp-eyed
bambi; I looked at him in surprise, and reproach. Until a month before he
had not been willing to hunt at all, and here he was shooting a creature that
would have made the cruellest man's finger hesitate on the trigger.

'It was hard,' he admitted sheepishly. 'I see it lying there in the little nest
that the mother make. I stop there for five minutes or more, thinking shall
I, or not?' He shrugged. 'Hunger won.' It was such a pretty creature with its
silky coat and soft eye; but at the same time the saliva was bursting out at the
prospect of supper. That we've all eaten lamb and veal was how we justified
the death to ourselves as we began to skin the fawn, and I've never eaten any
meat more delicious. It was so tender, that even the bones could be chewed
up and eaten.

Because the canoe was not drying out with any speed we built a large fire
next morning and propped the canoe up beside it. We then fibreglassed over
the holes, and I fixed another keel. By the time we had finished it was too late
to do another reconnoitre so we had a day off. Peter did some sketching and
I started to re-read parts of 'History of the World'. But I could not concentrate for long. I found my mind kept drifting off to thoughts of the world
outside the jungle. We were becoming bush-crazy and the idea of life away
from the jungle seemed more and more attractive. Entertainment, food and
drink, social life, girls, and a rest from all the repetitive toil. Sunshine was
something we missed, too. We had been living in gloom for weeks, and our
skins were pale and soggy.

I lay in the hammock thinking of food. Nothing very fancy (after all you
can't get anything much fancier than milk-fed venison), just good solid fare:
potatoes — fried, sauteed, baked or mashed — bread, eggs, cheese, fruit
juice, cakes, chocolate, a nice variety of puddings and some jam. Sweet things
were what we wanted more than anything else. Normally I'm a savoury man
myself, and rarely eat sweets and desserts, but now I was dreaming of
crumbles, chocolate, cakes, apple pies and biscuits. We joked that if we were
unexpectedly presented with the choice of a night in the best restaurant in
Manaus or a night with the most beautiful girl in Manaus it would be a tough
decision. Things were that bad.

I have to admit that despite my general familiarity with the jungle, on a
mental level I find it impossible to shake off a nostalgia for the people and
activities of home. The harder the going, the more escapist my thoughts.
Conversely, when life at home is dull and routine, my thoughts find their
way up Amazon creeks.

My yearnings now were for domesticity. Having reached the age of thirty-three without accumulating more worldly goods than could be fitted into a small saloon car, on sleepless Amazonian nights my thoughts were now dwelling upon how nice it would be to have more than one duvet cover; how my wardrobe really was scruffy and inadequate, and how I should invest in a clock radio and a machine to make me a cup of tea when I woke up.

Anyhow, next morning we had to get up without the aid of either, and before dawn, because we'd decided to push fast upstream on foot. To avoid returning to camp we took the minimum of gear with us for staying the night up there: our hammocks, some cooked rice, two small plastic sheets, the coffee pot and a couple of cooked monkey legs. It all fitted into one back-pack, and off we set. This was going to be the final push and exploration. If we found nothing that looked right by the end of it we would obviously have to conclude that we had gone wrong somewhere.

We donned our shorts just in case we bumped into somebody. Twice the previous day we had fired a volley of shots to try and attract the Indians we hoped might be in the vicinity. We needed their help now, and did not want to offend their sensibilities by arriving naked. On the other hand the canvas uppers of our shoes were flapping and separated from the soles, we were grizzled and hairy in appearance, pale from lack of sunlight and sickness, gaunt of face, and covered in a welter of scratches, scabs, infected cuts and pimples. We would certainly give any Indian a nasty turn if we took him by surprise. Our attempt to look decent did not last long. We had gone a couple of kilometres when I paused to rest on a log and smoke a cigarette. Peter began to laugh. Looking down I joined in. My shorts had been damp for so long that they had rotted and split during my exertions of clambering over logs. The split completely exposed my genitals in a manner that looked far worse than if I'd just been naked.

By mid-day we had passed the spot we had reached on previous walks and were now on new ground. The river was becoming more and more choked with vegetation, and we needed to cut our way through. We found one very small tributary coming in from the left − but it seemed too small to be likely and anyway it would have been impossible to get the canoe up, so we ignored it. There was then a long marshy section where the course of the stream had almost disappeared among grass and reeds. We squelched along with the mud sucking and dragging at our tired legs. It's strange, but I have never seen a leech in South America, and Martin and Tanis Jordan say the same. People associate them with rain-forests and we had expected to meet many in Amazonia. In South East Asia they are always present. A crossing of a marsh like that would have collected twenty or more. We should be thankful for small mercies.

By nightfall we had covered another six or seven kilometres and still could not see any mountain, but we realised we must be near the source of the tributary. By now it was less than 2 metres across and shallow. We slung our hammocks and had our supper, discussing the situation and knowing that tomorrow would be make-or-break day. It rained for over an hour. There had been cloud around all day and for the last week we had heard thunderstorms rumbling in the distance. The rainy season was overdue, and seemed to be on its way at last.

We started at first light and moved as quickly as we could. There were a few small hills to the north, which we climbed to get a view from the top. Nothing. On we went. There were a couple of little cascades, but these were small affairs. The stream would be too shallow for most of the way to float the canoe. Still no hills. We walked until after mid-day, then stopped for a smoke, some coffee, and a gloomy discussion. We were a tired and dispirited pair. There seemed no point in continuing. It would take several hours to walk back to camp, and if no hills were visible from where we were, it was probable they were not up this tributary at all. Where had we gone wrong? It seemed that we must have taken the wrong fork somewhere. But where? This one seemed to flow in the right direction, and we had followed our route approximately on our maps. When making the tracing of Elcio's 1:250,000 scale map, had we missed copying a crucial fork at the headwaters, or was that map no more accurate than the others? How senseless it would be to cut a trail before finding the hills which would assure us we were in the right place! We could, I suppose, have wandered off towards the north on foot to try to find the streams on the other side of the divide. But that would take a week at least, the cutting of a trail a fortnight, and the carrying of the gear another week. If we were on the wrong tributary it might be a 30-kilometre portage instead of fifteen. Even if we crossed to the Litanie, it was sure to be as difficult as the upper Mapaoni had been. We would certainly not arrive at Maripasoula, the first town of the French Guianan side, for at least two months.

We had only enough quinine and chloroquine for controlling one more malaria attack each and we would each be guaranteed more than one in those two months. We would be totally out of food in less than a fortnight. Did we wish to prove that we were more proficient in hunting than Raymond Maufrais had been? The jungle was an erratic provider. While we saw a lot of game when we were not particularly needing it for survival, not doubt it would immediately become scarce the moment we finished our last rice. The combination of weeks of very hard physical effort, sickness, and shortage of food would put us into that fatal survival trap that had killed Maufrais. Using all our dwindling reserves of strength to hunt, and rarely killing enough to replace the energy expended on the hunt, we would soon be reduced to a standstill. Our growing weakness would make portage of the canoe impossible, the malaria would rapidly debilitate us further, and the time spent just searching for food would leave no time for anything else. We would in all probability find ourselves camped for weeks in one place, unable to push on, or even to retreat, each day growing weaker.

The continuous toil of the past few weeks had already weakened our resolve. If we'd been sure enough of our position I am certain we would have cut the trail and completed our mission, yet all the uncertainty and fatigue had toppled the magic of crossing the Tumucumaque hills. What had seemed a noble objective at home as I pondered the map on a winter's evening, now seemed daft. Mark had been right, I thought, as I looked at the jungle around me. So what? What for? The work involved in cutting a trail over the hilly jungle was enormous. The carrying of a 40-kilo canoe and the equipment for 15 kilometres was sheer folly. If we had been fresher it would have seemed different, but we had been on the river too long already. Too much strength, enthusiasm and motivation had been eroded by exhaustion and ill-health. We wanted to get out. We were disappointed, and felt we had failed. But above all we wanted out.

We stumbled back to camp, only just making it before dark, and had a gloomy supper.

'If we was a big expedition,' Peter sighed wistfully, 'we'd radio for a helicopter to find the correct small river from high and tell us where we go wrong.'

'The pilot could drop us some malaria pills, some beers, and then go away,' I added. 'Hell, I don't want to turn back now. We're only 10 kilometres or less from the border with French Guiana, 250 kilometres from Maripasoula. It seems silly to give up after so long.'

Peter had calculated we'd been on the river for precisely 100 days, and had paddled over 650 kilometres against the current. That seemed an awfully long time and distance – only to end up thwarted and disappointed.

'The problem is we don't know where we make wrong,' said Peter. 'We can walk up every little river, and two more weeks would pass. I hate the idea of giving in, the same like you, but we know we have big trouble if we continue for two more months.'

He was sitting naked on the stool by the fire preparing some coffee. He'd lost most of his tan, and his skin had taken on an unhealthy yellow hue. The geologists had commented on that a month before, and said it was probable due to his liver being full of malaria parasites. Might he have hepatitis too? He was also having a lot of trouble from heart palpitations. He was always conscious of his heartbeat – fast and erratic – and complained of breathlessness. I had become aware of this a few nights previously when, with our hammocks touching, I had been listening to his breathing. It was noisy and fast, as if he had a fever. I asked him if he felt sick, and he replied, a bit surprised, that he felt okay. When I mentioned his breathing, he replied that he was having a spot of trouble with palpitations, but no worse than usual.

There was also one suspicion that I had not voiced. Among the cuts, scratches and sores on his forearms I had noticed two little ulcers with raised edges that looked alarmingly like leishmaniasis to me. This is a horrible disease spread by the sandfly, that starts off with skin ulceration and then spreads to attack the mucous membranes. The tongue, nasal and throat cavities become destroyed and obstructed, and death from seconday infection can be caused after years of suffering. It is difficult to cure. I felt a certain responsibility for Peter's well-being. After all, it was my crazy schemes which had lured him away from his original intention of hitch-hiking through South America. I knew that he had valued the experiences, but he seemed to be in danger of permanently ruining his health. The crossing of the Tumucu-maque certainly was not worth such a price.

Disappointment was therefore mixed with relief when we agreed to return to the geologists' camp at Molocopote and beg a flight out. The trip had not been a total failure. We had kept going and advancing over some pretty tough weeks. We had travelled one of the most beautiful rivers in the world, and seen most of the wildlife of the region. There was plenty to be grateful for, and not a little to feel proud of. The prospect of retracing our steps to Molocopote through all those tangles of vegetation and fallen trees yet again was not much fun. However, it had been sheer chance we had met the geologists there at all, and of course without their existence we would have been forced to continue.

We stayed put the next day sorting out our gear and chucking out presents for Indians that we had carried so unnecessarily for so long. As the fire consumed the cheap combs, and we dug a hole and buried the mirrors, we were grateful that we had been spared the embarrassment of handing over such gifts. We also dug the second shotgun out of the pack where it had been stored all the trip and found it seriously rusted. As we were hoping to pay for our flight out of Molocopote with the guns, we scrubbed it with sand and coated it with cooking oil. That did not make much difference to its appearance. We hoped the geologists would have some emery paper and gun oil.

There were a couple of heavy showers that day, and in the evening we had our first serious rain of the trip. Serious rain in the tropics is a miserable business for the camper. The clouds boiled up all afternoon, advancing, retreating and encircling, and by nightfall the distant thunder and lightning got us rushing our supper, and hastily repacking the rice and beans we'd spread out in an attempt to get rid of the musty, mildewed smell. The wind increased and the jungle began to sway and groan. This is when you begin to inspect the trees around your camp for the ones that are tired of life and might feel like lying down on you. Twigs and small branches often did fall near our camps, but nothing larger, although many times we heard large trees coming down with a sustained smashing noise as they toppled several others on the way, or barrelled down a hillside cutting a swathe of destruction. A couple of weeks earlier I had gone for a hunt and returned the same way to find a large tree had fallen since I had first passed. We hoped the storm would not blow a lot of new trees across the river to add to the enjoyment of our return trip.

We could hear the rain coming — the roar of millions of drops hitting leaves, advancing steadily towards us, louder and louder. Peter and I shouted our last messages and snuggled into our hammocks, pulling the blankets up to to our chins. The tarpaulin lifted and strained in the gusts of wind and the rain came, drumming and deafening. In a lot of books about rain-forest ecology, I have read that the jungle canopy is all-important to protect the thin soil from erosion. The rain merely hits the forest floor in the form of a fine spray, say some scientists who have obviously never sat out a storm in the jungle.

The noise of the rain makes conversation impossible. You just have to get lost in a world of your own, and it's quite pleasant to sit it out for as long as the hammock remains dry and snug. But there seems to be a limit of about an hour on the tarpaulin's impermeability, and then the water starts to creep up the ropes and gradually to soak the hammock, making it cold, clammy and uncomfortable. That night it rained for over seven hours without a pause.

13 The retreat

I awoke shell-shocked from the roar and din of the storm, feeling depressed by our decision of the previous day. The jungle dripped but the sky had cleared. I strolled sleepily to the river to collect water and let out a cry of surprise.

'Hey, Peter! Get out of your Swiss roll and have a look!'

'What,' he grunted, swinging his feet to the ground.

'Look at the river. The majestic Mapaoni!'

The river had risen at least 20 centimetres overnight, and was lapping around the items we had left on the sandbank. It had always seemed to me that after months of dry season when the jungle is tinder dry it would take several weeks of rain before the river level rose. I had been wrong.

'We go now easier downstream,' smiled Peter. 'We float over many logs.'

'Yeah, but there may be others we won't get under any more,' I countered.

We loaded the canoe and turned her round. No traveller likes to retrace old paths too soon, especially with the taste of defeat rank in his mouth, and we hesitated for a few minutes.

'Shit, this is a very bad day,' said Peter, and there was no denying the tears in our eyes. 'I'm thinking our journey deserves a better ending.'

'It sure does. One hundred and twenty kilometres back to Molocopote, over those same logs, through those same tangles. At least before we had the excitement of entering the unknown.'

We sighed, and began the gloomy wade southwards. We soon realised that those extra centimetres of water would make an enormous difference to our progress. Of course one or two logs we had squeezed under before were now impossible, but generally on the way up we had gone over far more logs than we had gone under. Also there were now no areas where the canoe could not float. We still could not paddle the canoe — we walked all day — but we covered over 7 kilometres. Three times the speed of our progress upstream.

In the afternoon I shot a monkey that fell mortally wounded but refused to die. I tried to insert a new cartridge to shoot it again, but the cardboard was damp and swollen and the spent cartridge would not eject. (This invariably happens when you need a quick second shot.) I tried to pick the monkey up by the tail to swing and brain it against a tree, but nearly got bitten. I searched around for a stick, but all the wood seemed rotten, so I used the gun butt on its head. Even that did not seem to work. It was a horrible experience — the monkey trying to drag itself away, emitting heart-rending little cries, with me in pursuit clubbing it with the gun-butt. In the end I could take no more. I lifted the gun up by the barrel and brought the stock crashing down on its skull. The skull fractured and so did the stock. I sat down and leant against a tree to roll a cigarette with shaking hands. I was close to tears. I had dealt with a Rasputin of the monkey world, participated in a murder where the victim keeps getting up. I had also ruined one of the guns. But at least the monkey had stopped making those cries. I was looking forward to leaving the jungle and being able to buy my meat dead, cleaned and cellophane-wrapped.

It rained again most of the next night and the river kept rising. The Mapaoni was transformed, and we only had to carry the canoe twice the next day, and once again covered more than 6 kilometres. If only we'd had this easier going during the previous two weeks — it's so difficult to choose the optimum period of ascending an Amazonian river by canoe. Go too soon after the rains stop and the river is still too full and the rapids too dangerous. Go too late and it becomes too rocky and shallow. There are only two months for the optimum balance: August and September.

We hoped to reach Molocopote on the evening of December 14th, allowing us nine more days to get there. We knew that all the geologists' team were leaving for Belem and Santarem before Christmas, and the 15th had stuck in our minds as the date the plane would come. We did not fancy having to wait there until they returned in January. Also, there was the risk that they might decide to leave for the duration of the rainy season, which would leave us over 500 kilometres of paddling back to Carecaru. This was a life-threatening prospect with our shortage of food and malaria drugs.

The morning after this lingers in my memory as one of the worst of the entire trip. The creek had deepened enough for us to have our first spells of paddling for over two weeks, but it also meant we had to leap out frequently into chest- or neck-deep water. It was a cloudy, drizzly day, and we were soon blue and shivering with cold. Our spirits reached a new low. We made a fire at lunch-time to get warm and stood around it like workmen round a brazier on an English winter's day. We continued to urinate dozens of times a day from all the immersion and it seemed a waste of such piping hot liquid to just spray it away: much better let it dribble in lovely warm streams down the thighs.

That evening we reached the place where we'd carried the canoe through the jungle to avoid the tangles, repeated the portage in reverse and camped. My temperature had risen to 102 degrees, so I swallowed some Fansidar, and sat wearily by the fire, reasonably warm at last. We had no meat to cheer us up at the end of an awful day — just a bowl of boiled rice. Boy, had we eaten a lot of rice. Peter and I had eaten more than 35 kilos of the stuff over those weeks, and surprisingly we still liked it. Our remaining 5 kilos had got damp and tasted sour and nauseating. We spooned it into our mouths stoically.

'How long do you reckon that portage was we did this evening?' I asked Peter.

'Oh, three hundred metres I think,' he replied, laying down his plate.

'Can you imagine carrying the canoe for fifteen bloody kilometres! What a crazy scheme that was!'

'We are too tired and old for those games. I'm only waiting to get to Belem and go into a supermarket and push a cart down those shelves full of beautiful things. I will take some bread, cheese, tomatoes, mayonnaise, chocolate, biscuits, cake, orange juice, jam . . . shit, I will take everything!'

'Imagine sitting in a restaurant, dressed in clean clothes, sitting on a real chair with a back to lean against – not like these stupid stools, and have someone cook a meal for us!' I dreamed aloud. 'Look at those two girls there with us, sweet-smelling, soft skin, velvety as peaches, laughing eyes, our knees touching under the table . . . '

'Yeah, okay, very nice,' interrupted Peter laughing. 'But what food do we order?'

'The big city,' I mused, drawing deep on my rank cigarette. 'Supermarkets, shops, restaurants, cinemas, bars, clubs, museums, beers, real cigarettes, noise, bustle, pollution, litter, squalor, degradation, filth, human misery and suffering. Mix it all together and you've got paradise. You've got Belem!'

That night it rained again, which gave us moderate pleasure – we needed the river to stay high for a while longer – but we were sick of the gloomy dripping jungle. We wanted unlimited horizons, fields and moorland. Once we joined with the Caripi the river widened out and the sun could reach us at last. I had to start from scratch with protective cream. All vestiges of my previous tan had vanished over the past weeks. We had the rapids to negotiate again, and they'd got much bigger and more menacing since the rains. But they did not delay us for long: we walked the canoe down some, lowered it empty on the rope down others, and the portages, if any, were brief. The extra water made the river unrecognisable. On the way up it had been bordered by or had flowed round numerous sandbanks. Now it must have been 70 centimetres higher and all the sandbanks had vanished. The water reached right up to the banks, and the Mapaoni looked a substantial river. She was still a pretty river, but she had been much prettier before. Or were we now looking at her with jaded eyes?

The beginning of the rains brings high mortality. Many of the sandbanks are riddled with wasps' nests in the dry weather – all of which are flooded out by the swollen waters. Hundreds of thousands of ants, termites and other insects must be swept away and eaten by fish. Plants that had misguidedly taken root on the sandbanks now stand forlornly doomed in swirling water. Though it is a bonanza time for fish, most animals must dislike the rains as much as we do.

In one pool we disturbed two adult giant otters with their two youngsters. We did not pause to watch these lovely creatures. We barely broke the rhythm of our paddling as we passed by. We had seen it all before, and nothing about Amazonia could any longer give us pleasure or excitement. Our indifference must have offended the adult otters, because they surfaced near the canoe, chattering and hissing. I had heard that they can be very dangerous when they have young, and certainly they are big and powerful enough to inflict serious injury. We kept on paddling, pulling a bit harder now while they swam around us, diving under the canoe and popping their heads up to hiss some more. They were getting uncomfortably close. We yelled at them, waved the paddles in their faces, and looked with alarm at those large, yellowed teeth. The otters would have been quite agile enough to climb into the canoe, and the idea of 2 metres of muscle hopping onto my lap made me stop to pull the shotgun within reach.

'Go away, you stupid animals!' I yelled at them. 'If you come in here I'll put your species even nearer to extinction. Go back to your babies!'

We had left the pool by now, but still they followed, and we were paddling at full speed. Gradually they dropped back and we could begin to relax. Or so we thought. We leant on our paddles for a breather and to look behind us at where we had last seen the otters, but they had disappeared.

'They go,' said Peter.

The words were no sooner out of his mouth than two snarling heads appeared out of the water 1 metre away and gave us a hell of a shock.

We paddled on. We were in mosquito country again, and had to put the nets back on the hammocks. The hammocks stank of mildew, dirt and urine, and seemed airless and suffocating. All our clothes were also in a filthy state — we'd got very lazy about washing them over the past few weeks. We only wore clothes in the evenings and at night, but they were covered in soot from the open fires, and of course we wiped our greasy fingers on our trousers. We had also spent many hot, sweaty, malarial nights in them. In short, they stank — but there seemed no point, or no time to wash them now.

We started to shoot a lot of the rapids, to save time, and through laziness, and, too, for the excitement. If they were short rapids we did not bother stopping the canoe to go for a reconnoitre, but just stood up in the boat, made a snappy decision as to whether they were possible, and if so, which line we should take. Quite frequently the quick look had missed some surprises and we shipped a lot of water. At least it gave us some excitement. In between the rapids we had long spells when we had no interruptions to our paddling. The number of times we had said upstream, 'Oh, for just one day paddling in the sun!' Now we'd got it, we found it hard in a different way. Our paddling muscles had grown soft, and although we paddled along at a brisk pace we found it both boring and strenuous. It also gave me hours in which to contemplate Peter's efforts with a critical eye. One of the inevitable consequences of sitting in the stern of a canoe is that I develop an obsession with my companion's lack of effort. I've sat behind five men on different trips, and not one of them did his share of the work. Each dip of their paddle produced a whirl of water that passed me on my left: feeble, little whirlpools that betrayed desultory paddling that had propelled them that way. I pulled hard on my paddle, and compared the magnificent swirl of water with their puny creations. I would scowl at my companion's back, growing bitter and savage as the ferocious sun caused my head to hum and as the hours passed. On a bad day I could work myself up into quite a state.

We stopped on a rocky islet to prepare a batch of pancakes with the last of our flour. It was my turn to cook and of course everything went wrong. The islet was just too small and uneven. I needed space for the bowl of batter, for the fire, for me to sit, for the plate with the finished pancakes. At first the fire was not hot enough, so the pancakes didn't cook right. Then the stones that I had placed around the fire needed shifting, and without thinking I moved one by hand and burnt my thumb. Soon the fire was too hot, scorching my hands and burning the pancakes. I'd had enough. I kicked the fire into the river and sulked. Peter, with infuriating Alpine calm, now took over from me, and turned out a dozen perfect pancakes.

'Of course he's not as tired as I am,' I thought to myself, 'he hasn't been paddling as hard as I have, has he?'

I always had to cajole him along during this period to do slightly longer days. I often felt like a school teacher chivvying along a reluctant pupil — and there was much sighing and casting of wistful glances at camp places after 2 pm. I felt much more urgency. I preferred to paddle an hour or two longer every day rather than run the risk of missing the flight out by a day just because we felt tired and lazy. But they were long, long days — we were covering 25 kilometres a day on the lower Mapaoni.

However, at least we ate well, because we were in prolific fishing waters once more. As long as we had some bait, fishing was laughably easy. We'd stick the bait on a large hook with some fencing wire for a trace, attach that to a nylon cord, heave the whole lot into the current, and tie the cord to a tree. Within five minutes, before we had even got the hammocks up, the branches would be shaking and we would have landed a trairao of 2 kilos or more. It was hardly great sport, but gave us large pots of fish stew and soup.

Fruit was not very abundant at that time of year, but we experimented with any we found. In case they were poisonous we took it in turns to have one good bite, and wait for any unpleasant reactions. Occasionally we got stomach ache, more often the taste would make us discard the rest, and very occasionally we found something delicious. We found some orange-coloured soft fruits reminiscent of apricots, and it was my turn to be guinea pig. I took a bite. 'Mmmm, great!' I said, resisting the temptation to eat more. 'Let's gather a lot to take with us.'

We filled our largest saucepan and carried on paddling. When an hour had passed, and I was still alive, we began to tuck into the fruit, putting aside twenty for supper but eating the rest. We agreed they were the nicest thing we had eaten for weeks.

About one and a half hours later, I felt the call of nature, and told Peter I'd have to pop into the jungle for a moment. I emerged five minutes later.

'That was a profoundly moving experience,' I commented as I picked up my paddle.

Ten minutes later it was Peter's turn, and then mine again, and then his. Each time was becoming more painful, and by the fourth, we were clutching our abdomens as the cramps shook us. There seemed no point in continuing our travels. We found a convenient branch to sit on and hang our bums over and waited for the thing to pass.

'Bloody fruit,' groaned Peter.

'We've made a discovery for science,' I said. 'The world's strongest natural laxative. Move over senna, your days of supremacy are over.' It was over three hours before we could safely leave that branch.

On the eighth day after turning back we collided with a tapir. The dumb beast lumbered into the water followed by her youngster, fixing us with an unseeing eye, submerged and swam straight underneath us. We stopped paddling, but she suddenly realised we were there, and tried to get out. The broad, muscular back rose below the canoe and keeled it over sideways, half filling it with water. The tapir then panicked, dived again, made a bee-line for shore and finally belted off into the jungle. Her youngster meanwhile ended up on the far bank, and knowing tapir they probably never found each other again.

If the truth be known we were not particularly expert at paddling downstream. We had adjusted our skills to the slow pace of upstream travel when there is ample time for manoeuvre. Swept along by a swift downstream current, we often found that making an unexpected sharp turn to avoid a tangle of thorns and creepers ended us smack in the middle, scratched and cursing. Frequently we shot alarmingly under fallen trees with only a centimetre or two to spare. Peter is smaller than I, so he could crouch down lower. Several times I failed to get low enough and scraped my back on the log as we skimmed under. At other times I would lean backward over the stern of the canoe and go under the log in limbo style, praying I had gauged it right and would not be decapitated.

At midday next day when we thought we were still about 20 kilometres from the Jari we rounded a bend and emerged abruptly into the wide river. It came as a total surprise, but we now knew we could easily reach Molocopote that night, dead on schedule — it was December 14th. We stopped for lunch and caught some piranha to grill. After that was the very boring paddle down to the camp. The Jari was so deep and wide and incredibly dull after the small streams we had grown used to. It rained heavily but we paddled on. Rain on the river is pretty. Each drop causes a droplet to jump above the surface, and the effect is of a sheet of bouncing pearls. However, we were not at our most appreciative that afternoon. We were cold, and the rain stung our bare skins. Moreover, we had paddled or walked over 120 kilometres in the past ten days. We just wanted to arrive at Molocopote, tie up the canoe, and never paddle again.

We recognised a small rapid which we knew to be a kilometre from camp (Peter had thrown up his breakfast hereabouts), and quickened our pace. Round a couple of bends and there it was. No canoes were moored there, so it looked as if everyone was still at the gold-workings. We were relieved. What we had feared was that we would find all the canoes and no hammocks. That would have meant they had already flown out. With a last shove of our paddles we ran the bow up onto the sandy shallows, and grinned wearily at each other. We'd made it and in damn good time. Christmas in Belem!

14 The long wait

Confident that the place was empty we had not bothered to put on our shorts, but as we stepped out of the canoe we were surprised by a welcoming greeting. It was Fernando, standing with a blanket over his shoulders, hugging himself in the sunlight and looking far too ill to be shocked at our nakedness. We had met Fernando from our stop there over five weeks before, but he was a shadow of the jaunty twenty-year-old joker we had known. He loosened his warming self-embrace for a moment, letting a chink of cold air through the blanket long enough to stretch out a hand to us, and then retired to his hammock.

We grabbed a few things from the canoe and followed him up the slope to the hut where we found three more men cocooned in their hammocks. Malaria was now rife in the camp. When we had passed before there had been none. It is very hard to stop the spread of the disease in a jungle camp like that. Elcio, the manager, had pursued the policy of making everyone sleep under a net and isolating anyone with the sickness. Perhaps since he had left everyone was more careless. Or perhaps Peter and I had been responsible for bringing it here? Anyway, we learnt that ten men had already been flown out for treatment, and these four were waiting for the next flight.

We sat and chatted with them and they commiserated with us for not having achieved our goal, but agreed we'd had a good stab at it. We also learnt that there would possibly be a flight to Santarem on the 18th, and certainly two to Belem on the 23rd. It seemed we need not have hurried quite so much. One by one they ceased talking as they embarked on their evening ordeal of the rigours that, as one man commented, came regularly at six o'clock 'like cocktails'. Knowing they would prefer to endure the attacks alone and hearing four sets of teeth chattering and the hammock strings vibrating, Peter and I took ourselves off to raid the cashew fruit trees along the airstrip. It is a peculiar fruit — apple-shaped, some red, some yellow, bursting with juice and with an appealing bitter-sweet taste. They also have the added bonus of a cashew nut at one end — but these we discarded as they needed to be roasted.

The presence of the sick men was something of a disappointment. We had hoped that we would be alone at Molocopote if we were to wait a few days for a flight, so that we could wander around naked and be spared the friendly curiosity, questioning and efforts at conversation. After weeks and weeks of solitude it takes a while to be at ease among groups of people. We cooked up some rice for ourselves as no one else was interested in food, and flopped into our hammocks. We were exhausted, and it was a good feeling to know we would never have to make or unmake another camp. We didn't even have to get up the next day and paddle. If we so wished we need never have to paddle again.

We were awoken at midnight by the arrival of another canoe-load of men waiting to take a plane which apparently was due the next day. This had been requested over the radio from the gold-camp. It looked as though there'd be no room for us, and the number of men with malaria had risen to seven. For consolation they had shot a paca on the way down and we sat around the fire preparing and eating a late-night stew. We were up at first light to get our gear more organised, in case we were able to squeeze on the plane. Everything was filthy and in a chaotic state. We gave our clothes a good bashing on the rocks, stitched up the rips in the seat of our pants, and felt we were perhaps now ready for the bright lights of the city. We cleaned the two shotguns with emery paper and diesel, and they looked quite presentable at the end, apart from the broken stock. We then sorted through all our belongings and distributed what we did not need any more — torches, batteries, fishing line and hooks, rope, plastic sheets, etc, and some of the more useful (and less dangerous) items from our medical kit. The men enthusiastically grabbed the ampoules of local anaesthetic, and used some on the spot to extract someone's tooth with a pair of pliers.

The men all had lousy teeth — what few were left — and most smiles would reveal large gaps in the front. It's strange how the absence of teeth can transform a handsome man. After one smile you feel a sense of relief when the lips close over the wreckage. Others had a form of decay that ate all round the edges of each tooth, making them look as if they were widely-spaced. Glen, an Australian dentist with whom I had travelled on the Rio Verde, called it the 'rip-saw smile'. When you see the amount of sugar they eat, you understand why the teeth go. Coffee without at least four spoonfuls of sugar provokes indrawn breaths and puckering of the lips, as if you had offered them a lemon to suck. 'Muito amargo (very bitter),' they say, and add two more spoonfuls.

Well, things were very 'amargo' at Molocopote. They had run out of sugar and we only had one cupful left. There was no tobacco, either, so they pounced on my remaining stash and that was gone by the end of the day. It seemed the time had come at last to kick the weed; at least until we got out of there. There were seven people wanting to go on the plane to Santarem, and the others were waiting for the Belem flight. The plane could take 700 kilos if the pilot agreed, and as the Brazilians were small, light-weights there was some hope.

'What happens if the pilot only agrees to take one of you?' one man asked. 'Who stays and who goes?'

Peter and I looked at each other. We'd grown close over the past few months . . . but . . .

'John, would you stand aside and let Peter take the place?' he continued. I fidgeted uncomfortably on my stool.

'Well . . . I'm sorry, Peter, but I don't think I would, no.' I answered.

'Dear me, John, what selfishness!' He turned to Peter. 'How about you?' Would you do the decent thing and insist John go first?'

'Not a chance,' smiled Peter. 'We decide with a coin I think.'

In any case the plane did not arrive that day: a disappointment, but we were still confident it would not be long. There were some nice people in the camp – above all Mineiro and Cabeca Branca. Mineiro's real name was Ernesto – he was called Mineiro because he came from the state of Minas Gerais. He had been a student of physics until the previous year, but when the bank he used went broke he had to give up his studies. He had a lot of easy-going Brazilian charm, and the ability to converse easily with everyone whatever their background. He had been at school with one of the investors in this project who invited him to take the job as supervisor. Ernesto regarded the whole thing as a holiday and an adventure, writing notes on his impressions, and making a collection of jungle curios.

Cabeca Branca (white head), was a prematurely-grey man of forty-five who was in charge of one gang of workers. In contrast to Ernesto, he was illiterate, but with a native shrewdness and intelligence. He had an impish smile and amused us every morning by singing songs in the *repentista* manner. A simple melody is used and the lyrics are inspired by the events of the moment and the people around. In the northeast of Brazil you see incredible performances of this art that needs continuous rapid thinking for half an hour without hesitation, all the time choosing the words for the rhyme. Cabeca Branca was an amateur, but his witty and acidic comments on our situation got us up with a laugh. He was also the best hunter in the group and was passionate about it. He wanted a lot of information on the Mapaoni, saying he was thinking of taking a canoe up there and becoming a gateiro. I could well imagine him returning with plenty of furs, so I deterred him a little with the addition of at least twenty major rapids. That did not seem quite enough to kill the sparkle in his eye, so I invented a contact Peter and I had had with a fierce band of Indians. I think the jaguars, ocelots and giant otters of the Mapaoni owe me a drink, because like all these men he was scared stiff of Indians.

Round the fire that night we talked about Indians for several hours and I found in them a sad, blind ignorance and prejudice on the subject. Indians were 'dirty', 'thieving' and above all 'treacherous'. The original American frontier clash was being reenacted 150 years later in the southern hemisphere. The Indians and the rough, tough adventurers would not find a way to live without conflict, and, their undeniable qualities apart, these characters were ill-suited to the delicate mission of first contact, trust and compromise. They all had some second- or third-hand account of treachery and murder to back up their intolerance, and my appeals fell on deaf ears. The fact that we had supposedly had a contact with Indians and emerged unscathed and without having killed any aroused a mixture of admiration and consternation. Of course it had all been a lie, but from what we knew of the two tribes in that area — the Wayana and the Akuriyo — it seemed we would in fact have been in little danger.

The Akuriyo were totally nomadic until the early 1970s, hunting and food-gathering in the forests of southern Surinam, French Guiana and across the border in Brazil. They avoid the big rivers, being unable to swim or build canoes, and move around in the forest staying at the most a couple of weeks in any one place. Hunting and fishing provide the Akuriyo with protein and fats, and additional food is provided by honey, palmfruit, palmnuts and various tubers. They are able to distinguish some thirty-five kinds of honey and are constantly in search of nests. As these nests are often located high in trees, falls are a major cause of death.

The Akuriyo are unable to make fire, so the women of the tribe are responsible for carrying the precious embers from camp to camp. If the fire of a band is extinguished, there remain only two possibilities: to get fire from another band quickly, or to die. According to Peter Kloos who has lived and worked among them, the expression 'His fire has gone out' is a euphemism for 'He is dead'. Since the early 1970s most of the Akuriyo have moved into the Trio and Wayana settlements and forsaken their nomadic, stone-age existence. However, there are thought to be one or two small groups who have chosen to remain in the forest, and there would have been a slight chance of our bumping into them on the Mapaoni headwaters, although they would probably have merely spied on us from a distance.

Hunting and fishing were extremely poor around Molocopote, due, we supposed, to the past proficiency of the Indians in these pursuits. Fishing around the camp was almost totally unprofitable. Lots of us tried it for several hours, day or night, and we caught nothing, not even a piranha. This was extraordinary on the Jari. To catch fish you had to go to the two small rapids a kilometre upstream. I got my first taste of the equally poor hunting that day when I went for a short walk. I saw a small troupe of capuchin monkeys, which scattered in every direction, bounding from branch to branch, while I was still well out of shotgun range. These monkeys really knew that man was bad news. Otherwise the jungle seemed strangely empty.

Having plenty of time on my hands I walked fast to put distance between me and the airstrip, hoping to enter less-trodden pastures. I found a tree that had been dropping its large fruit — and there were four toucans and a mob of green parrots tucking into the crop in the canopy. A lot of discarded pieces had been chewed by monkeys, pacas and agoutis, and there were tracks of deer and wild pig. I seemed to have hit a well-visited tree.

I remembered an Indian technique for attracting animals, and cut a sapling. The idea was to imitate the fruit being blown off the tree by a breeze. The falling fruit would hit a few leaves — so you swished the vegetation twice — it might hit a branch — so you knocked one — and it would make a good thump as it struck the ground — like that. The idea was that the agoutis and pacas in their burrows would rush out, but I felt pretty self-conscious and foolish as I slapped the leaves and branches and stamped my foot for 15 minutes to no avail.

The next morning being Saturday, we were informed that the pilot would not be coming, as he was a Seventh-Day Adventist and did not work on Saturdays. The morning passed fairly quickly as we got up late and made breakfast for everyone. There was quite a lot of farinha so we made fried farinha cakes which everyone was curious about, but which no one really liked. Brazilians are pretty conservative about food. If it's not meat, fish, rice, beans or orthodox farinha they are suspicious. Apart from the farinha there was not much food left at Molocopote for so many of us. We had 2 kilos of rice, a little spaghetti and beans. However, with so many men either out hunting or making fishing trips along the river in the motorised canoes, we ate a lot over those first few days. Each time someone caught a fish, or shot a monkey or bird, it would be cooked immediately and everyone would partake, filling the meat out with farinha which swells up in the belly giving a warm, bloated feeling for a while. That way we ate nine or ten times a day.

Molocopote was situated on a bend in the river, and round the corner from the main camp was an attractive sandy beach where few people went. At first I thought it would be the ideal place to be alone. However, when I went there with a book to do a bit of sunbathing I found that thousands of little ants drive you off the beach within half an hour. It was Amazonia in a nutshell: relaxation marred by insects. So to get a bit of privacy Peter and I would go hunting or for walks along the airstrip and around the old Indian clearings. It had been a very large site – there were many acres of old plantations that had now run to secondary growth. Scattered around were the ruins of the old huts and some old graves, several of which showed clear signs of the disturbance caused by Ernesto in his 'archaeological digs'. In fact one had been left almost open with a bone protruding from the soil. I commented to Ernesto that should any warrior come down to put flowers on Mum's grave he might be a bit upset to find it like that.

As predicted, the plane did not come on Saturday, nor on the Sunday, and time was really beginning to drag. We sat around and chatted, had a few swims, re-read a little of our well-thumbed books, tried to write and ached for tobacco. One guy went round collecting all the old dog-ends and emptying them into a cigarette paper. I confess that I had sunk so low I too queued up for a few puffs of that tarry, germ-filled cigarette. A period of such prolonged inactivity is not ideal for breaking the smoking habit. Once 3 pm had come and gone each day, we knew the pilot would not be coming because he would not have time to get to Santarem or Belem in daylight. So then we would wander away from the camp to hunt. The bulk of the time we just lounged in the hammocks, trying to resist the temptation to sleep during the day as it would cause insomnia in the night.

Next day, the 19th, was a Monday and we all got up optimistic that a plane would arrive. The more confident among us untied our hammocks and rolled them up and sat with ears cocked for the distant drone. Peter and I discussed which of the restaurants we knew in Santarem would receive our custom that night, although clearly we had no cause for much hope unless two planes came. We were way down on the waiting list.

Fernando was the only man still ill from malaria. I had handed out a lot of Fansidar, and it seemed to do the rest of the men good. Mind you, with the dosage they took it was kill or cure. The doctors advise three at one time and no more for a week. These prospectors perferred to take four the first day, three the second, two the third and one the fourth. All survived. Yet poor Fernando showed little sign of improvement – he carried on getting a fever and the shakes every night, and his companions told me he had been ill for over a month and taken over forty Fansidar in that time. I thought of giving him some of my remaining quinine tablets, but decided to leave it for a while. I was due an attack of malaria and did not want to leave myself with no effective treatment.

Mid-day came and went, and our optimism began to fade. We replaced our hammocks so we could lounge in them. Later I went down to the river and chatted for a couple of hours with Ernesto while we swam, shampooed and sunbathed. He was one of the men who had been suffering from malaria, but far from being concerned with the several kilos he had lost in weight, he was delighted.

'This is fantastic,' he chuckled, running his hands over his flat stomach. 'I must have twenty pairs of trousers that were too tight for me before. Now I look like a teenager again. I think I'll ask a chemist to prepare me some malaria pills so every time I want a quick diet I just pop one down, retire to bed for three days, and shake and sweat it off. Malaria is the best slimming aid ever.'

He was thinking of spending Christmas there by himself – he had no real desire to spend it in civilisation and looked forward to a period alone. He was pondering whether to quit the job in January.

'This garimpeiro stuff is only worth it if you earn big money. I mean a lot of money – six or seven times what you could get out there in the wide world. It's not worth doing for less. Think of all the things we miss out on – girls, entertainment, good food, music, comfort – for six months at a time. If you earn a fortune it's worth the sacrifice.' He submerged to rinse the shampoo out of his hair. 'There's gold up there – but not in big quantities. None of us has earned much yet, and I don't think we'll ever earn enough. So once you've experienced the garimpeiro life and had your adventure – it's best to go back home. That's what I say.'

They had all the necessary machinery upstream, and Ernesto explained the method they used. They have two motors, one more powerful than the other. One pumps water from the river under pressure to break the gold-bearing shale and the second sucks the rock and water and squirts it into an inclined trough with metal grids to separate the large pebbles. The trough is lined with sack-cloth to catch the gold. (This is a method used since ancient times, and in ancient Europe a sheepskin was used instead of sacking. This is believed by some to be the origin of the Golden Fleece.)

There was also one diver in the team who would take the hose down to the river bed so that gravel could be sucked up to a trough mounted on a raft. Cabeca Branca had been a diver on the river Tapajos, and although the water was not usually more than 10 metres deep, it was a dangerous job owing to the strong currents. Once he had lost the mouthpiece that supplied him with oxygen and had passed out before the team on the raft realised anything was wrong and hauled him up. Generally the men worked in teams of six or eight, and were provided with the machinery, their food, and rewarded with 50 per cent of any gold found. Other prospectors preferred to work for a daily wage of about $15 a day, which is four or five times the usual wage for unskilled work in Brazil.

A few men wander off to explore new areas, and retain vestiges of the old romance of gold-prospecting, at least to the uninitiated observer. Certainly their ability to survive in the jungle with the absolute minimum of provisions is a lesson to most of us. All they seem to take with them are sacks of farinha and cans of kerosene. (I have never met a caboclo who bothered to light a fire without a cupful of kerosene to help him.) Their proficiency at hunting and fishing guarantees them enough food. Although Peter and I had journeyed in a very unsophisticated and uncluttered way, we had a comprehensive medical kit, and many, many more luxuries than they. These men had no doubt covered every river and creek in Amazonia with no fanfare, and some had probably disappeared unnoticed.

Certainly some gold prospectors in Brazil make considerable fortunes judging by their subsequent spending sprees in the nearby towns. On the other hand, there is no shortage of people ready to relieve them of their fortune, from the pilot who flies them the 70 kilometres for $200.00 one way, to the whores, and the stores where a bottle of beer costs $40.00 and a chicken $100.00. In a way, it does not seem to matter, because to many the idea of making a fortune and getting out with it is considered bad form. One should treat one's friends to a party with glorious girls and luxuries flown in from Rio, or as one man did a few years ago, have a Cadillac flown in from the States to drive up and down 100 metres of mud at the camp. In short, the pattern is two or three years of backbreaking labour in the jungle, with a handful of malaria attacks, only to return penniless after a week and start all over again.

All previous gold finds shrunk into insignificance recently with the discovery of a bonanza at Serra Pelada (east of Maraba on the Brasilia–Belem road). It is estimated that over 50 tons of gold a year could be extracted from this area 2 kilometres long and 300 metres wide. Twenty-five thousand prospectors flocked there before the government began to impose rigid controls. Mainly it wanted to make sure that the gold was sold to the Central Bank, rather than through illegal channels, but it was also feared that so many men with so much money at stake threatened serious violence. Now, no more prospectors are permitted, and a police force is on the spot. One man found

19 kilos of gold in one day and sold it for $190,000, and several others have found over 100 kilos each in their time there, but of course many others don't even manage to pay their way.

In 1983 the prospectors of Serra Pelada won an extraordinary victory. A group of powerful mining concerns were pressuring to be allowed in to work the area more efficiently (it is estimated that at least 40 per cent of the gold at present ends up on the slag heaps owing to the inefficient methods used). Other groups argued that with the Brazilian foreign debt standing at such an enormous figure, sentiment about the livelihood of a few thousand prospectors should not stand in the way. However, President Figueiredo promised them that they could stay — at least until conditions got too dangerous to continue with their present methods. This was an extraordinary triumph for the little man, especially in the South American context.

Well, the plane did not arrive that day, or the next, or the next. The men were infuriated by the delay. They had requested a plane for a handful of sick people and it seemed that the pilots could not be trusted to appear promptly when summoned.

'What would happen if we had a serious accident?' they asked. 'A broken limb, or appendicitis? Just because the pilot can earn more money doing a run elsewhere they leave us until last.'

On December 21st, a week after our arrival, we at last saw the first plane circle the camp before landing on the strip. Could we get on it and escape from this boring place? Everyone said we should go and speak to the pilot and beg a flight. He was a glum fellow and his eyes were invisible behind the mirrored sunglasses so favoured by a certain type of South American. He answered that he was already taking six and could not arrive at Belem with any more passengers. It was against regulations. We had heard of this, so I countered that he could easily take us as far as Macapa where he would have to refuel, and where controls were lax. He refused, and when I attempted to persuade him by pleading ill-health and urgency, he was unmoved.

'You came up here through choice. So you can get yourselves out again the way you came up.'

In the mirror of his glasses I could see myself fighting the urge to punch him on the nose and rip the stupid, affected, tough-guy things off his face and stamp them into the dust. Reason won. He might be returning in a day or two, and we could not afford to antagonise him. I turned on my heel, walked back to camp and kicked hell out of a tin can.

Ernesto saw our impatience and disappointment and apologised for not helping us out with a word to the pilot. He told me that it had been the owner of the Aero-Taxi firm, and not one of the usual pilots who were more prepared to bend the rules. I asked him if he really thought we'd manage to get out before Christmas, and he assured us that there was no doubt of that. Only two more days.

That night we watched, to our dismay, the arrival of another canoe-load of men, swelling the numbers yet again. Many were sick and must have had a miserable two days' journey, especially as the canoe had overturned in a rapid. One of the least attractive prospects I could imagine was to be dumped in cold water in the middle of malarial shivers and forced to swim for your life. They had also lost a lot of provisions. So now we were almost out of food. We had been eating so insanely since we arrived that the prospect of reduced rations seemed quite attractive. As I wrote in my diary on December 20th 'Now mid-day of yet another exciting instalment in this waiting game. So far have eaten three times – beans and farinha, fish and farinha, and just now another catfish and farinha – and I turned down an offer of monkey and farinha. Everyone has round little bellies, Pete and I included, and we no longer feel the healthy, fit, lean creatures that arrived here six days ago. And we haven't even got to a place with beer, cakes, chocolate, biscuits and everything else yet!'

We passed the morning of December 22nd in increasingly futile hope, and when nothing had come by 3 pm I set off in our old canoe to go fishing with the Brazilian I'd sold it to for $10. I had already begun to regret giving this guy so much stuff – he had been greedy and grasping when we had been sorting out our stuff while the others had been more retiring. I later learnt that he had sold off a lot of the gear that I had intended for everybody. He was unpopular and over the past week we had seen why: he was lazy, never stirring to hunt, fish or prepare food, but leaped out of his hammock with agility when it was time to eat. He then piled his plate to overflowing with all the best pieces.

This man had been cajoled into going fishing for once, and feeling in need of some exercise and wanting a last paddle in our canoe I went with him. We set off the 3 kilometres to a rapid downstream, and after half an hour I was regretting it. All my muscles were already lazy and out of condition, and the Brazilian was not pulling his weight. It was a morose, ill-tempered fishing excursion, especially when he had the nerve to tell me he had just sold the canoe to Ernesto for twice the price he had paid me. I was livid. He had told me that he really needed a canoe, and all the time it was only for him to trade. The frustrations and irritation of this week of emptiness came pouring out of me and I yelled and swore at him, and he answered in kind. We almost came to blows in the canoe. 'No one speaks to me like that,' he shouted, 'not even my father.'

'If your father had done it more often you might not be such an unpleasant, lazy, selfish son of a bitch,' I replied.

We arrived at the rapid, and he was obviously expecting us to stop above it to fish from the rocks. However, out of a perverse need to scare him and get a bit of excitement after so many days of tedium, I headed for the worst section and yelled at him to paddle. We had nothing in the canoe except the shotgun, and that was tied on, so even if we overturned not much would have happened to us, but I got a kick out of the scared, wide-eyed glance he gave me over his shoulder before we swept, bucking and bouncing, over the waves that slapped over his lap and put 15 centimetres of water in the canoe.

MOLOCOPOTE

He was nicely quiet and subdued after that.

'Crazy gringo bastard,' I heard him mutter as we pulled to the shore and tied up. We then fished for two hours, caught nothing and paddled wearily home against the current. On the way he asked me if I had any drugs to control epilepsy, as he had run out of the tablets that he had been taking for the last fifteen years. He said he had been trying all the drugs in our medical kit, and had found some bitter-tasting ones. That was enough for him. His epilepsy tablets tasted bitter and these tasted bitter, so they must work the same he thought. When I got back to camp I found several quinine and chloroquine tablets were missing. Also Peter had lost his Swiss Army knife, and my sheath knife had disappeared. Peter went up to him and accused him outright of thieving, which was a good sign that the strain was telling on him too and soon the knives were miraculously 'found' in some place where we had never used them.

December 23rd, and we were all up bright and early. Two flights were due that day, and we were all going to be in Santarem wining and dining that night. Cabeca Branca composed a witty little song about us all and we were as excited as school kids. The grizzled prospectors dug out little slivers of mirror and rusty razors and retired to the river to perform their grooming. Unruly hair was wetted and combed flat, moustaches were trimmed, fingernails were cut, and out came the hats. Generally around the camp people wore old straw hats or went hatless, but for the return to the city suitable headgear was required. These must have normally been preserved in plastic bags and moth-balls, but that morning was The Day. Stetsons, Hombergs, Fedoras, were lovingly brushed and placed at jaunty angles. The garimpeiros were going to town. Sadly though, only a couple of men had the sort of face to carry off the panache. The rest looked a bit silly. What is more, they bore the flashing sign on the head to all who lay in wait: 'I'm a garimpeiro. Fleece me.'

At 9 am the drone of an engine was heard by the other men several minutes before Peter and I could hear anything, and we grabbed our gear and raced up to the airstrip to try to fight for a seat. It was not that important to get on the first plane, although a restaurant lunch and some cold beers would be nice. The plane taxied to a stop and a different pilot stepped out. This was the Seventh Day Adventist apparently, a young man in his late twenties, and we jostled good-naturedly around him.

He said he was taking nine people with him this flight, which seemed a full load — only fourteen of us wanted to fly out, so we had expected him to take seven each trip. Then he dropped the bombshell.

'I'm not going to do a second flight today,' he announced. 'I'm afraid the rest of you will have to wait until January 5th when I'll be back.' Those of us not included in the nine, stared at him in horror. Twelve more days here? Christmas Day here? New Year's Eve here?

Peter and I had Fernando dangling between us with his arms around our shoulders. He was too weak to walk unaided by this time.

'Aren't you going to take this guy?' I asked. 'He's had malaria a long time.'

'He hasn't got enough money,' was the reply, 'and anyway, I'm full already.'

The red mist came slowly filtering down over my vision.

'These men are all wanting to spend Christmas with their wives and families and girlfriends,' I said. 'They've been in the jungle for six months. Most of them are sick, this man particularly, and maybe he'll die before you return.'

No one else said a word. Brazilians perhaps are accustomed to being let down, to the cruel whims of fate, or the callousness of the powerful. I was the lone voice. I knew it. And I went over the top.

'They tell me you're a Seventh Day Adventist,' I went on, gathering momentum and bile as he shrugged his shoulders indifferently. 'You should know that there's more to Christmas than praying and church-going and Bible-beating. It's a time to lend a hand, to help the sick, to re-unite families, to put aside the thought of profit, and to be altruistic and caring.'

He got into the plane, but not before I had seen a twinge of guilt flicker in his eyes. The departing men shook our hands and looked embarrassed — the reprieved leaving the condemned.

Peter and I carried the boy back to camp, laid him in his hammock, and tried not to look up as the plane roared overhead heading south. We just wanted to cry.

15 Christmas

Twelve days! Another twelve days with nothing to do, nothing new to read, and not much to eat. It was the excruciating boredom that had really eaten into us during that past week. The waiting, those blank hours swinging in the hammock curbing our impatience, the sudden inactivity after months of adventure. We were so bush-crazy and suffocated by the jungle that we were beginning to crack up. How could we survive these extra twelve days just hanging around? We deserved a Christmas in civilisation, and Molocopote was no place for festivities.

Ernesto and three others decided to head back up to the goldfields for the next eleven days and urged us to accompany them.

'There's food up there,' Ernesto argued, 'and hunting and fishing are much easier. We won't be able to leave you much stuff here and you'll go hungry.'

We were too depressed to be persuaded. Partly because if we had to spend another twelve days hanging around, we would prefer that everyone left so that we could be by ourselves. Partly because we were expecting more malaria, and it seemed likely that one of us would have a canoe trip while suffering from it if we went with Ernesto. Partly because there was an outside chance that another plane might arrive before January 5th.

'You won't even have a functionable canoe,' Ernesto went on. 'We're taking all of them with us — including yours — except for that one over there that has a big hole in it.'

We didn't care. We had two shotguns, lots of cartridges, fishing tackle and there were always the cashew trees to stop us starving altogether. Ernesto left us 2 kilos of pasta, 2 kilos of farinha, 1 kilo of beans, 1 kilo of wheat-flour, and a small tin of powdered milk. That lot, rationed carefully, would go quite a long way.

However, we would have the sick youngster, and to our dismay Epileptic announced he would be staying too. (I later learnt that he stayed because Ernesto had refused to take him.)

'Are you sure you want to stay?' Ernesto asked us as we said goodbye.

'Yes,' I replied. 'We'll be okay.'

'We'll be back on January 4th,' he said, started the motor and departed.

I went down to the rocks to do a bit of sunbathing and to try to shake myself out of depression. I did not succeed. If we had known we were going to have more than three weeks waiting at Molocopote, we might perhaps have continued over to French Guiana, or even have carried on paddling to Care-caru downstream. Both these courses of action would have been foolish. We had made the right decision, but in our black mood either alternative seemed preferable to continuing this enforced inactivity.

After a couple of hours I returned to camp and found Peter making a big stack of pancakes, and with a lot of milk on the boil. I controlled my temper with difficulty, but in my diary I wrote, 'Barely three hours after a good lunch, and Ernest leaving, Peter used up half the wheatflour and a third of the milk. It pissed me off quite frankly, especially as he is becoming really fat and lazy — hasn't been hunting or fishing once since he arrived — just swinging in his hammock like a big cuckoo waiting to be fed. At this rate all the food will be gone in two or three days, and then what?'

Not having been for a hunt or fished, Peter couldn't really understand just how difficult it was at Molocopote. He had grown accustomed to a bountiful river and forest and simply assumed there would be no problem even if our stocks were finished.

The next morning we were awoken by a shaking of the hut that made all our hammocks shudder. It turned out to be Epileptic having a fit while lying in his hammock. We checked that he did not swallow his tongue, but it was a mild affair and he was in no danger.

Peter went over to the fire and finished off the rest of the flour with another batch of pancakes. Oh well, I thought, he'll learn soon enough. But we put aside the rest of the powdered milk for Fernando who by this stage could not eat much in the way of solids. In fact he could not get out of his hammock unaided, and seemed to be deteriorating fast. I felt guilty withholding the quinine from him, but I knew I would need it myself. It was a horrible decision to make, and one I still live with. Would ten quinine tablets have made any difference? Was it only malaria he had, or did he also have hepatitis? Certainly he was very yellow, but that may just have been due to prolonged malaria.

I went for a long hunt and saw some monkeys and spent three-quarters of an hour stalking them. I was getting better at this game, and sneaked along in true Indian fashion. I wriggled under bushes and from the cover of one tree to another until I was below them. They still had not seen me and were stuffing their mouths with some berries. Feeling overconfident, I got a second cartridge ready — hoping to bag two, cocked the gun, took a bead on a plump one and pulled the trigger.

'Phutt' went the dud cartridge, a billow of smoke erupted and the lead shot went up 2 metres then showered about me. I snapped open the breech to eject, but no luck. The monkeys chattered in alarm and disappeared, leaving me hopping up and down in a fury.

I returned dejected to camp and found there was a big pot of spaghetti cooking on the fire. This time I rounded on Peter. 'We had a bloody big breakfast — so why do we need another meal so soon? Why not save it for tonight?'

'I didn't cook it,' he answered. 'It was Epileptic.'

'Didn't you say anything and try to stop him though? You've got a tongue haven't you?'

I went up to Epileptic, and with icy rage asked him why he needed to finish all our food so soon. He grew sullen.

'Ernesto left us this food. For me too. I'll eat it when I damn well please.'

'Oh, no, you won't,' I countered, and the control slipped away. 'You'll eat it when we decide, and unless you pull your weight you won't eat at all. We're prepared to share what we hunt and fish with you, so long as you share some of the work and control your greed. But we owe you nothing, we don't like you and you're dependent on our charity. It's us who make the rules.'

'Who the hell are you to give me orders?'

I put my face up close to his.

'I'm a big, mad gringo,' I answered comically, although no doubt I didn't look too comic at that moment, 'I weigh 20 kilos more than you, and I'm 12 centimetres taller than you. I could knock your head into the river. You're also an epileptic,' I added cruelly 'and if you want to make sure I pull you out of the fire or the river when you have a fit, you'd better obey me.'

And so it went on. I felt mad and violent. The concept of rationing was alien to the Brazilian mind, and seemed to be alien to the Swiss mind too. You ate what you had, and only worried when it ran out I turned on Peter. I was furious at him for saying nothing when the Brazilian had begun to cook the spaghetti. Now it was I who laid down the rules, who became hated, while Peter emerged smelling of roses.

'I know it's a Swiss custom to sit on the fence and not take part in any conflict around you. But you're not in Switzerland now, and there's no room for neutrality. If you got off your arse for a change and went for a hunt, you'd see why we have to go easy on our food.'

A few minutes later he picked up the shotgun and went off, and while he was gone I felt bad about shouting at him. I seemed to be alienating everybody. I need not have worried about Peter, however, because he returned empty-handed and from then on his attitude changed.

A bit later, Epileptic asked if he could use the shotgun. I agreed reluctantly because there was a risk that he might have a fit while in the jungle. I wasn't worried that he might shoot himself, but that he might lose the shotgun.

He'd been gone about half an hour when we heard two shots in quick succession. We waited eagerly to see what he would bring on his return. It was Christmas Eve after all, and a bit of meat would be welcome — otherwise it would just be boiled pasta. Epileptic emerged into the clearing and the sun struck the plumage of the dead macaws he carried. He had them by the legs and their wings hung limply open, dragging the ground. I had not realised that the red and blue macaws were quite so beautiful until we examined these two closely. How sad to kill such gorgeous creatures. By the time we had finished plucking them the ground was brilliant with blue, yellow, green and red feathers, and we were left with two skinny little carcasses that made their murder even more poignant. Brazilians and Indians often shoot these birds, the Indians more for the feathers than the meat.

Of course old Epileptic was quite insufferable in his triumph at being the breadwinner for a change, especially so soon after my tirade. I got a little pleasure however out of informing him that he had shot two birds that retail illegally in the States for $1000 apiece. Live macaws of course. The meat in fact was so tough that it was hard to gnaw it off the bones without loosening our teeth, but at least we had something for our Christmas Eve dinner.

We fed the broth to Fernando and I sat and chatted with him for a while. He told me he was engaged to be married, and had come to the jungle to earn money for the wedding. He was twenty years old and lived in Santarem. He reached weakly into his pocket and pulled out a well-thumbed photo of a plump negress with a mischievous grin, who he informed me was his fiancée. Tears ran down his cheeks as he talked about her and the five years they'd known each other, the house where they were going to live and the six or seven children they planned to have.

'I don't think I'm ever going to see her again,' he sobbed, 'I'm going to die before the plane comes back.'

'Oh no you won't,' I answered with forced cheerfulness. Secretly I agreed with him. I was more and more convinced that there were some complications beyond the malaria. His urine was very brown, the whites of his eyes were very yellow and he was very anaemic. But my lack of medical knowledge left me helpless. I gave him two chloroquine, two quinine and two Fansidar to see whether there would be any improvement the next day. If there was we would give him more. If not, all we could do was to get some nourishment down him and hope he survived the next ten days.

I turned in at about 8 pm because the mosquitoes were fierce. Now that they were concentrated on just four of us instead of the fifteen who had been in the camp before, Molocopote was becoming a very unhealthy place. Even if Peter and I only had one strain of malaria each when we arrived, we were certain we would have a second before we left. That proved to be true.

Christmas Day. I went for a walk to savour the early morning coolness and to enjoy the view of the mist over the river. This blanketed the Jari every dawn and lasted until 7 am, by which time it would be burned off by the sun. We wished each other a happy Christmas and then tried hard to forget what day it was. This we almost succeeded in doing apart from one unwise discussion of Christmas fare in England and Switzerland, which drove us hunting and fishing in the urgent attempt to find something good to eat. Using damp farinha as bait on a little cane rod with a bent safety pin as a hook, we managed to catch eighteen little fish. These we gutted and grilled over the fire and shared out four and a half each. They were bony and tiny — but that was Christmas dinner. As we ate we discussed the pilot.

'I bet the son of a bitch is in church for most of the day,' we snarled, 'thumping the Bible, holier than thou, feeling self-righteous and one of God's chosen. He's probably put us out of his mind and his conscience feels sweet and pure.'

Fernando was showing no signs of improvement that day from the pills

I'd given him. While I was feeding him there was the sound of liquid falling to the ground. He had urinated in his hammock. He didn't seem to notice, and it was an indication of how weak he'd become. From then on, we cleaned, washed and changed him several times a day.

I went for a hunt that afternoon and had more bad luck. I wounded a monkey, and again the cartridge failed to eject and it got away. A few weeks before I would have felt unhappy about a wounded animal escaping and suffering, but now I was just unhappy that lunch had escaped. In fact the way I had shot at it marked a departure from usual practice. It had been a bit outside the safe killing range, and on the run, but I had snapped off a shot in the express hope of wounding it and slowing its flight. Hunting had reached such a degree of necessity that there was now no room for either sentiment or sportsmanship. We needed to kill, and if animals sometimes were wounded and escaped, that was just too bad.

As soon as it was dark we climbed into our hammocks and tried to sleep. The more we could sleep the better, and the days would be shorter. Epileptic had two annoying traits to add to all his other faults. He farted explosively dozens of times a day and each fanfare would reduce him to helpless mirth. Peter and I were hardly prudish, but we found everything about Epileptic tasteless and irritating. The other thing he liked to do was swing in his hammock singing in the most tuneless voice imaginable the most trite, maudlin collection of ballads penned in Brazil over the last ten years. We told him to shut up. We ourselves had stopped singing long since, and we could see nothing to sing about, especially with his voice.

The next day we busied ourselves repairing our back-packs, clothing and mosquito nets. After that we went hunting for cashew nuts. When we had fifty or sixty nuts Epileptic showed us how to roast them. Using our old, solid frying pan, he heated them over the fire, and there were little puffs of smoke as they began to release their oil. He stirred them around as they began to blacken and until the bottom of the pan became lined with oil. He then deliberately let it all catch fire, which it did explosively with the nuts letting out jets of burning gas and oil until all the shells were blackened and charcoaled. They were then ready to eat. The shells could be crumbled away to reveal the delicious nuts inside.

That first time we made the mistake of sitting around the pile of nuts eating communally. Definitely a mistake when dining with Epileptic. His tempo rapidly increased until he ended up eating most of them. From then on we counted the nuts and shared them out equally so that we all ate the same and could eat them with leisurely enjoyment.

Later Peter went out for a hunt and shot a monkey. It cheered us up and we kept Epileptic on tenterhooks all afternoon while we forced ourselves to wait until the evening before we ate it. When it came time to serve up, there were more scenes of brotherly goodwill when our friend helped himself to both legs and an arm and was forced to return them to the pot for a more equable share-out. We had to watch the bloke like a hawk. He took his plate to the other side of the hut in what we assumed to be a sulk, but which we discovered the next morning had been a planned move to enable him to finish off nearly all the farinha without us noticing.

I think we would have hit him, had our discovery of the theft not been just as he was having a serious fit, kicking up the dust and writhing and foaming on the floor. Much as we hated the guy it was no time to thump him, and anyway he was really rather appealing in the hour after the attack. He never had any memory of having had a fit (the normal aftermath), and would wander around afterwards as if in a drunken daze. However many times we guided him back to his hammock and suggested he rest, he got up again and came stumbling over to us.

'Who are you?' he would ask.

'I'm Joao and this is Pedro.'

'You are my friends, and I am your friend,' he would murmur charmingly, and put his arm around our shoulders like an affectionate child. We felt quite warm towards him at these moments, but unfortunately the fits just were not frequent enough.

On December 28th we finished the last of the food that Ernesto had left us, Epileptic having already eaten the few grams of farinha we had expressly put aside for fishing bait. From now on we would be totally reliant on hunting, the cashews, and the slim chance of catching a fish on a spinner. (In all the time we had spent at Molocopote the spinners had produced nothing.) It promised to be a hungry eight days. Peter and I made plans to go fishing in the old canoe that we had caulked up with rags, and to try our luck at the rapid upstream where perhaps spinners were a novelty to the fish. However, that night I got malaria again and spent such a miserable night that I could not face the exertions necessary for such an expedition. I told Peter and wrapped myself up in my blanket and surrendered myself to my sufferings. I heard Peter depart, punting the canoe as we had no paddles, and assumed that Epileptic had gone with him. When I peeked my head over the edge of my hammock a couple of hours later however, I saw Epileptic was still there.

'Why didn't you go with Peter?' I asked.

'I didn't feel like it,' he answered.

Ah, Jesus, give me strength, I thought, as I lay back. Peter hadn't said anything, so why should I? Bugger the lot of them.

Contrary to most of my malaria attacks of the trip I did not feel any better the morning after. The fever lasted all day and increased that evening. At least I was not feeling hungry though, and did not mind when Peter returned in the afternoon having caught nothing. We ate three cashew fruit each, and Peter pulped some for Fernando and fed him.

'He is looking worse,' he told me. 'Only just conscious and his temperature is 104 degrees.' He tucked the blanket around him to keep out the cold and damp, and got up in the middle of the night to change him and feed him some warm milk.

Epileptic also got a malaria attack that night and made quite sure we all knew it. He groaned theatrically and noisily all night, keeping us both awake, but getting no sympathy from us.

'Oh my God in heaven, I'm going to die,' he groaned at one point, and in one voice Peter and I answered, 'Well, for Christ's sake die then, you son of a bitch.'

'I've got malaria,' he cried, 'I feel so sick.'

Hell, as if we needed to be told how sick malaria makes one feel! Peter and I were very reserved and stoical in our suffering. Northern European stiff upper lip and all that. The occasional whimper or groan would slip out, but no more. Epileptic was just less inhibited. He let it all hang out, and being the unpleasant character he was, groaned to an indifferent world.

Piranha

16 Last days

December 30th, and 1983 was coming to a close. I made a chart at the back of my notebook of the remaining days, and each morning savoured the small pleasure of crossing out one more day. One week to go. We were pinning our every hope on January 5th, but there were doubts that the plane would arrive even then. After all, most of the men had departed with malaria and two weeks might not be enough for them all to have recovered completely. Perhaps they would decide to prolong their holiday a bit, in which case the pilot was unlikely to fly up to Molocopote empty just for us. Money was their prime concern it seemed, and such a trip simply would not be economic. Still, we had to pin our hopes on something.

I decided to set off for another hunt, soon to realise how much the malaria had sapped my remaining strength, and of course three or four cashew fruits a day do not provide much energy. At the airstrip, I saw a commotion in a distant tree-top where a troupe of spider monkeys were feeding. Big, gangly, 10-kilo beasts they were. Malaria, hunger and all, I broke into a trot. They had seen me coming and were already in retreat. The only hope seemed to be to run as fast as I could in the attempt to get within range. I floundered through the jungle, tripping and scrabbling in the undergrowth, and with only a pair of underpants on I was soon scratched and bleeding. My heart was thumping in my chest, there was a bitter dry taste in my mouth, and my empty stomach was flapping against my spine, but I was gaining on the monkeys. The chase went on for several hundred metres, until I staggered within range. One monkey was running along a branch and about to leap to another tree when I fired. It was a hurried snap shot, but the monkey faltered as it was about to leap and missed its handhold, toppling head first 20 metres down to the jungle floor.

Between me and the place it had landed was a fallen tree, and I needed to sit down and rest before I could go on. When I did, there was no sign of the monkey. I walked around searching for half an hour. This was a cruel blow. Either the monkey had been not too badly wounded and had dragged itself away, or else it had missed its handhold from shock at the sound of whistling pellets, recovered, and nipped up another tree. At all events, it was our last hunt at Molocopote. After that we conserved our strength by spending most of the time in our hammocks, with the odd foray to the cashew trees.

In the evening when I took some of the last of our milk to Fernando I found him lying with his eyes closed and his breath rasping from his open mouth. His thin face with the adolescent beard was gaunt and shiny with sweat. His lips and the corners of his mouth were caked with dry white spittle.

Down the ropes of his hammock ran a column of ants. They crossed his cheek and disappeared into his open mouth. I recoiled in horror, then called Peter over. We brushed the ants away and bathed the boy's face. We squeezed some water into his mouth. But apart from the occasional groan he did not react. We sat helplessly by his hammock for the next few hours as his breathing became noisier and noisier until it rattled deep in his chest. Finally, at about ten o'clock, the breathing faltered, his chest quivered and then relaxed. He had gone. We pulled the blanket over his face and went to our hammocks. Poor boy. We hoped the Good Lord had written a little entry alongside the pilot's name for the Day of Reckoning, to greet him when he turned up pompous and pious and oh so sure of his appointed place in heaven.

Next morning we awoke to find Epileptic had been busy. Somehow he had manoeuvred the body out of the hammock and laid it on a board between two trestles. Candles burned at head and feet, the hands were crossed on the chest, and he had wound a bandage around the boy's jaw to keep it closed. The face was horribly yellow and the ants were back. I wiped them off the cold skin with a shudder.

There was no way we could leave him unburied for long in that climate, so after an hour or two we grabbed shovels and set about digging the grave. We looked for a place with some nice views around, and where the soil might be less compacted and easier to dig. The best places were near the Indian graves, so we began to dig there. It was back-breaking work, especially as the sun rose high, and weak as we were from three days of cashews, we suffered badly from having no pick with which to loosen the soil. We got down to 1 metre, when Peter and I began to argue that it was deep enough.

'Oh, no,' said Epileptic, 'a good grave should be at least 2 metres deep. Otherwise animals can dig up the bones, and it is disrespectful to the dead.' Typical, I thought. When Fernando had been alive Epileptic had done nothing to look after him. Now he was dead, everything had to be by the book.

By late afternoon we finally finished, and it was a fine job. Two metres deep, sheer, smooth sides, and 2.5 metres long. We leant on the shovels and admired it. 'Seems a shame to fill it again,' I muttered, and went down to the river to wash off the sweat and dust. An hour later, as the sun was setting, we lifted the boy up in his hammock and carried him up the hill. It was a rather scruffy funeral cortège — the three of us just wearing shorts or underpants. Peter got down in the grave and we passed the body down to him to lay in the bottom. He uncovered the face for a moment while we all said our farewells, recovered it, and filled in the earth. Peter picked some flowers to lay on the top and the job was done.

'One down, three to go,' I commented sickly on the walk back. 'Who next? and giggled. A reaction to the exhaustion and the death, I suppose. Peter looked shocked and angry at my lack of taste, but I could not stop. 'At least there'll be one less waiting to get on the plane now — our chances are better. Imagine if the plane had come this morning! They'd have laid him out flat, occupying at least four places. We couldn't have really sat on

him, could we, or rolled him up in a ball?' Then, after a pause, 'Pete, I want
to tell you that if I'm next, don't bother going down more than a metre, eh?
I wouldn't regard it as a lack of respect — and I know you'll be weak and
tired. But, could you put a piece of wood over my head and face before you
fill it in? I don't like the idea of all that weight pressing down on my nose.'

Ah, it was a festive New Year's Eve. We ate some cashew nuts — six each —
and then turned in. We were not waiting up for midnight to sing Auld Lang
Syne. My last shaft of brilliant wit to Pete before I fell asleep was 'I think a
plane will come next year.'

Over the next four days we only got up to drink water, urinate or do a
shuffling tour of the cashew trees. The fruit was now very scarce — only two
or three each a day. Yet by now we no longer felt the same ravenous hunger;
just an emptiness and lack of strength. In fact many times I have felt a lot
hungrier in England by the mid-morning tea break. Nature's safety valve I
suppose. Peter and I both suffered more fevers in those days and that reduced
our weight even further.

We may not have been ravenous but we did think and talk of food a lot.
I particularly remembered the ten-week cycling trip I had done with a friend
the summer before down to Sicily. We had eaten unrestrainedly to fuel our
muscles, and what magnificent spreads they were — cheese, paté, fruit,
raisins, dates, figs, crusty bread, croissants, butter, jam, salami, milk, fruit
juice. That was a real holiday. All the same, our hunger was easier to bear
than the crushing boredom. We should have liked a fat novel or two as much
as a meal.

Epileptic began to have a fit per day, and we had to keep an eye on him
when he went near the fire or the river. He became quieter and quieter, as we
all did, and we all lay for hours on end in our hammocks without exchanging
a word. The rain continued to fall frequently, approaching the rainy season
pattern of a fierce storm every evening. The river continued to rise. It was
over a metre higher than when we arrived.

On the evening of January 4th Ernesto returned with three others.

'My God, you look like shit,' he said when we got up to greet them. 'So
skinny.' He glanced around and noticed Fernando was missing. 'Didn't make
it, eh?' — and he took me by the arm and informed me in a whisper that the
boy's father was among those who had just arrived with him. He then went
over to one of the men and led him away from the camp to stop by the
water's edge and talk. I saw the face crumple into tears, and he sat down
abruptly and stayed there sobbing for a long time after Ernesto returned to us.

'Let's go for a walk, John,' he said. 'I want to talk to you and I fancy a
cashew.'

'You'll be lucky to find one,' I answered, but we set off slowly. The slope
up to the airstrip seemed steeper every day, and my heart hammered in my
chest. Ernesto slowed his pace to match mine, and I told him our news.

He found one ripe cashew that we had missed, and we sat under the tree
and chatted — about Epileptic mainly. I learnt that he had been sacked from

the goldfields five weeks before for laziness, and had been hanging around at Molocopote since then waiting for a flight. However the pilots refused to take him without payment.

'I've brought some food with me from the goldfield, but we've only a little and I've decided that Epileptic is not going to have any.'

'What'll he live on then?' I asked.

'That's his problem. He should have thought about that before he turned everyone against him by thieving, and by doing damn all to help. At least six men have come to blows with him. We're just not prepared to look after him any longer. It could be another ten days before a plane comes and . . . '

'What?' I cried, snapping out of my contemplation of Epileptic's fate and thinking of my own. 'Ten days! But there's one due tomorrow isn't there?'

'Well, it might come, but I can't imagine those sick men being ready to return just yet. Anyway,' he smiled, 'if that same pilot comes back he might not take you after the things you said to him. They were well said, I never liked those evangelist bastards — but you upset him, and he's a powerful man.'

I was on the edge of tears and my voice shook.

'Oh, Christ, Ernesto. I don't think Peter and I could take another ten days of waiting here. We'd go crazy. We're not too good now, but we've managed to hang on in the hope of getting out tomorrow. Hell, we'll buy the canoe back off you and paddle downstream — anything's better than staying on here.'

Ernesto looked at me, a bit concerned and a bit amused.

'That would be stupid. At least we've got some food here now so it won't be so bad for you. It's only ten days after all.'

'It's not hunger, Ernesto — you just don't understand. We've been here twenty-three days already, and another ten days would be just too bloody much.'

I was pacing up and down shouting — and Ernesto got up and put his arm around my shoulders.

'Well, let's wait and see if the pilot comes tomorrow or not, before you go paddling off heroically downstream or put the shotgun in your mouth, okay?'

We returned to camp and told Peter the news. He reacted much as I had done. 'Ten more days! No way, John! Impossible! We would go crazy!'

We had a supper of paca meat that the men had hunted on their way downstream, and turned in with our bellies full for the first time in ten days.

When we got up the next morning Peter and I were nervous, but still forced ourselves to act with confidence. We untied our hammocks and rolled them up, gave away our mosquito nets and blankets, gave the shotguns one last polish, and packed everything away. We were leaving that day, we reminded ourselves optimistically. 'Tonight a good steak with fried eggs, potatoes and salad. Six cold beers and a chocolate dessert.'

We sat around for the next four hours, and finally one of the men cocked his head and announced, 'Plane coming.' We hadn't heard it, but we let out a whoop of excitement, grabbed our gear and began to scramble up to the air-strip. We'd only gone a few paces when a figure raced past us carrying a shotgun. It was Fernando's father. 'Stop him,' I yelled, shrugging the pack off my shoulders and beginning the chase. 'He'll shoot the pilot!'

That was evidently the man's intention. As far as I was concerned, he could do the deed whenever he pleased in Santarem, but not here leaving an unmanned plane. I gained on him and tripped him with a rugby tackle. The gun flew out of his grasp.

'Leave me alone, gringo!' he shouted, twisting and fighting furiously. 'I'm going to kill the son of a bitch. He left my boy to die.' Peter and Ernesto joined me and helped to hold him down.

'You can't do that,' Ernesto told him. 'It wouldn't bring your son back or change anything. It would just put you in prison for ten to fifteen years. Think of your other children — the ones who are still alive and need you.'

The man weakened and his struggles subsided. Soon he was sobbing and safe to let go. We continued up to the airstrip and the plane taxied up to us. To our relief the pilot was a new face to us and were were able to calm Fernando's father with the news.

'You're the gringos old Cabeca Branca has been telling me about,' the pilot said with a smile before we'd even introduced ourselves. 'He's been pestering me every day, persuading me to take you out. You've got a persistent friend there.'

'Are you going to take us then?' I asked nervously.

'Yeah, I'll take you.'

Peter and I did a little dance of joy.

'He told me you would pay with two shotguns,' he went on. 'Have you still got them?'

We showed him the guns and he seemed content enough, though he muttered 'Out of all the rich gringos in Brazil right now, it's just my luck to end up with the only two poor ones.'

We loaded our packs and heard Epileptic pleading with the pilot to be taken.

'Have you any money?' the pilot asked him.

'No.'

'I'm not a charity,' the pilot retorted. 'If you get on a bus you'd expect to pay, wouldn't you? Why should a plane be different?'

'He's not very well,' I said. 'He's got malaria and has finished his pills to control his . . . (I paused) . . . his illness.'

It suddenly occurred to me what it would be like to have to deal with an epileptic fit in a small, crowded plane. If Epileptic was taken I vowed to sit very close to him. 'No money, no travel are my rules,' said the pilot, slam-ming the door and starting the engines. Peter and I and the other passengers averted our eyes from Epileptic who stood forlornly on the grass. Our intense dislike turned to pity.

The plane taxied to the far end of the strip, revved its engines into a rivetpopping crescendo, released the brakes and bounced down the runway into the air. As it dipped its wing to turn southwards we caught a final glimpse of the hut where we had spent so many days and the little figure of Epileptic trudging dejectedly down the red smear of the trail.

Postscript: It was confirmed in Europe that Peter did, in fact, have Leishmaniasis — as well as Falciparum and Vivax malaria, and he spent a long period in hospital. I got off lightly with only two strains of malaria.